Hidden in the Household

HIDDEN IN THE HOUSEHOLD

Women's Domestic Labour Under Capitalism

Edited by Bonnie Fox

The Women's Press

Canadian Cataloguing in Publication Data
Hidden in the household
ISBN 0-88961-065-7 pa.

1. Women – Economic conditions. 2. Home labor.
3. Women – Employment. I. Fox, Bonnie, 1948-

HD6053.H52 331.4 C80-094259-0

Cover and book design by Liz Martin

Lithographed by union labour at Alger Press Limited, Oshawa, Ontario, Canada

Printed and bound in Canada
Published by the Women's Educational Press, Toronto, Ontario, Canad

CONTENTS

CONTRIBUTORS

Emily Blumenfeld is a doctoral student in sociology at the University of Toronto. She is currently writing a dissertation on the question of a Marxist analysis of the mother-child relationship and the possibility of the collective organization of childrearing.

Linda Briskin is active in the women's movement, teaches women's studies at Sheridan College, Toronto, and is finishing a dissertation on the family, capitalism and women's consciousness.

Bruce Curtis is an Assistant Professor of Sociology at McMaster University in Hamilton, Ontario, specializing in the comparative history of elementary education.

Bonnie Fox, who has just completed a doctoral dissertation on married women's involvement in wage work, has taught sociology at York University and the University of Alberta and is a member of the Women's Press collective.

Susan Mann is a doctoral student in sociology at the University of Toronto. She is a member of Organized Working Women and, in addition to her work on women's oppression, she has published articles on the political economy of rural development.

Wally Seccombe is a doctoral student in sociology at the Ontario Institute for Studies in Education, writing his dissertation on the reproduction of labour power under capitalism. He is the author of previous articles on domestic labour, which appeared in *New Left Review*.

INTRODUCTION

Bonnie Fox

The writers came together in the fall of 1977 to write a book that would carry forward the discussion of domestic labour that began with such promise in the late 1960s. In so doing, we hoped to help develop the Marxist theory of women's oppression that is an essential tool in the struggle for women's liberation.

The importance of the roles of mother, wife and "housewife" in defining women's social identity today is clear. And while being a housewife does not always involve being a mother or even a wife, having children and being married both entail a host of household chores and responsibilities. Indeed, domestic labour—broadly defined and including child care—is most women's primary responsibility and it is also often exclusively *their* responsibility. In fact, being adult and female means involvement in domestic labour for all except perhaps bourgeois women. Moreover, domestic labour is basic to society: it involves the reproduction of daily life itself. Therefore, in order to understand women's position in the family and in society, we must look to the organization of their daily work in the home.

If the material conditions of women's household work are central to the determination of women's social position, then an understanding of them is key in formulating a strategy for women's liberation. The struggle must begin from an understanding of the structural features of the household that are most oppressive to women, the origins and sustaining foundations of these household features, the ways in which the household is changing and the obstacles to significant social change.

An understanding of the material situations of working-class and middle-class women requires sifting through the details of their daily lives: the emptiness of the early morning home with its unmade beds, dirty dishes and universal chaos; the energy drain caused by growing kids with boundless energy and unceasing demands; the escapist relief offered by the soap operas; the psychological onslaught waged by the ad men and the idiocy of the directions on their products. For some, it also means the conflicting demands of a double workload—in the home and at a waged job. In the early days of the women's movement, much attention was focussed on women's experiences of these conditions of their daily lives. The personal perceptions articulated in countless consciousness raising sessions contributed to a collective understanding of the oppressive features of women's common experience. However, questions about the sources and sustaining structures of women's oppression cannot be answered through immediate experience alone.

Because appearances are especially deceptive in capitalist society, we need a rigorous analytic approach to questions about women's condition. For example, the true source of the value of commodities (namely labour), is mystified under capitalism so that commodities' useful characteristics and their exchange appear to give them value. Similarly, the real relations between the part of the production and reproduction of society that occurs in the household and that productive sphere known as the economy are hidden and mystified.

Marx successfully penetrated the surface of the appearances of capitalist commodity production, revealing its basic structure and historic tendencies. He focussed his attention on production because he assumed it to be the ultimate basis of social organization and ideology. In writing about this materialist conception of history, Engels argued that

> the determining factor . . . is, in the final instance, the production and reproduction of daily life. This, again, is of a twofold character: on the one side, the production of the means of existence, of

> food, clothing and shelter and the tools necessary for that production; on the other side, the production of human beings themselves, the propagation of the species. The social organization under which the people of a particular historical epoch and a particular country live is determined by both kinds of production. . .[1]

This statement suggests that without an understanding of the organization of the household we will not fully understand the organization of society. It also points out that women's domestic role involves a type of production. Only the implication that the conceptual separation of the production of the means of existence and of human beings is paralleled by a physical separation of their production—between the economy and the household—makes the statement less than definitive. For part of the means of daily existence are produced through domestic labour and labour power is partly produced by workers outside the household. Furthermore, this conceptual vagueness preceded the subsequent omission by both Marx and Engels of any analysis of the production that occurs in the household, as it develops under capitalism.

Nevertheless, Marx's method of historical materialism makes clear the importance of domestic labour as the other half of the production and reproduction of daily life and a necessary counterpart to the capitalist production of subsistence goods. And a systematic use of Marx's methods can disclose the key features of that labour process. In order to analyze capitalist production, Marx abstracted from its details and thus isolated its determinant elements; he then slowly reintroduced the detailed specifics of capitalist development. This sort of theoretical abstraction reveals dynamic tendencies in society that are mystified by appearances. Therefore, such theory is not only essential, it is also a powerful tool in the struggle for change.

So, a theoretical analysis of women's domestic labour is called for. This analysis must clarify the *particular nature* of domestic labour and thus women's oppression *under capitalism.* Those attempts at an analysis of women's oppression that begin with the assumption of women's universal subordination are inherently limited. In ignoring the marked historical and cross-cultural variations in women's position, these analyses abandon the search for causally related material and social factors before it has really begun. Yet, a clear understanding of the factors influencing women's social position must account for variations in that position and the relation of these variations to other aspects of the society.

Under capitalism, most women and men are oppressed by a social order that separates them from the means necessary to produce their own subsistence, from the products of their labour and from each other in their daily work lives. Additionally, however, women are oppressed in special ways when the dominant mode of production is capitalist. Not only is the sexual division of labour highly elaborated, it entails the relegation of women's chief productive role to the household, which is separated from the sphere of socialized (or cooperatively organized) labour, where capitalism's dominant form of production occurs.

In stark contrast with capitalist production, in which the direct producer is clearly compelled by necessity to sell his or her capacity for work, domestic labour presents itself as a labour of love. Instead of being mediated by a market sale between two formally contracting parties, domestic labour accompanies a personal commitment to family members. While work for the capitalist is physically and temporally separated from the rest of daily life, household labour is interwoven with "personal life" and totally enmeshed in the worker's most intimate personal relationships. Consequently, while the wage worker is caught up in a clearly delimited process of production for sale, the household worker is perpetually striving to meet personal needs.

That household work is a privatized labour has consequences for the workers' class consciousness and implications for their ability to organize for collective action. Furthermore, the fact that no wage is paid to the worker affects her or his social status and power within the household. It is not surprising that labour occurring in the home, creating no clear product, drawing no obvious payment and performed in a society where wage work dominates, appears to be non-work and confers on the worker little social recognition.

Nevertheless, domestic labour, as one of the major ways that the means of daily living are produced, is of primary importance: it not only produces the next generation, it also produces and continually reproduces the working capacity of the wage earner(s). In an economy based on the historic dispossession of people from their means of production, the majority of adults is left with only one saleable possession, the capacity to work. Because that same historic process of dispossession entailed the commoditization of the means of subsistence, the household depends for its survival on the continual sale of this labour power. In selling labour power to capital, the worker submits himself or herself to a routine that drains his or her energies and returns only a pay cheque. Physical nourishment, recreation and relaxation, emotional development, intellectual stimulation, the cultivation of personal relationships—in short, most of what human living and growth comprise—must occur outside of work. "Personal life" must be found in the time left over from wage work. Yet, personal life depends upon successfully earning a wage; and not only the wage worker's personal life but also his or her family's continued existence depends upon that wage. Nevertheless, the worker could not return to work without the material and emotional rejuvenation he or she experiences at home, at the end of each day. Should he or she fail to recover, at home, from the daily wear and tear of work, his or her work capacity and even his or her life expectancy will shrink.

Much of household work involves meeting the needs of the wage earner, in obvious ways (e.g., feeding him or her, clothing him or her) and in ways that are more subtle (e.g., providing a rewarding home environment and family life). Of course, much of this contribution towards the reproduction of labour power by the domestic labourer involves spending the wage for commodities that require her or his labour before they are ready for consumption. So, she or he unites the labour of those wage labourers who produce consumer commodities with her or his own in order that the wage worker might continually return to work and that the family might survive.

From the perspective of capital, wage labour is the source of profits. Consequently, the production and reproduction of labour power must be of concern to capital. It is, then, somewhat paradoxical that the domestic work process has fallen progressively behind the capitalist production process with respect to productivity. The work continues to be carried out by the individual working alone, a situation that precludes elaboration of a division of labour and consequent increases in productivity. Actually, the long-term trend has been towards a shifting of the burden from the shoulders of several household members to the shoulders of one. Its continued privatization largely explains why domestic labour continues to be time consuming despite its increased mechanization over the last several decades.

While the consequences of privatization are fairly clear, the basis of the peculiar coexistence of the capitalist economy and the private household is not well understood. Whether the private household is only one of many formations possible with capitalist development, or whether it is a structurally necessary component of an economy dominated by capitalist production is unclear. Similarly, the nature of the continued relationship between the daily work that occurs in the domestic sphere and capitalist commodity production remains at issue. The answers to these questions are crucial: they will indicate the extent to which changes in the position of women are possible under capitalism.

Subsumed under this broad question are more specific and immediate questions. The fact that married women are increasingly involved in wage work raises the question of how capital activates the reserve labour pool latent in the household. The trend towards a double work day for most women also raises the question of whether the relationship between the household and capitalist production is changing. Similarly, the increased assumption by capitalist production and the state of more and more of the tasks involved in the reproduction of labour power, a trend related to the influx of married women into the labour force, may have a significance as yet unexplored. Is the socialization of domestic labour in fact possible under capitalism?

Equally crucial is the issue of the relationship between patriarchy and capitalism. The way in which class relations shape the relations between the sexes demands the attention of all struggling for women's liberation. The question is not only whether the demise of the capitalist organization of production is a precondition for women's liberation, but also what specific changes must be made subsequent to that transformation before women will be truly free.

These are the key questions addressed by the articles in this book. They are not addressed here for the first time, however. The women's movement of the late 1960s and early 1970s generated an array of serious, if often crude, discussions of the sources and specific shape of women's oppression under capitalism. The writing that focussed specifically on domestic labour set the context within which we all work now.

Past Contributions

Margaret Benston's article, "The Political Economy of Women's Liberation," opened the Marxist debate on domestic labour and persisted as one pole on the continuum of positions.[2] Benston based her analysis of household production on an examination of the nature of its obvious products and the quality of its social relations. To Benston, domestic production is a "pre-market," "reduplicative, kin-based, private" mode of production of use values, standing outside the sphere of market mechanisms.

In describing the household as a separate and parallel mode of production, a holdover from pre-capitalist times, Benston took the position that there is no organic relationship between the household and the sphere of commodity production. Rather, the functions of the family that meet the needs of capital provide the link between household production and capitalist commodity production. Specifically, the nuclear family serves as the "production unit for housework and child rearing," the "ideal consumption unit" and the source of satisfaction of male (wage workers') emotional needs. Moreover, according to Benston, "the amount of unpaid labour performed by women is very large and very profitable to those who own the means of production," because male wage earners and not capital pay for domestic labour.[3] Of course, in making this argument, Benston neglected the fact that wages must pay for the subsistence of the working class or the system would not endure (because labour power would not be reproduced), and that wages are a cost to capital.

The tight functional "fit" between household and economy, posited explicitly by Benston, leaves no room for contradictions or change. Contradictions between the two spheres of production are, however, implicit in her analysis—because in reality they exist. Nevertheless, the contradictions implied in Benston's theory of domestic labour, when spelled out, only indicate shortcomings in the analysis. For example, Lise Vogel later argued that in producing use values women have "access to a vision of a life of unalienated productive activity."[4] Men are coming to see this "vision" and the contrast between alienated wage work and unalienated household work because they are beginning to share the burdens of domestic work. So Vogel argued. Unfortunately, there is evidence that men are not, in fact, sharing domestic chores more as women increasingly work outside the home.[5] More to the point, domestic labour is hardly rewarding work.

Benston argued as well that women represent a distinct class: they are the "people who are responsible for the production of simple use values in those activities associated with the home and the family."[6] The domestic labourer's relationship to her means of production was not explicitly analyzed, even though Benston stated that "women as a group do indeed have a definite relation to the means of production . . . and this is different from that of men."[7]

The argument that women represent a class is both inaccurate and misleading. If there were a *structural* condition whereby all women were forced to submit themselves to continual exploitation, we could argue that sex represents a condition similar to class. For the crux of the working-*class condition* is the structural necessity to perform work for wages for the owner of the means of production who appropriates part of that labour without recompense. Women as a group are not in a similar position: no necessity forces them to marry, keep house and raise a family in order to survive. There are clearly social pressures promoting such a course of action, and it is certainly the case that unless women bear children the human race will not be reproduced. However, since there is no personal necessity for the individual woman to reproduce or to do housework for others in order to survive, and since dependence on a man's wage is also not strictly necessary for women under capitalism, women's position cannot be seen as a class position.[8]

Neither are all women similarly oppressed under capitalism. The class differences among women are reflected in the ways women experience the responsibility for the daily maintenance of the family, for example. The weight of the burden is greatly reduced if domestic help can be afforded, if dry cleaners and restaurants can be used regularly; it is greatly increased if the woman must additionally work outside the home for wages. Even the effectiveness of state control over the means of birth control and abortion varies considerably for women of different classes. Ignoring these obvious effects of class differences among women means not only that the particularities of the conditions they face are glossed over. It also means that one possible route for uncovering the deep-seated sources of women's oppression—the way in which class relations, based on production, shape the relations between the sexes—remains unexplored.

The possibility of a class analysis, as well as an abstract value analysis, of domestic labour was established with the notion that domestic labour reproduces labour power. Such an assessment of domestic labour was made by Peggy Morton in 1970.[9] Most of the discussion that followed involved attempts to analyze the household work process at the abstract level of value relations and from the perspective that domestic labour reproduces labour power.

An early analysis by John Harrison was fraught with internal inconsistencies.[10] Harrison's approach was to assume value production by domestic labour without determining the way in which the work is involved in commodity production and how the market mechanism affects it. In fact, Harrison began his analysis by asserting that household production is a mode of production of use values.

The notion that the domestic labourer produces value dominated Harrison's argument nevertheless. He stated that the *value* of labour power depends not only on the socially necessary labour time involved in the production of commodities under capitalist social relations but also on the actual time spent by the household worker producing *use values* consumed by the wage worker. Moreover, Harrison argued, the domestic labourer performs surplus labour if her work time exceeds the work time involved in the production of her means of subsistence. Capital appropriates this surplus labour by paying a wage lower than the value of the labour power being purchased.

The main problem with Harrison's analysis is his apparent assumption that surplus labour is simply appropriated from the private household sphere in the same way that it is under capitalist commodity production, despite the absence in the former sphere of those elements that enable the appropriation of surplus labour in the latter. It is only in the process of labouring for the capitalist, in exchange for a wage, that surplus value is created and appropriated. Harrison was attempting a Marxist analysis, but with substantial confusion, and for an overriding purpose: he set out to show the functional aspect of domestic production for capital.

Jean Gardiner's first article seemed to make a more subtle argument than Harrison's (although her later critique of her own work implied that it was essentially the same).[11] In that first article, Gardiner maintained that the value of labour power is determined by the value of commodities necessarily purchased by the wage (i.e., the labour time socially necessary to produce subsistence goods), but that the "subsistence level" of workers is determined by the contribution of domestic labour (and the state) as well. Therefore, presumably because this labour becomes generalized and thus reduces socially necessary labour time involved in the production of necessary subsistence commodities, "the contribution which domestic labour makes to surplus value is one of keeping down necessary labour to a level that is lower than the actual subsistence level of the working class."[12]

Gardiner also discussed, in a third article, the class position of "housewives."[13] She argued that housewives, though not a class themselves, share particular interests. First, they face the capitalist class as a whole only indirectly, through the price mechanism or via the state, and their surplus labour is appropriated individually and voluntarily on the basis of personal commitments (to their husbands). Second, they are economically dependent on their husbands.

Gardiner, Himmelweit and Mackintosh offered the following reason why some work is retained (by an all-powerful and plotting capital) as privatized household work even though the drive of capitalist accumulation is to invade and take over production processes.[14] A woman's subordination to her husband in the household, and the absence there of a mechanism that would equalize the division of the wage between the two, means that the wife receives less than what is necessary for her own subsistence from the husband's wage packet. In other words, capital pays less than it would if the woman were doing the same work for wages.

Focussing less attention on the inequality in the relationship between husband and wife, Wally Seccombe offered a highly provocative argument about the relationship between the household work process and capitalist production. He argued that domestic labour is part of the total social labour directly or indirectly governed by the law of value.[15] For Seccombe, household labour is a form of petty commodity production, the product of which is labour power. The woman's labour in the home "becomes part of the congealed mass of past labour embodied in labour power. The value she creates is one part of the value labour power achieves as a commodity when it is sold."[16] So, this past domestic labour embodied in labour power is "brought into relation with the average labour of society via the wage"; it is abstracted.[17]

The amount of value created in the household is determined by the value of the domestic labourer's necessary means of subsistence–not by the amount of time she works. Moreover, according to Seccombe, this value finds its exact equivalent in part of the (man's) wage. In other words, there is no surplus labour and all her labour is paid.

Although he assumed that time is not important in determining the value that is produced in the household, Seccombe argued that the law of value indirectly impinges on domestic labour.[18] Consequently, he maintained that value provides the mechanism distributing women's work time between the household and wage work. "Tracing the flow of value right through the reproduction cycle of labour power–as wage goods enter one side of the household unit and renewed labour power bound for the market comes out the other–is the vital link in connecting domestic labour to women's wage labour."[19]

How does the law of value allocate women's time between household and paid employment? Domestic workers compare the amount of time it would take to produce necessary use values in the household (with the man's wage, purchasing necessary commodities) with the amount of time it would take to procure the same amount of use values earning a wage. Therefore, the relative productivity of the two production sectors is behind the growing allocation of women's work time to wage work.

These, then, are the major positions so far articulated in the attempt to analyze domestic labour.[20] They have focussed, to the exclusion of other issues, on the definitional question of whether or not household production is value production, probably because of a desire to locate domestic labour theoretically squarely within the process of capitalist accumulation and exploitation. However, abstract definitional purity is not as crucial as an understanding of the ties between the household and the wage labour process; the contradictions within the domestic sphere and between it and the process of accumulation of capital; and the structural determinants of women's oppression. Unfortunately, these key questions were too often neglected in the approaches offered so far. We hope that our arguments will be more fruitful.

NOTES

My gratitude extends to all of the writers in the book for advising me with respect to organization and content at various stages in the writing of this introduction. Jane Springer, as copy editor of the book, deserves special praise and thanks. Without her early encouragement and active support, as well as that of Meg Luxton and others at Women's Press, the book would not have been published. As well, Jane contributed to the book in ways that extend far beyond the boundaries of editing. Finally, I should like to thank Judy Oleniuk and John Fox for helpful editorial comments, and note that despite the considerable advice I received, the arguments herein—and their weaknesses—are my own.

1. Frederick Engels, *The Origin of the Family, Private Property and the State* (New York: International Publishers, 1942), pp. 71-72.
2. Margaret Benston, "The Political Economy of Women's Liberation," *Monthly Review*, 21 (Sept. 1969), pp. 13-27.
3. Ibid., p. 207.
4. Lise Vogel, "The Earthly Family," *Radical America*, 7 (July-Oct. 1973), pp. 9-50.
5. Martin Meissner, Elizabeth Humphreys, Scott M. Meis and William J. Scheu, "No Exit for Wives: Sexual Division of Labour," *Canadian Review of Sociology and Anthropology*, 12 (Nov. 1975), pp. 424-40.
6. Benston, p. 201.
7. Ibid., p. 199.
8. Biological reproduction, while in the interests of the human race, is in many ways opposed to the interests of individual women. (See Simone de Beauvoir, *The Second Sex* trans. H.M. Parshley, (New York: Knopf, 1953), for a vivid discussion of this point.) Moreover, because wage earning jobs have been available for women since the beginnings of capitalist development, strictly speaking, dependence on a man's wage is not necessary.
9. Peggy Morton, "A Woman's Work is Never Done," in *Women Unite* (Toronto: The Women's Press, 1972), pp. 45-69.
10. John Harrison, "The Political Economy of Housework," *Bulletin of the Conference of Socialist Economists* (Winter 1973), pp.35-52.
11. Jean Gardiner, "Women's Domestic Labour," *New Left Review*, 89 (Jan.-Feb. 1975), pp. 47-59. Later, Jean Gardiner, Susan Himmelweit and Maureen Mackintosh, "Women's Domestic Labour,"

Bulletin of the Conference of Socialist Economists, 4 (June 1975), pp. 1-11.

12. Gardiner, "Domestic Labour," p. 54.

13. Jean Gardiner, "The Political Economy of Domestic Labour in Capitalist Society," in Diana Barker and Sheila Allen, eds., *Dependence and Exploitation in Work and Marriage* (London: Longman, 1976), pp. 109-121.

14. Gardiner, Himmelweit and Mackintosh, 1975.

15. Wally Seccombe, "The Housewife and Her Labour under Capitalism," *New Left Review,* 83 (Jan.-Feb. 1974), pp. 3-24.

16. Ibid., p. 9.

17. Ibid.

18. Wally Seccombe, "Domestic Labour—A Reply to Critics," *New Left Review,* 94 (Nov.-Dec. 1975), pp. 85-96.

19. Seccombe, "Reply," p. 87.

20. I have omitted consideration of Mariarosa Dalla Costa's *Women and the Subversion of the Community* (Bristol: The Falling Wall Press, 1972) because her usage of Marxist categories restricts them to the status of metaphors. My omission should not be interpreted as an underestimation of the extent to which Dalla Costa's highly polemical work has stimulated discussion and theoretical analysis.

DOMESTIC LABOUR
AND THE WORKING-CLASS HOUSEHOLD

Wally Seccombe

Implicit in the debate on the issue of domestic labour is the question of the usefulness of Marx's theory of capitalist development and the laws of motion of capitalism for understanding women's oppression. In this article, Wally Seccombe considers the limitations of the analysis employed by Marx and Engels, but attempts to extend its insights, after raising specifically feminist issues. A lucid discussion, as extensive as it is systematic, the article should be useful especially to those seeking a general introduction to the Marxist discussion of women's domestic labour.

Seccombe argues that a mode of production can only be understood from the standpoint of its continuous production, that is, its reproduction through time. From this vantage point, he describes the twenty-four-hour cycle of labour power's consumption in capitalist production and its replacement in the private working-class household. The proletariat is thus conceived to be the product of two labour processes, conducted at two sites.

Seccombe's argument then attempts to establish the relationship between capitalist production and the isolated household. After exploring the practical limits of the private ownership of household property for proletarians, Seccombe identifies the two-generation nuclear family as the normal (but by no means universal) living arrangement in the formation of working-class households. He then uses the household/family distinction to conceptualize the relation of capitalism to patriarchy. Seccombe insists that the domination of the husband-father in the working-class family is grounded materially in his possession of the primary wage, and he describes the power that this form of petty entitlement confers upon him as head of the household.

Introduction

The working-class household is a non-capitalist unit located in a subordinate position in developed capitalist social formations, but it is by no means an unimportant unit for capitalism.[1] Its unpaid labour makes an indispensable contribution to the production and reproduction of labour power on a daily and on a generational basis; that special (living) commodity whose "incessant reproduction . . . is the sine qua non of capitalist production."[2]

Marxists have had a great deal of difficulty relating the private domestic labour of women in the working-class household to the capitalist labour process. In *Capital,* by far Marx's most developed analysis of the capitalist mode of production, the private household and the necessary labour conducted therein receive only infrequent and cursory attention. It is true that Marx and Engels did not neglect to include descriptive accounts of the proletariat's (squalid and chaotic) living conditions in their work. Such accounts, often very insightful, can be found in several places in *Capital,* and especially in Engels' pathbreaking work, *The Condition of the Working Class in England.*[3] However, such description was never transformed into a distinct theoretical component of their overall conception of the capitalist mode of production.

The essential task which Marx set himself in *Capital* was to elaborate the laws of motion of capital. His marginalization of the private domestic sphere, which Marx termed the sphere of "individual consumption," does not appear to have had serious adverse consequences in the pursuit of this objective (yet even here we should note Marx's own caution that "for a full elucidation of the law of accumulation, his [the proletarian's] condition outside the workshop must also be looked at; his condition as to food and dwelling").[4]

From the standpoint of comprehending the full working and living conditions of the proletariat, however, such an omission *is* devastating. Leaving out of account women's primary labour role; failing to analyze in detail the domestic household sphere within which this labour is conducted; unable to relate women's labour in this sphere to wage labour (male and female)—most Marxist analyses have been unable to come to grips with the core material condition of women's oppression under capitalism. The complex position of women within the proletariat has been skimmed over. It is only in the past decade (thanks, in large part, to the new rise of the women's movement), that this omission has begun to be frontally addressed.[5]

The filling in of such a vacuum in an interdependent theoretical structure rarely proceeds smoothly, however. This can never be merely an additive process, like finding the long-lost piece in a jig-saw puzzle and happily inserting it in the formed space left waiting for it. For the surrounding categories of a complex discourse have invariably suffered a reductionist compression in the process of obscuring this omission. One of the essential tasks therefore, in inserting domestic labour in the working-class household into an overall analysis of the capitalist mode of production, will be to salvage the essential categories of Marx's political economy from a reductionist tendency. It is to this preliminary task of category reworking that I now turn.

Production from the Standpoint of Reproduction

Let us begin with the most fundamental category of Marxist political economy: mode of production.[6] It is very common for Marxists to reduce the mode of production to a conceptualization of the unit of production, taken by itself—be it the capitalist factory, the slave plantation or the feudal lord's manor. This conception derives from a faulty, if understandable, reading of Marx's *Capital*, which was an unfinished work.

Volume I, the only book finished by Marx himself, looms large in our conception of the capitalist mode of production. Marx was aware that the view taken of capital and the capitalist mode of production in Volume I was partial and isolated, a necessary starting point for his exposition but by no means an adequate conception in itself. In Volume II, he expands his framework from the individual (industrial) capital of Volume I to the reproduction of total social capital. He writes:

> So long as we looked upon the production of value and the value of the product of capital individually, the bodily form of the commodities produced was wholly immaterial for the analysis. . . . What we dealt with was *the immediate process of production itself,* which presents itself at every point as the process of some individual capital. . . . This merely formal manner of presentation is no longer adequate in the study of the total social capital and of the value of its products [emphasis added].[7]

> The annual product includes those portions of the social product which replace capital, namely social reproduction, as well as those which go to the consumption fund, those which are consumed by labourers and capitalists, hence both productive and individual consumption.[8]

It is at the level of the reproduction of total social capital that the capitalist mode of production must be conceived. And here, Marx is explicit: the individual consumption by the labourer of the material means of subsistence via the wage is an integral component of the analysis of total social capital.

This expanded conception of the capitalist mode of production, in contrast to the standard version based on "the immediate process of production itself" (i.e., on Volume I), is fully consistent with Marx's general formulation of the mode of production concept. He repeatedly speaks of the mode of production "of material life," "of social existence," "of social life itself," etc. In the following passage from *The German Ideology,* Marx and Engels explicitly include the production of the new generation of labour power, though at this stage they had not yet clarified the distinction between labour and labour power.

> Production of life, both of one's own in labour and of fresh life by procreation appear at once as a double relationship. On the one hand, as a natural and on the other, as a social relationship. By social is meant, the co-operation of several individuals, no matter under what conditions, in what manner and to what end. It follows from this that a determinate mode of production . . . is always bound up with a determinate mode of co-operation and this co-operation is itself a productive force.[9]

Engels is perfectly explicit on this in the following famous passage from *The Origin of the Family, Private Property and the State*:

> According to the materialistic conception, the determining factor in history is in the last resort, the production and reproduction of immediate life. But this itself is of a two-fold character. On the one hand, the production of the means of subsistence, of food, clothing and shelter and the tools requisite therefore; on the other, the production of human beings themselves, the propagation of the species. The social institutions under which men of a definite historical epoch and of a definite country live, are conditioned by both kinds of production: the stage of development of labour, on the one hand, and of the family, on the other.[10]

Despite Engels' very promising formulation here, Marxists have generally failed to analyze the specific way in which "the production of immediate life . . . the production of human beings themselves" is socially established in different modes of production. Too often this dimension is left out, and the inevitable result is that subsistence relations are permitted to collapse back into their own biological sub-strata. They are dehistoricized and treated as eternal species-processes, bound up entirely with instincts, "natural" needs and "natural" divisions of labour. This is highly ironic, since it was precisely such a historical naturalism that Marx's critique of classical political economy was designed to defeat. And yet, we often see naturalist assumptions creeping into historical materialism through the unanalyzed back door of subsistence relations.

There are several closely related pitfalls here: (a) a tendency to assume, and not to socially explain, the specific way in which the major classes in a given mode of production appropriate and consume their means of subsistence, and, in the process, reproduce their labour power from one day and from one generation to the next;[11] (b) a tendency to consider subsistence, when it is considered, merely as goods consumption and to fail to socially explain the specifics of the reproduction of human life itself in different societies;[12] (c) a tendency to conceptualize a mode of production purely synchronically, failing to investigate its reproduction through time.

If we are preoccupied exclusively with material goods production at the primary production site and analyze the organization of production statically, on a single working day, then the specific way in which the producers restore their labour power, to be able to labour again the next day and over the next generation, becomes entirely peripheral to our concerns.

A mode of production can only adequately be conceived at the level of its production over time, its continuous production, that is, its *reproduction*. The replacement/restoration of all productive forces directly consumed within its dominant production sphere must therefore be included as an integral part of its conceptualization as a mode of production. I hold this to be a general principle, applicable to the correct theorization of all modes of production.[13]

Prevailing modes of production tend to replace/restore their productive forces, including labour power, in their own characteristic way. Distinct modes of production are not eclectic about the subsistence form of their labouring classes; to the contrary, they exhibit strong tendencies to seize and to reorganize pre-existing subsistence forms in accordance with the distinct way in which labour power is harnessed and consumed in the predominant sphere of their material goods production. For this reason, the subsistence forms of the labouring class must be included in the theoretical construction of the mode of production under study, and not left to merely descriptive notation, as an afterthought in the analysis of concrete social formations.

Marxists, from Marx on, have always considered that the specific social mechanism by which a given ruling class extracts the surplus product from its labouring class is the secret of its entire mode of production.[14] But the underside of this same mechanism is the specific way in which the labouring class secures and consumes its (necessary) part of the total social product and reproduces its capacity to work again in the production of that product. This subsistence dimension has received much less attention and analytical care.

We can distinguish four interrelated facets of the mode of the labouring class' subsistence in any mode of production: (a) the mode of appropriation of the necessary product by the producers; (b) the mode of its distribution among producers; (c) the mode of its consumption in the domestic group; and (d) through (c), the mode of labour power's production, both on a daily and on a generational basis. In this article, I will attempt to clarify these facets for the proletariat in the capitalist mode of production. Before proceeding it may be useful to consider the kind of questions raised by each of these elements in turn.[15]

1. *The Mode of Appropriation*. The total social product is divided up between the classes in struggle, into its necessary and its surplus parts. What are the mechanisms of this division? What is the form in which the producers retain or regain the necessary product?

2. *The Mode of Distribution*. The producers do not consume the necessary product *en bloc*. It is divided up among them. How is this accomplished? The producers are organized into small domestic units or households where, for example, food is eaten communally and people rest and sleep under the same roof. How do these units form, endure and dissolve and how do they lay regular claim to a definite portion of the fruits of their labour? How is the necessary product divided up or shared out between households?

A second aspect of distribution is the division of the product within households. There is the question of ownership and disposal rights over durable household property at marriage (dowry) and at death (inheritance). There is also the problem of sharing out consumables on a daily basis among the members of the domestic group. In addition, definite arrangements must be made for the care and upkeep of those household members who consume (in use values) more than they produce—infants, the aged, the infirm and the sick. What provisions exist for these dependents?

3. *The Mode of Consumption.* The personal consumption of the means of subsistence involves, in all societies, certain expenditures of necessary labour time by members of the domestic group. Over and above the labour of goods production, there are domestic labours of food preparation, house cleaning, child care, etc. These labours may be completely intertwined with goods production or they may be quite separate, but I find it useful to distinguish them analytically, even in cases where they are intermingled with goods production, in order to investigate, for example, the sexual division of labour. How are domestic tasks and responsibilities allocated among members of the domestic group? How is domestic labour coordinated and supervised?

4. *The Production of Labour Power.* In order that a society continues to produce, the labour power of the producers must be reproduced from one day to the next among those already labouring, and from one generation to the next to replace the older generation's labour power as it deteriorates and wears out.

The problem of the generational replacement of labour power is an absolutely critical one in two ways: first, all societies must establish an overall relation between the schedule of labour power's exhaustion in production and its demographic replacement through the medium of its small domestic groups. The way in which this relation is regulated (and upset) furnishes an important insight into the dynamics of the society as a whole. Secondly, the position of women in any society is closely bound up with the social construct of wife/motherhood. How does a particular society deal *socially* with the biological fact that women bear children and lactate and men do not? Since this is a pre-eminently social question, it requires an historically specific explanation.

A mode of production is generally defined as a set of productive forces in specific combination/contradiction with a given ensemble of production relations.[16] What becomes of the categories, "forces" and "relations" of production under the foregoing treatment of the mode of subsistence? [17] In each case these categories must be stretched to incorporate the subsistence dimension.[18] Productive forces must include both the technological means of production and the capacities of the producers. Both energy and knowledge must be produced and transmitted in requisite forms. In order for labour power to be harnessed effectively in production, the producers must be prepared and motivated to work within the social relations established at the site of production and enforced by the ruling class. From the standpoint of the ruling class, therefore, the alignment of subsistence relations with production relations is critical. The producers, for their part, will generally strive to preserve whatever autonomy they can in the sphere of subsistence and safeguard it, as much as possible, from the dictates of their relations with the ruling class in the sphere of production. Thus, the class struggle itself is played out, in part, in a struggle around the relative autonomy of the labouring class' subsistence arrangements.

Recently, many Marxist feminists have begun to use the term "reproduction" in counterposition to "production" to denote the specific sphere of labour power's production. I find this usage far too restrictive. All forms of continuous production in all spheres entail definite cycles of reproduction, by which the founding conditions of that sphere's production are repaired, restored, replaced and expanded. Reproduction, therefore, should refer to: (a) these particular cycles; and (b) more broadly, to the dynamic operation of the system "in full swing," as Marx put it.

The dualism of production-reproduction models has arisen in positive response to the arbitrary compression, within

Marxism, of the conception of production—its reduction to material goods production. Employed as the tool of an initial break-out from this conceptual strait jacket, "reproduction" has an undeniable merit. It clearly registers the distinct character of this separate household sphere and the labour of its ongoing social construction. The problems with it, however, are rapidly becoming manifest.[19] It promotes a conceptual dualism which, in many ways, adapts to the phenomenal separation of these two spheres under capitalism instead of uncovering their underlying connection. It also renders static the concept of production, leaving the reductionist compression of this category intact instead of attacking it head-on.

One of the strongest features of Marx's mature economic work, in spite of his marginalization of the subsistence sphere, is his dynamic treatment of all processes of production as processes of reproduction. Thus, his attempt in the second volume of *Capital* to work out simple and expanded reproduction cycles for various fractions of capital is methodologically instructive in analyzing domestic labour as a part of the reproduction cycle of labour power.

Marx considered all production processes, dialectically, to be processes of consumption and all consumption processes to be processes of production. From a Marxist standpoint it is quite incorrect to treat the consumption of the means of subsistence as if it were not, at one and the same time, the production of labour power. From the standpoint of human beings as consumers, their individual consumption may be the last act in a long labour chain, the satiation of their needs and consequently an end in itself. From the standpoint of analyzing a continuous economic process, however, the failure to turn individual consumption around and see it as the production of labour power vitiates the analysis of a society in full swing.

Although Marx's treatment of this in *Capital* is in no sense adequate, he does write:

> [T]he individual consumption of the working class is, therefore, the reconversion of the means of subsistence given by capital in

> exchange for labour-power, into fresh labour-power at the disposal of capital for exploitation. It is the production and reproduction of that means of production so indispensable to the capitalist: the labourer himself. The individual consumption of the labourer . . . forms therefore a factor of the production and reproduction of capital. . . . The fact that the labourer consumes his means of subsistence for his own purposes, and not to please the capitalist, has no bearing on the matter.[20]

These enlightening comments, and others in a similar vein, are made by Marx in a short chapter in Volume I entitled, "Simple Reproduction." It is no coincidence that it is from the standpoint of reproduction that individual consumption comes to be considered, unambiguously, a process of production.

The Location of the Proletariat in the Capitalist Mode of Production

In the capitalist mode of production, personal subsistence and goods production are locationally divorced from one another. They take place in two distinct spheres of production/consumption—the sphere of capitalist industry and the sphere of private households.

It is essential to distinguish between capitalist production and the capitalist mode of production. Capitalist production refers to the specific sphere of the production of material goods and services for profit, organized directly by private capital. Thus, the household is non-capitalist. But this does not imply that this non-capitalist sphere of proletarian (and bourgeois) subsistence is somehow *outside* the capitalist mode of production. Indeed, it is a component of this mode.

From the standpoint of capital, the proletariat lives outside capitalist production in order to be able to return continually to work inside it. From the working class' standpoint, it is just the opposite—its members work in capitalist production so that they may be free to live on their own outside this sphere, beyond the direct authority of capital. The proletariat's independent living conditions, sustained by the wage, in combination with its own private labour, is an integral part of what makes it a class of free labourers. The unique situation of the proletariat in the entire history of the world's mass labouring classes cannot be fully grasped unless the material conditions of its living independence from capital are addressed in detail. Marxism's economic categories and analytical field must be stretched beyond the immediate confines of capital-in-motion (the spheres of capitalist production and exchange) to include, integrally, the entire field of the proletariat's necessary self-activity and private self-reproduction as a labouring class.

It is, of course, true that the proletariat's insertion into capitalist production is the determinant foundation of its overall position in capitalist societies, but this unquestioned fact cannot be used to justify or excuse the omission of "the other half" of the proletarian condition. For this forgotten half is key to gaining an adequate grasp of this class' interior gender antagonisms and the potential strategic processes of their resolution.

The proletariat as a social class is constituted at two locations, not one. It cannot live without working for wages; it cannot work for wages without living in a definite place outside capitalist production where it restores its capacity to work. For the proletariat *both* locations are spheres of production/consumption. In capitalist production, the proletariat's labour power is consumed and its monetary means of subsistence, in the form of the wage fund, produced. In its private household residence, the material means of subsistence are consumed and its labour power on a daily and a generational basis is produced. A balanced, comprehensive study of the proletariat must analyze the social relations within which this class lives and labours at *both* locations; and, most importantly, their changing relationship with one another.[21]

The residential sphere of the proletariat is structurally subordinate to the sphere of industrial production where capital (or the capitalist state) presides directly over labour. While the proletariat works for wages in order to live on its own, free from direct capitalist control, it is, nevertheless, equally freely compelled by its poverty in the means of production to return to work for capital. This free compulsion (the paradoxical expression of the proletarian condition) enforces the subordination of the independent sphere of private working-class life to the sphere of labour's direct incorporation into capitalist production. The subordination of the non-capitalist subsistence sphere to the capitalist production sphere underpins the subordination of female to male workers within the sexual division of labour of the working class.

The mainstream discourse of Marxist political economy has been riveted on "the point of production"—that is, the point of *capitalist* production of goods and services. In this discourse only half of the proletarian condition is retained within the theoretical problematic. This distortion in the analysis of capitalist societies is part of a more general distortion, which has seriously marred Marxism's grasp of the human labour process in all societies, and in particular, women's role within this process. The "two great classes of labour," the labour of material goods production and the labour of producing human life itself in socially definite forms, have been practically reduced to the former.

This tendency to collapse the labour of direct subsistence into the labour of goods production has also marred the strategic dimension of Marxist thought. It was the common belief of classical Marxists that the emancipation of women would come about more or less directly as a result of their mass entry into socialized production; the rearguard private sphere of domestic labour would be integrated into socialized production through the entry of women into industry.[22] As the history of all societies that have overthrown capitalist rule has made painfully clear, the one does not follow from the other. The split double day of labour remains a stubborn and oppressive feature of women's condition in these societies, as it does in industrial capitalist societies.

The Simple Reproduction Cycle of Labour Power

The capitalist mode of production provides an historically unprecedented leeway to its labouring masses in arranging their means of subsistence. Nevertheless, workers make their arrangements within real limits. In specifying the simple reproduction cycle of labour power, we can clarify these limits.

How does the harnessing, consumption and release of labour power by capital circumscribe the ways in which the proletariat can organize its subsistence apart from capital? What are the *outer boundaries* of the proletarian condition, given the commodity form its labour power must assume? Once these boundaries of proletarian subsistence have been situated, then at a later stage of the analysis we can analyze the *predominant forms* adopted by the proletarian masses within the range of subsistence possibilities afforded them by the capitalist mode of production.[23]

We will therefore consider the reproduction cycle of a single proletarian, employed by a single capitalist, for one twenty-four-hour period. We are here concerned only with the simple replacement of that labour power consumed in capitalist production, by a capacity of the same quantity and quality. Left out of account at this point is the typical family form of the labourer, the question of the sexual division of labour within this cycle, the propagation of a new generation of proletarians and the state's role in education, health care, etc.

We begin by asking: what are the minimal requisites of labour power's simple replacement from one day to the next? The cycle begins with the worker's appearance in the labour market as a prospective seller of her/his labour power, searching for a buyer.[24] Because we are describing a circuit which returns to its starting point, it may appear as if our point of departure is merely a matter of descriptive convenience. But this is not the case. The proletarian condition is produced and reproduced by means of the *worker's separation* from the means of production. It is this lack which drives the proletarian into the labour market as a seller. She/he has nothing else to sell. She/he is devoid of any means of producing other commodities. Taken on its own, the worker's labour power has no economically viable use value to the worker her/himself. It only has utility for another—the capitalist. It must be *alienated* (sold) to be of use. Since this is the foundation of the proletarian condition, it is the logical starting point for our exposition of the labour power cycle.

The second condition of her/his market appearance is the real prospect of finding a capitalist, an employer, who will purchase her/his labour power, in order to use or consume it. The proletarian had best ensure then that her/his labour power is in usable form for capital, because the utility of her/his labour power for capital is her/his sole attraction as a seller. And, since she/he finds her/himself in a buyer's market, where the supply of needy sellers chronically exceeds the demand of buyers, she/he must offer her/his labour power to capital *competitively,* in both its exchange value and its use value aspects. That is, the worker's asking price must be competitive with other workers whose labour power is of comparable utility.

The proletarian appears in the market under her/his own compulsion. In other words, she/he is *freely compelled* to seek out the capitalist on her/his own account. This is the key to the natural and reasonable appearance of the proletariat's subordination to capital. Upon a labourer's objective separation from the means of production, a subjective compulsion is immediately engendered, wherein the worker has no choice but to submit to capital voluntarily. "Freely compelled" and "forced to volunteer"—these are logical antimonies within linear thought. They make the proletarian condition extremely difficult to think about, since the mind boggles and seeks to resolve the paradox one way or the other. Is the proletarian bound, or is she/he free? Which is it? The answer is that she/he is both—in peculiar combination. I shall explore this paradox in the next section.

In the market, the proletarian seller seeks a capitalist buyer. Unlike most markets, where buyers go to sellers, in the labour market sellers go to buyers. The internalized compulsion to sell in a buyer's market is generally sufficient to ensure a ready supply of labour wherever the employer sets up shop. The first labour of the proletarian is therefore to locate an employer and to secure employment.

The two commodity owners meet in the labour market and bargain as juridical equals. They strike a renewable deal into which they both enter voluntarily and which either can terminate unilaterally at her or his discretion. Both were free to pursue other protagonists of the same class and both chose, nevertheless, to make a deal with each other. Hence it is a formally free and equal exchange.

There are many obscured asymmetries to this exchange: the most fundamental, of course, is the despotic rule of capital in the adjacent sphere of production, which appears as a condition of the sale itself. In the act of sale, the worker "entitles" the capitalist to exploit her/his labour power in production as the latter sees fit. She/he agrees to relinquish any claim upon the fruits of her/his own labour, which become the uncontested property of the capitalist. These crucial prerogatives appear as a natural part of the agreement of the sale of labour power. They are so taken for granted, in fact, that they are rarely specified.

The second inequality is intimately related to the first and reinforces it. Both parties to the renewable agreement can terminate it freely, but the consequences of exercising this legal prerogative are drastically unequal. Quitting the capitalist's employ is generally an extremely serious step. The competition of the unemployed for scarce jobs is fierce and the worker forfeits her/his wage as soon as she/he quits. By contrast, the consequences of firing an employee are often directly beneficial for the capitalist. The performance of other workers is usually improved by exemplary discipline. The employer now has a chance to hire a more industrious and docile worker, and/or a cheaper one, to take the former's place, and he saves the former's wage in the meantime.

But there is a third basic asymmetry to the deal that the capitalist and labourer strike that is seldom recognized. What does each receive and each forfeit? The worker receives a wage—a definite amount of exchange value—and she/he gives up her/his use value to the capitalist for a definite period. The capitalist receives the use value, and pays out a definite exchange value. The end result is that the capitalist ends up with something he can use, the worker ends up with something she/he cannot use—but can only exchange. In order for the money wage to become the use value of her/his own subsistence, she/he must perform an *additional* labour, after working for the capitalist all day—the private domestic labour of proletarian subsistence. There is no escaping the necessity for this second labour. The fundamental genesis of "the double day of labour," which an increasing proportion of modern working-class women perform, lies here, in this drastic inequality in the character of the exchange between labour and capital.

When the deal has been struck, the capitalist takes his purchase and leaves the sphere of exchange to consume it. Because of the peculiar character of this commodity, the seller and the buyer do not go their separate ways at this point; instead, the seller must accompany the buyer in person into the latter's consumption sphere. The proletarian enters the capitalist's private premises and comes immediately under his authority. She/he becomes both a part of the firm (formally) and an integral cog in the production process (substantially). She/he becomes a part of capital, the elastic, variable part. Through this direct incorporation, the proletarian's labour power is consumed according to the rhythms and discipline of capitalist production.

In the process of becoming a part of capital, the worker's labour is *abstracted*—that is, she/he is forced to become actively indifferent to the concrete working conditions and the character of her/his work process and product. The critical point is not what one produces concretely but how much surplus value one's labour posits for capital in the form of its product. The wheels of production turn for one overriding purpose—the self-expansion of capital. The alpha and omega of capital accumulation is thus the money form of capital—the universal abstract equivalent.[25] The whole means of production are seized by this implacable drive to the heaping up of ever greater quantities of exchange values. The logic of capital accumulation enforces an active indifference to the use value limits of the means of production, including the physical limits of particular workers who are expendable as long as fresh labour power can be found.

Inherent in the process of capital accumulation is the danger that labour power will be consumed in such a way as to jeopardize the proletariat's capacity to replace it in a durable fashion. The short-term drive of individual capitalists, in competition with one another, to extend the capacities of their workers beyond recuperation, is thus in contradiction with the long-term interest of capital in ensuring the stable reproduction of the entire proletariat's labour power.[26] As we shall see later, it is the external agency of the state which is compelled to intervene in defence of the long-term interests of capital-in-general, against the immediate interests of particular capitalists, by limiting the normal working day of wage labour through legislation.

The proletarian is paid by the capitalist at the *end* of her/his shift. In most market transactions, the buyer and the seller exchange the commodity and its money equivalent simultaneously. But the commodity labour power can only be alienated by its seller gradually and only in the sphere of production. Until this alienation is accomplished, the buyer is under no compulsion to hand over its monetary equivalent.

The worker quits the capitalist's premises, his property and his authority at the end of her/his shift. In doing so, she/he relinquishes the entire fruits of her/his day's labour to the capitalist. Her/his labour power is depleted, but she/he is richer in pocket one day's pay. Her/his wage takes a monetary form—a definite amount of the universal equivalent. The proletarian is "entitled" to this money. She/he now owns it personally, having "earned" it. The wage is the first form of the proletarian's means of subsistence.

Because the worker is paid in money, the universal equivalent, she/he is legally free to purchase anything that money will buy, limited only by the wage's size. Her/his money is no different from the capitalist's. She/he only has less of it to spend. Her/his subordination to the capitalist thus appears to be only a matter of the size of her/his bank rolls.

I mentioned earlier the right the worker grants to the capitalist, in handing over her/his labour power to use as the latter sees fit. When the capitalist hands over the worker's pay cheque, he grants in return the right to quit his premises after the day's labour and to "go free." Once the wage is paid, the employer washes his hands of his worker's subsistence. This is the worker's private affair, to look after as best she/he can. She/he is free, as far as her/his employer is concerned, to live and sleep where she/he wants, eat and drink what she/he wants, socialize with whomever she/he wants, etc. This prerogative—the very basis of Marx's insistence upon terming the proletariat a "class of free labourers"—permits a real discretionary leeway in how workers arrange their subsistence.

But what can the worker do with this leeway? Her/his freedom is contingent upon her/him reporting punctually back for work in sixteen hours, ready and able to repeat the same exhausting labour process all over again. In other words, this "free time" *must* be spent restoring the labour power consumed today in order that it can be drained again tomorrow. There is no choice in this because the wage has not enabled the proletarian to gain possession of a viable means of production. Instead, it must be spent on consumables to restore her/his only commodity to a saleable state. She/he will find her/himself tomorrow morning in the same needy condition as she/he found her/himself this morning, seeking out the capitalist under the compulsion of her/his own hunger and empty pocket.

In the interval between quitting time one day and starting time the next, the worker faces the necessity of providing for her/his own food, lodgings and rest. This is a personal responsibility determined by the personal ownership of the commodity labour power and the personal possession of its monetary form on leaving the employer's premises and jurisdiction at quitting time.

Because the wage takes a monetary form and is of no use except for exchange, the proletarian is immediately forced back into the market, this time as a buyer of commodities. The worker began the day with nothing to sell but her/his labour power. She/he now finds her/himself dead tired, with nothing to eat but her/his pay cheque! She/he is still in a position of being privately compelled by her/his own needs to go to market.

When she/he was a seller (of labour power) she/he had to go in search of a buyer. Now that she/he is a buyer (of consumer goods and services), do the sellers come to her/him? No. She/he must seek them out. *Both* of the proletarian's market activities therefore involve her/his own active search for commodity deals. This entails a considerable expenditure of time and energy in the two spheres of exchange, over and above the labour time necessary in the two spheres of production.

In the consumer market, the worker purchases the commodities which will comprise her/his means of subsistence. These wage goods are the second form of the proletarian's means of subsistence.

But still the worker's day of labour is not complete. Most of the commodities she/he has purchased are not in immediately consumable form and she/he must leave the marketplace to complete the labour necessary to consume them. Some form of private household residence is therefore necessary, wherein these commodities can be made into a consumable form and the worker can consume them and rest until her/his next shift. This is the third and final form of proletarian subsistence. Its physical structure is some form of housing accommodation; its property form is private; and it is sustained by personal unpaid labour of the proletariat on its own time.

Only in this third form can the proletariat consume its means of subsistence and satisfy the elementary needs which drove its members into the market in search for employment in the first place. Only after domestic labour has been expended can the proletarian live and relieve her/his needs. She/he is compelled, in other words, to make a personal arrangement or provision to ensure the consistent exercise of this labour.

All that remains, after falling exhausted into bed after this double day of labour, is to rise punctually in the morning and travel to her/his place of employment to begin the cycle all over again. We note in this final step, the market implication of the fact that "labour goes to capital." Place of employment limits the place of residence; travel time to and from work is private unpaid labour time; and transportation costs are assumed by the worker.

The Nature of The Proletarian Condition

The proletarian is a free labourer, "free in the double sense that as a free man [or woman] he can dispose of his labour power as his own commodity and that on the other hand he has no other commodity for sale; he is short of everything necessary for the realization of his labour power."[27] What is the nature of this freedom which, in the first instance, is shared by both male and female proletarians? To begin with, the proletariat is free or separated from *both* the means of production *and* subsistence. Had its members possession of either of these, in a sustainable form, they would experience no compulsion to sell their labour power to capital. In his general statements concerning the propertyless condition of the proletariat, Marx was entirely correct to include the workers' lack of the means of subsistence in the first instance.

What he then failed to do, however, was to go on from this first premise, to analyze in detail how the proletarian actually came into possession of the private means of her/his subsistence and established a *property right* to her/his means of "individual consumption."

Private ownership of the means of subsistence becomes for the proletariat the stable basis of its retention of ownership over the commodity labour power. Of this latter ownership right Marx was unambiguous:

> [L]abour power can appear on the market as a commodity, only if, and so far as, its possessor, the individual whose labour-power it is, offers it for sale, or sells it, as a commodity. In order that he may be able to do this, he must have it at his disposal, must be the untrammelled owner of his capacity for labour, i.e., of his person. . . . The continuance of this relation demands that the owner of the labour power should sell it only for a definite period, for if he were to sell it rump and stump, once for all, he would be selling himself, converting himself from a free man into a slave, from an owner of a commodity into a commodity. He must constantly look upon his labour-power as his own property, his own commodity, and this he can only do by placing it at the disposal of the buyer temporarily, for a definite period of time. By this means alone can he avoid renouncing his rights of ownership over it.[28]
>
> . . . .
>
> If the owner of labour power works today, tomorrow he must again be able to repeat the same process in the same conditions as regards health and strength. His means of subsistence must therefore be sufficient to maintain him in his normal state as a labouring individual.[29]

In these famous passages from Volume I, Chapter 6, "The Buying and Selling of Labour Power," Marx proceeds at the level of the *individual* proletarian. This is the same starting point I have taken in tracing out the simple reproduction cycle of labour power. Marx does not adopt this perspective merely for purposes of simplicity in exposition, but because this level of exposition corresponds to the material *fact* that the proletariat, as a necessity of its class position, takes possession of its only commodity personally, at the level of its separate members. This is the form which the commoditization of labour power enforces upon the proletariat.

Individual proletarians sell, or fail to sell, their labour power daily. This class is moved in and out of production, hired and fired, as individuals. Its members are forced to compete against one another for scarce jobs. The manner in which the proletariat receives its portion of the total social product is also individual. The wage is a payment to a person. It is claimed and legally owned by that person. It is then exchanged in order to obtain consumer goods which are, in turn, selected and consumed individually. The commodity form of this exchange reinforces the privatization of individual consumption and discourages cooperation or communal living based upon wage-sharing arrangements beyond the nuclear family.

In individual consumption, labour power is replenished privately. Only in this way does the proletariat "avoid renouncing its rights of ownership" over its sole commodity. This avoidance is the *sine qua non* of the proletariat as a class of free labourers. It determines a definite form—the personal private property form—in which the proletariat constitutes and maintains its living independence from capital.

Proletarians require a residence, a domicile of some sort, in order to satisfy their personal needs on their own time, and to recuperate their labour power for capital's use the next day. This is the home base of the worker's living independence from capital. It may be as meagre as a lockable rented room in a boarding house, retainable only by means of the payment of rent from next week's pay cheque; or it may be as comfortable and relatively secure as a privately-owned house on a private lot, completely paid for. But a private domicile in some form or another is an indispensable condition of stable proletarian existence. Anything less precipitates an open crisis of subsistence, with the likelihood that the person will soon cease to be able to sell her/his labour power, and will thus sink beneath the class condition of proletarian existence.

The formation of a private household residence is not at all secondary or incidental to the stabilization of the proletarian condition, and the labour–domestic labour, overwhelmingly women's labour–which sustains its residences as living centres, as centres for the reproduction of its only commodity, is not incidental to the life existence of the proletariat. The proletariat cannot *be* a full proletariat, a doubly free labouring class, unless it constitutes its means of subsistence apart from capital; and it cannot do so without working within its own dwelling places.

When the production of labour power is considered from the standpoint of its *reproduction,* then it becomes impossible to forget about domestic labour, just as impossible as it is for the living proletarian to forget about it! The proletariat is constituted as a labouring class, by means of its labour at two distinct production sites. These sites are owned and managed by the two opposing classes of the capitalist mode of production–the bourgeoisie and the proletariat.[30]

While the former class rules over the latter, it does not do so without a struggle. The capitalist's production sphere and the proletariat's living sphere are bound up in an antagonistic relation with one another, which capital dominates through the former sphere, but not without resistance from the proletariat from its base in the latter. This is an essential dimension of the class struggle, which is too often overlooked or inadequately understood, as a consequence of failing to clearly grasp the bipolar situation of the proletariat.

The antagonistic relation between the two classes reveals itself clearly in their perspective on the two spheres. For capital, the proletariat lives at home in order to return to work. The proletariat, for its part, works for wages in order to be able to live on its own apart from capital. It struggles to *minimize* its exertion on capital's behalf and to *optimize* its living comfort on its own behalf. Capital's imperative is exactly the opposite: it consumes labour power under the competitive compulsion to maximize labour's exploitation and to minimize the wage payment necessary to sustain the proletariat's independent subsistence.

Struggles for the eight-hour day; against compulsory overtime; for higher wages; sickness benefits; maternity and paternity leave; and retirement benefits and holiday time—all of these familiar working-class struggles take on added meaning when they are viewed as struggles for proletarian autonomy, to strengthen its living independence from capital, on its own time and under its own roofs.

The struggle for subsistence is ultimately a matter of life and death for proletarians. This undoubtedly seems like an extreme statement in the modern context of the welfare state. But it was only the struggles of the workers themselves, and the subsequent intervention of the state, that furnished working-class households with the time, space and resources to replenish their labour power on a stable, expanding and long-term basis. The private consumers of labour power function under no compulsion to ensure the replenishment of the living commodity upon which their profits rest.

In the event that the working class is so weak and disorganized that it is unable to defend itself in an elementary sense, and the state is not pressured to intervene, the reproduction of this class' labour power by means of the private wage system is not assured.

In the Third World today, many employers recruit cheap labour from rural and sub-proletarian urban populations, and do not need to preserve the labour power of the proletariat already employed from one generation to the next. A similar pattern of labour turnover and high mortality rates among the working poor was very much in evidence in the period of the industrial revolution in England (1780-1840). The proletariat of the major industrial centres was formed and reconstituted during this period mainly by rural depopulation and mass migration to the cities, not by indigenous growth of the labouring poor in these centres. The average life-expectancy for men in Manchester in the mid-nineteenth century for example, was only 24.2 years, while for England as a whole the rate was 40.2 years.[31]

Appalling working conditions in the factories played a role in this difference. But the primary cause of the mass human carnage was grossly overcrowded and unsanitary living accommodation. Housing, taking the form of a private commodity obtained through the market, made a major demand on family budgets. The struggle for liveable and affordable housing was a life and death question. In Glasgow, the crude death rate of families living in one or two rooms was two and a half times the rate of those living in five or more rooms.[32]

The more exhausting and debilitating wage work is, the more critical it is to eat well, rest and recuperate in the intervals between shifts. To do this, workers need not only a sufficient wage, but the time, space and energy to restore their health. None of this can be accomplished at work, on the boss' time. It must be achieved at home, in the worker's "leisure" time. However, shift scheduling and the capitalist labour process are designed to enhance the employers' profits and not to facilitate the domestic rehabilitation of labour power.

The structured indifference of employers to the reproduction of labour power is nowhere more glaring than in the case of women who are pregnant or are nursing infants. The great majority of women in this condition are forced to quit work by the utter failure of their employers to provide child care and by the extreme danger that most capitalist work environments pose to the health of their infants and themselves.[33]

Leaving the paid labour force to bear and rear children seriously undermines women's future earning power. They lose seniority and their bargaining position in the labour market is weakened. To make matters worse, the labour movement has traditionally supported the strict seniority principle, and has not effectively challenged sexist employment practices of last hired, first fired.

The problems women encounter in trying to combine wage work and childbearing go to the heart of the capitalist system. This mode of production engenders a powerful antithesis between the production of the human species and the production of its material means of subsistence. Capitalist development drives these two labour processes apart, forcing them into opposed spheres, and so thoroughly antagonizes their recombination that popular demands which seriously pursue this objective rapidly become revolutionary—demands for the transformation of the system itself.

Unlike the slaveowner, the capitalist does not have his capital tied up in the *person* of his workers. This is the peculiar virtue of free labour as far as he is concerned. He can run his present workers into the ground, if he can get away with it, and then replace them with fresh ones while never having to sell the deteriorated workers on the market. To get rid of them, he merely ceases to rehire them, and the responsibility to re-establish the value of their labour power with another capitalist falls "naturally" back on the shoulders of the workers themselves. Thus, once the reserve army of the unemployed is constituted, labour flows through the capitalist economy with an ease that is unique to this mode of production.

The personal insecurity of the proletarian condition (even where relatively comfortable living standards have been achieved) is rooted in this structural irresponsibility of the private consumers of labour power to ensure its stable replacement. It is impossible under capitalism for workers to become permanently indispensable to their employers, and therefore to be assured of a regular means of subsistence in the future.

The independence of one's private life apart from capital is always relative, limited by the compulsion to return to work in order to secure wage income. Despite the fact that the worker's private life is her/his own, conducted on her/his own time, according to her/his own tastes, these non-capitalist use value criteria are ultimately subordinated to the exchange value imperative of producing labour power for purchase and use by another class. Even in her/his own home, the worker is "bound to his [her] owner by invisible threads," as Marx so graphically puts it.[34]

The proletarian is freely compelled to choose an employer.[35] The subtle dialectic between internalized compulsion and free choice is the essence of the proletarian condition. It is worth exploring this in some detail.

Behind every free proletarian choice lies a compulsion, individually experienced. It is this obscured compulsion that permits the choice to be an open one for workers as individuals, and at the same time, one that fulfills capitalist commodity relations. The first proletarian compulsion is to enter the labour market. The first free proletarian choice is therefore one of employers.[36] Given the chronic oversupply of labour power relative to jobs in the market, this freedom is largely formal for the great bulk of the proletariat, but that does not mean that it is illusory or unreal. The failure to maintain this distinction has marred a great deal of Marxist analysis of the character of capitalist relations, particularly in bourgeois democracies. Proletarians are legally free to leave the employ of one capitalist and to go to work for another. The fact that many individual workers do so all the time merely confirms to the proletarians as well as to everyone else that this freedom exists.

Proletarians are also perfectly free to take leave of their class position and become petty capitalists, any time they are able to do so. A trickle of upwardly mobile proletarians is forever proving that this freedom exists as well. It is in the nature of market freedoms that they engender a spontaneous confusion between legal prerogatives and the capacity to exercise them.

The apologists of the bourgeoisie are quick to collapse the exercise of this prerogative into its formal right (i.e., "free enterprise"). This is no reason for Marxists to counter reductively by collapsing the second into the first (i.e., terming these freedoms "a sham"). Since the market prerogative of the proletariat is a defining condition of this class, in relation to all other labouring classes in world history, it is somewhat ironic to find Marxists treating this prerogative as illusory.

Although the proletarian condition is formally an open one, the great mass of this class cannot escape its class position even though, as individuals, they are free to try. They are kept anonymously in their place by the impersonal discipline of the market, because they calculate, accurately, that if they quit their present jobs they would not be able to secure more favourable ones; they are held beneath their bosses' authority by means of their own appreciation of the chances of securing alternative employment. This establishes an intimate link between the anonymous discipline of the market and the personal authority of the boss, exercised on the job. The existence of the reserve army of the unemployed, actively seeking work, is thus an integral component of the proletarian condition, since it permits employed labour to be firmly held within the grip of capital while being legally free to leave at any time.

The first freedom of the proletarian condition (employer choice) sets up the second. For if this particular labouring class will come on its own to be exploited by particular employers, then it can be released to live on its own in the interval between the periods of its exploitation. Because of this, the bourgeoisie has no need to preside directly over the proletariat when it is not labouring in capitalist production. The specific form of subsistence autonomy that the proletariat achieves is thus the second distinguishing characteristic of this labouring class vis-à-vis other labouring classes in world history.

As with the first, this second freedom is predicated upon the same bedrock compulsion to return to work for capital. The nature of that work determines a great deal about how workers can use their "leisure" time. The hours of work dictate the intervals between shifts; the character of the job determines the way in which workers' labour power is exhausted and therefore the way in which it must be refurbished, etc. This then sets the outer practical limits of the worker's free market choice in subsistence. A worker may live wherever she/he pleases, but the location must be convenient to her/his place of wage work. A worker can do whatever she/he pleases in her/his own time (eat and drink what she/he pleases, sleep when she/he wants, etc.), but she/he had better be able to work the next shift, up to the employer's standards, or risk being fired.

Both the first and the second proletarian freedoms are ones of personal choice for individual members of that class. (The class as a collective group has no choice at all, except to rise up and expropriate the capitalists, to put an end to its peculiar form of bondage.) These individual choices matter a great deal to workers. They have *no choice* but to be vitally concerned with the choices they must make as proletarians. This is why it is hopelessly abstract and sectarian for socialists to deride non-socialist workers for the energy they invest in thinking about and exercising these options. The root to collective proletarian action must proceed *through* the individual insecurity workers experience concerning their personal situations and their desire to seek collective redress. Solidarity that is rooted in the experience of the proletarian masses finds its soil in large part in the myriad of their personal insecurities, which are held in common, but not often shared. It is equally abstract and futile to appeal only to those insecurities and injustices which are generated by wage work. A great deal of the personal anxiety that workers suffer is based upon the other half of the proletarian equation—insecurities on the home front. And this is precisely where the question of women's oppression and proletarian insecurity intersect.

The Character of Proletarian Possession of the Means of Subsistence

I have maintained that the proletariat not only gains access to but actually gains ownership rights over the means of its personal subsistence. This possession is the normal condition of the regular appearance of labour power in the labour market. The personal ownership of labour power and the private means of subsistence must be materially linked if the proletariat is to live and work in a stable condition. The proletariat, while a propertyless class in the first instance, becomes a privately propertied class in the means of its subsistence, by securing a regular wage income and establishing with it a regular private household domicile.[37] This property condition is a very peculiar and tenuous one. I want to specify its limits here.

The first limit is that it is entirely conditional upon securing regular employment and regular wage income. This is why the wage *must* be the first form of proletarian subsistence. Without it, the second form (consumer goods) cannot be obtained, and the third form (the household), established through previous labour, will soon fall into jeopardy. The commodity labour power is never sold once and for all. It must be sold over and over again. Consistency in this repetition is the precondition to maintaining private property in the means of subsistence.

When proletarians are thrown out of work for more than a brief period, they become dependent upon some form of state subsistence to maintain access to consumer goods. But the price of this wage-replacement is a partial loss of their domicile rights to privacy. The state's agents (social workers, welfare officials, etc.) can now enter their premises; and the refusal to admit them may result in termination of support. Thus, the second proletarian freedom–to conduct one's private life as one sees fit–is undermined. Now the welfare officer makes a legal state intervention into the sphere of private subsistence. Similarly, the first proletarian freedom is also undermined. Unemployment insurance officers may now coerce individuals into the arms of particular employers, forcing them to take certain jobs or risk having their benefits cut off. These are unmistakable encroachments, by the state, upon the proletarian prerogative to sell its labour power in a free market.

Despite the fact that in the twentieth century, a larger and larger percentage of the total population of capitalist countries finds itself divorced from the means of production, this great proletarian mass has been continuously shedding peripheral populations which are no longer wholly sustained by means of the private wage. Increasingly the aged, the sick, the unemployed and youth have become, to one degree or another, dependent upon state subsidization for their subsistence, a diminishing proportion of which is covered by the take-home pay of the private wage. The absolute swelling of the proletariat's ranks has thus been accompanied by a steady shrinkage in the size of the average household unit and a decreasing capacity of the proletarian wage to cover non-waged dependents, especially if they do not labour usefully in the home. These non-waged sections of the proletarian mass are thus losing, to one degree or another, the proletarian prerogative of private subsistence.

While private ownership of the means of subsistence is a necessary condition for the stable reproduction of proletarian labour power under capitalism, this linkage never becomes an identity. The reserve army of labour loses effective ownership of the means of private subsistence and becomes state-dependent, but it nevertheless must remain in possession of its capacity to labour usefully for capital. State subsidization of the unemployed mass is therefore designed to prevent the use value of its labour power from deteriorating too much, allowing it to remain competitive with the employed labour force. At the same time, this support must not be so large as to reduce the internally experienced proletarian compulsion to seek employment. The state must subsidize the reserve army just so much and no more. The minimum and maximum levels within which it must manoeuvre are historically determined variables, requiring continuous fine-tuning by state authorities.[38]

One of the difficulties in analyzing the private property rights of the proletariat is that we are steeped in a powerful tradition of bourgeois thought that treats property rights as absolutes. Within this framework, the question, "Does the proletariat own private property in the means of subsistence? " can only be answered "Yes" or "No."

But this is a completely false and reified conception of property. Private property forms express the prerogatives of different parties within conflicted social relations. They are therefore always relative to the forces expressed through these social relations. In stable periods, established property rights may go largely uncontested and therefore appear absolute, but they are always conditional upon the capacity of the owner to maintain and enforce them.

The formal symmetry of the bourgeoisie and the proletariat in relation to their private property should thus be appreciated. Marx emphasized one side of their juridical equality—both were commodity *owners* who met in the marketplace as equals. We are now in a position to add another dimension of formal equality—both are *owners* of private means of subsistence. While the materially pivotal private property in capitalist society is property in the means of production, the ideologically pivotal property form is private property in the means of subsistence. The latter acts as the general multi-class cover for the former. The vast majority of the bourgeoisie own their own homes (often several), while the majority of workers rent accommodation; both are nevertheless entitled to the private possession of their domiciles. The effect of this formal symmetry in obscuring class divisions is considerable. The household is the one genuinely *mass* unit of private property in capitalist society, and the only form which is broadly popular among the working class.

The desire among working people to become home-owners is often considered to be a desire for upward mobility and status, but it is also, just as importantly, a need for living space, security and stability which rental accommodation usually does not afford.[39]

The struggle of proletarians to constitute, maintain and enhance their private property in the means of subsistence is thus a permanent one. It is a constant battle to maintain wage income at a rate and a regularity sufficient to sustain a grasp on private property. The fact that a great proportion of the wage is spent on immediate consumables, as opposed to consumer durables, insures that the viability of the private living unit, should its regular income be curtailed, will be short-lived. This proletarian insecurity has not been ended by "the age of affluence." The contemporary level of unemployment is staggering. It is true that unemployment insurance, savings and credit provisions provide a cushion today that did not exist in the nineteenth century; but it is also true that it is more difficult now than it was a century ago to intensify domestic labour for direct use or initiate entrepreneurial income-producing activities "on the side" in order to compensate for lost wage income.

In conclusion, there is a proletarian form of private property in the means of subsistence, gained by means of the wage and domestic labour combined. Only those sections of the proletarian mass which are able to secure a regular wage income can sustain it and it is a profoundly tenuous form of private possession and property right. It is not internally self-generating. It does not accumulate a savings fund of any description. It is unconvertible (with occasional exceptions) into entrepreneurial forms of property.

Nevertheless, having underlined its fragility, it would be a mistake to deny its material reality as a private property form. For this has real consequences within the proletariat in engendering conflict between breadwinners and dependents, home-owners and tenants, ethnic groups by neighbourhood, etc. In a society in which all social power is ultimately based upon private property, property differences within the proletariat are critical factors in generating its internal stratification. The distribution of household property is highly unequal within the working class–it is owned mainly by men and not by women; by wage workers and not by their dependents; by the top half of the working class (steadily employed) and barely, or not at all, by the bottom layers and the lumpen proletariat; by indigenous strata and not by immigrants and racial minorities. The implications of all such asymmetries for the divisions of the working class require further investigation. In the next section I will address the male-female relation as it pertains to the wage and to household property.

Patriarchy and The Working-Class Family

So far I have been attempting to delineate the class boundaries of proletarian subsistence. In this chapter I want to begin to analyze the mainstream patterns of subsistence which have congealed within these limits for the majority of proletarians in developed capitalist societies.

In moving from limits to norms, we are shifting from one level of analysis to another; we are moving off the plane of the capitalist mode of production, conceived in abstraction, apart from other major determinations which operate in capitalist societies. From the sexless and epochal abstraction of the capitalist mode of production, we are now moving toward the sexist and historically periodized concrete of developed capitalist societies. We are moving from the household, conceived as a necessary part of the capitalist mode of production, to the nuclear family, the predominant form for recruitment to and maintenance of private households.[40]

But before proceeding, let us review what has been established thus far at the conceptual level of the capitalist mode of production. We have established: (a) the necessity of the private household domicile as the primary site of the daily reproduction of labour power which is consumed externally in return for the monetary wage which funds this domestic unit; (b) the effective possession of and entitlement to household property by the regular wage earner; (c) the necessity of private domestic labour conducted within this unit on a daily basis, to organize the household and to convert the money wage into the immediate consumables of personal subsistence for all household members—the necessity, therefore, of the double day of labour.

Within each of these parameters we have *not* established the following three mainstream patterns: (a) the nuclear family form that normally constitutes the private household units of the working class, the co-residence of married couples and their legitimate offspring; (b) the fact that men overwhelmingly own household property and exercise the accompanying prerogatives of being househeads (above all, the ultimate control over the family budget); (c) the fact that women, overwhelmingly, do the domestic labour which privately reproduces the next generation of proletarians and which keeps most working households functioning.

In sum, it is the particular form of patriarchal family relations prevalent in capitalist social formations which has not been and cannot be established solely at the level of the capitalist mode of production.

In all periods of capitalist development, minority subsistence arrangements have been sustained among the proletarian masses: single parent households (mostly female); single persons living alone or in groups with other single people and doing their own housework; unmarried couples; couples who remain childless by choice; couples who share the domestic labour more or less equally; women who own household property and genuinely control their household's income, etc. In all of these cases the people involved are able to fulfill their proletarian duties, and they remain exploitable by capital. It is not easy to live in these ways. For the majority it is preferable to take the path of least societal resistance, to get married and establish nuclear family households. But one can live as a proletarian against the grain of its subsistence norms. Nothing in the capitalist mode of production excludes it.

In the present period various minority household arrangements are growing and, proportionally, majority family norms are weakening. While this "crisis of the family" certainly places serious strains on capitalist societies, it does not violate the relations of capitalist production nor halt the accumulation of capital. Today we see the ranks of the proletariat swell, as its mainstream family forms weaken. We will be unable to comprehend the various effects of this family crisis on the overall stability of capitalist social formations unless we comprehend *both* the linkages of the nuclear family form to capitalist production relations and the genuine leeway these relations provide the proletariat in developing alternative arrangements.

I do not deny the vital reinforcement which the capitalist mode of production gives to the patriarchal family norm— in fact, in this chapter, I want to investigate several ways in which this reinforcement takes place. But I do insist that the way in which private capital harnesses, consumes and releases labour power does not uniformly impose the patriarchal family on the ranks of the proletariat. Therefore, the concept of the capitalist mode of production is not sufficient to explain it. To simply derive patriarchal relations from this concept would be to seriously overreach its explanatory power and, in the process, to oversimplify and to collapse into one the many determinations which comprise the concrete structures of capitalist societies.[41]

The absence of patriarchy in the concept of the capitalist mode of production is considered by many feminists to be a fatal flaw in Marxism. In all capitalist societies without exception, after all, women are systematically subordinated. Surely Marxism should be able to reflect this material reality in its fundamental concept of capitalist society.[42]

This kind of argument displays two idealist misconceptions that are also shared, not coincidentally, by many Marxists: (a) that the workings of a society as complex as modern capitalism are ultimately reducible to a single core determination, which can thus be reflected theoretically in a single (albeit complex) concept; (b) that the acid test in the dialectic between the abstract and the concrete in a system of thought is located at the point of its highest abstraction.

Marx touches on both these problems in the following passage from the *Grundrisse:*

> The concrete is concrete because it is the concentration of many determinations, hence unity of the diverse. It appears in the pro-

> cess of thinking, therefore, as a process of concentration; as a result, not as a point of departure, even though it is the point of departure and hence also the point of departure for observation and conception.[43]

Capitalist society (in the concrete) is a concentration of many determinations. These determinations are irreducible; the unity of their result is therefore complex—a unity of the diverse. The concrete whole cannot be adequately reflected by means of a single conceptual abstraction—mode of production—however well elaborated. The point of departure for observation and conception must reflect many determinations if it is to approach an adequate conception of the concrete society under investigation. The mode of production concept, however pivotal, cannot be expected to carry the explanatory load for every important feature of life in capitalist social formations. To suppose that it can, or should, is theoretically unilateral and idealist.

The capitalist mode of production is not merely a concept, of course. It is an immense material force, active in the development of capitalist societies. Its effects are pervasive and overriding. But this does not obliterate the action of other powerful determinations, such as patriarchal relations.

Patriarchy, as well, has a pervasive impact in capitalist societies. It, too, must be analyzed in its historical specificity. From a materialist standpoint, the nature of the phenomenon under study ultimately conditions the methods and concepts of its appropriation in thought. Patriarchy thus requires methods and concepts which are particular to its nature as a phenomenon. Their development will require sustained historical study and theoretical reflection, which has only just begun.

The term "patriarchy" has been used in many different ways in feminist studies.[44] My own use of the term here will be relatively restricted, and, I hope, precise. It will by no means capture all of the dimensions of women's social subordination in class societies, but it will focus on what I consider to be the core determination of that subordination in the family.

Patriarchy, for me, refers to a system of male househeadship based on the domination, in the family household, of the father/husband over the mother/wife and the resident children. It is founded upon three intimately coupled, material cornerstones:(a) effective possession of, entitlement to and ultimate disposal rights over family property, including income, on a daily and/or an intergenerational basis; (b) supervision of the labour of other family members; (c) conjugal rights of sexual access to and possession of one's spouse in marriage and custodial rights over children.

One of the cornerstones of historical materialism, as developed by Marx and Engels, was the association of property forms with the division of labour and hierarchy and power in social relations. Thus, they noted a connection in pre-capitalist households between patrilineal property inheritance and the direct control and supervision of the labour process of the family by the father/husband. The loss of this property prerogative within the new-born proletariat—as a function of its divorce from the means of production—was thus accompanied, symmetrically, by the loss of direct supervisory control over domestic labour, as men were forced to absent themselves from the household for long periods every day to work elsewhere for wages. And, after a brief transitional phase of family hiring, women's work outside the home was also no longer under the control of their husbands and fathers.

Marx and Engels saw the English working-class family in the mid-nineteenth century to be in serious crisis, close to collapse. They perceived its turmoil to be partly rooted in the breakdown of the former patriarchal stability of the pre-capitalist household and partly in the demands of modern industry for female labour. As the old household's property form had been eroded, its interior authority relations had become unhinged.

I find this appreciation to be essentially valid—as far as it went. What Marx and Engels concluded from this was, however, profoundly mistaken. They thought that the proletariat, as a propertyless class, was incapable of re-establishing a material (property) foundation for durable patriarchal domination within the family in the bourgeois epoch. Marx writes in the *Communist Manifesto*, for example:

> The proletarian is without property; his relation to his wife and children has no longer anything in common with the bourgeois family relations.[45]

Patriarchy therefore remains, in Marx and Engels' conception, a relic amongst the proletariat, sustained ideologically by the accumulated muck—to use their term—of past epochs. As Engels comments in *The Origin of the Family, Private Property and the State*:

> The last remnants of male domination in the proletarian home have lost all foundation—except perhaps for some of that brutality towards women which became firmly rooted with the establishment of monogamy.[46]

Marx and Engels thought, therefore, that the patriarchal household was destined to wither away with women's mass entry into socialized production, despite resistance among male workers, which would perhaps be tenacious for a period. How wrong this appreciation has proven to be!

There were two decisive errors here. In the first place, Marx did not anticipate (although he theoretically allowed for it) that male wages could be raised sufficiently (while capital continued to accumulate at a viable pace) to permit any significant percentage of working-class families to withdraw women from the labour market for prolonged periods. He thought the spread of modern industry involved the irreversible replacement of male with female labour power. He therefore did not anticipate the subsequent development of the single male family wage which could stabilize the sexual division of labour and consolidate the domestic housewife role as a "natural" vocation.

Marx and Engels also made a key theoretical error in their conceptualization of the modern proletariat which led to this erroneous prediction. They thought that because this class was propertyless in the first instance—hence its compulsion to sell its labour power—it remained in a propertyless condition upon securing a regular wage income. In this sense they failed to clarify the differentiation which emerges with the formation of the proletariat between property in the means of production and property in the means of subsistence.

And, because the transfer of household property through marriage and inheritance no longer played much of a role in the working class, they reasoned that there was no material basis for the continuation of any form of private property in this class, nor for the durability of patriarchal dominance in the working-class family. Engels writes in *Origins*:

> But here [among the proletariat] all the foundations of classical monogamy are removed. Here there is a complete absence of all property for the safeguarding and inheritance of which monogamy and male domination were established. Therefore, there is no stimulus whatever here to assert male domination.[47]

Engels here ignores the formation of household property among the modern proletariat. While regular wage income did not permit the vast majority of working-class households to establish a viable means of production (and thus to escape the proletarian condition), it did permit them to stabilize the private property household, owned and controlled by the primary breadwinner. This ownership was the concrete material basis upon which the domination of the husband/father, as the househead, could be reasserted over the disposal of the household's resources and the conditions of his wife's domestic labour. We thus have, with the rise of the modern proletariat, the eventual consolidation of a new form of household property (contingent upon the regular sale of labour power) and a new mode of patriarchal domination. I have termed the latter "breadwinner power."

But before exploring the specific nature of patriarchal domination in the proletarian family, it will be useful to obtain a clearer picture of the historical contrast between the fully proletarian family household and its typical peasant and proto-industrial predecessor. The pre-capitalist household in Western Europe tended to be characterized by the following.

1. There was a highly variable mixture of production for direct use and production for sale. There was also an absence of a strict sexual division of labour between these two labour-sets, although there was a tendency for men to work more intensely on production for sale. And, since women combined goods production with family maintenance tasks directly on site, domestic labour was an embedded and intertwined component of the family's total labour process.

2. Wage income was not the principal means of subsistence for the majority of households. External employment was on a seasonal, irregular and day-labour basis. Payment was often partially in kind and employment arranged through social networks in the community and not through an open labour market.

3. Production within the household was of the manufacturing type—hand and foot-powered tools, natural fuels, hand-drawn water, etc. State-supplied infrastructure was absent or absolutely primitive.

4. From the age of about six on, children were expected to work as part of the household team, and by the time they were adolescents, their economic contribution to the household would normally cover their own upkeep.

5. Apprenticeship and property inheritance both played important roles in differentiating the occupational destinies of offspring from one generation to the next. Both skill and property transmission were generally based on principles of patrilineage and primogeniture, with girls and later-born receiving inferior portions of the household's lot, if they were lucky enough to receive anything at all.

6. The labour-intensive household unit generally contained, at one point or another in its life cycle, relatives and non-relatives beyond the immediate two-generation nuclear family. These people performed indispensable labour roles during the time of their residence.

By contrast, the fully proletarian household, in its mature form, is characterized by the following.

1. With the absence of production of goods for sale, labour in the household is reduced to the strict conversion of wage goods into the daily and generational reproduction of the family member's labour power, fit for sale and consumption outside the household. Domestic labour therefore emerges as a separate, distinct labour-set. Women do not normally combine it with revenue-producing labours in the household; and men, basing themselves on the legitimacy of their breadwinner role, do not normally do much housework at all. The household becomes, for them, the primary site of their leisure time, and their work is now located outside the home.

2. There is a near-total reliance on wage income in money form as the means of acquiring goods necessary for the subsistence of household members. This, therefore, necessitates regular year-round employment for the primary male breadwinner, and supplementary employment, on a less sustained basis, for the female wife/mother. Since conditions in the labour market are critical for the household, the industrial business cycle, as opposed to the seasonal agricultural cycle, becomes pivotal to family fortunes and fluctuations in labour intensity.

3. Subsistence goods are increasingly commoditized; the scope for the working-up of raw materials into domestic products within the household is reduced to a minimum. Baking, gardening, cloth and clothes-making, preserve preparation, etc., all have been largely replaced by commodities purchased with the wage. In addition, the scope for supplementing family wage income by means of selling goods or services in the immediate neighbourhood has virtually disappeared. The taking-in of laundry, of boarders etc., for a fee is largely ended, and door-to-door junk dealers, knife sharpeners, fruit sellers, etc. are largely past history, along with the corner grocery store. In all of these ways, the proletarian (wage) basis of the household's livelihood is purified. The substantive tasks of household

maintenance (washing, cleaning, cooking) are now accomplished through the use of machines and power tools, and the urban residence is supplied by a state infrastructure of serviced land with electricity, running water, flush toilets, telephones, etc.

4. The household unit is normally constituted by a couple and their children. Neither relatives, domestics nor boarders normally reside with them. This unit, on average, has two children, reproducing itself on a simple replacement basis.

5. The children will be an economic drain on the household through their entire stay in it. As soon as they become productive economically, they will leave and set up households on their own. Nor will they be constrained or expected to support their parents once they leave, through wage remission or any other reliable support mechanism. Obversely, inheritance is negligible and property inheritance and skill apprenticeship will not play a significant role in determining occupational position or the future living standards of children within the working class.[48]

The fully proletarian nuclear family household, whose profile I have sketched out here, was by no means an immediate or automatic byproduct of the industrial revolution and the initial appearance of the mass factory proletariat. This family form was gradually consolidated and its pre-capitalist features shed, one by one, for a full century and a half after the first wave of mass proletarianization. In the developed capitalist countries, the industrial sector led the socioeconomic revolution and the transformation of the household sphere lagged behind. It took a century and a half in these countries for the sphere of proletarian subsistence to come into full congruence with the sphere of capitalist industry. Such is the uneven and combined "progress" of the bourgeois revolution.

The first shocking impact of the industrial revolution on the fledgling proletariat was to break the back of its old patriarchal households. As the full logic of private production for profit was unleashed in the burgeoning factory system, all aspects of family life were thrown into chaos. Marx comments in *Capital*:

> Modern industry, in overturning the economic foundation on which was based the traditional family, and the family labour corresponding to it, had also unloosened all traditional family ties.[49]

In *The Condition of the Working Class in England,* Engels graphically depicts the squalor and turmoil of proletarian living conditions that resulted from the boundless appetite of private capital for the exploitation of labour in the factories and its complete indifference to the imperatives of the double day of proletarian labour, especially as it affected women with nursing infants. There was nothing internal to the logic of capital accumulation that ensured the stable reproduction by the proletariat of a future generation of able-bodied, exploitable labour power. The unfettered drive of private capital to maximize profit was a short-term drive, and by its very nature made industrial capitalists remarkably short-sighted. Engels shows how the demands of private capital (as yet unchecked by state legislation in the long-term interests of capitalist reproduction, or by the effective resistance of the organized working class) were actively disintegrating the working class family, and ruining its members' health.

> The employment of women at once breaks up the family; for when the wife spends twelve or thirteen hours every day in the mill, and the husband works the same length of time there or elsewhere, what becomes of the children? They grow up like wild weeds; they are put to nurse for a shilling or eighteenpence a week, and how they are treated may be imagined. Hence the accidents to which little children fall victims multiply in the factory districts to a terrible extent. . . . That the general mortality among young children must be increased by the employment of the mothers is self-evident, and is placed beyond all doubt by notorious facts. Women often return to the mill three or four days after confinement, leaving the baby, of course; in the dinner-hour they must hurry home to feed the child and eat something, and what sort of suckling that can be is also evident.[50]

The traditional basis of patriarchal authority in the family was also upset by the demands of capital for adult female (and child) labour. Thus Engels also recounts:

> In many cases the family is not wholly dissolved by the employment of the wife, but turned upside down. The wife supports the family, the husband sits at home, tends the children, sweeps the room and cooks. This case happens very frequently; in Manchester alone, many hundred such men could be cited, condemned to domestic occupations. It is easy to imagine the wrath aroused among the working men by this reversal of all relations within the family, while the other social conditions remain unchanged.[51]

He then tells the pathetic tale of an unemployed working man who is discovered by his mate doing housework. A more poignant portrait of the devastating psychological consequences of sex-role reversal on the male ego can scarce be imagined:

> He found him in a miserable, damp cellar, scarcely furnished . . . there sat poor Jack near the fire and . . . mended his wife's stockings with the bodkin; and as soon as he saw his old friend at the doorpost, he tried to hide them. But Joe . . . had seen it, and said, "Jack, what the devil art thou doing? Where is the missus? Why is that thy work?" And poor Jack was ashamed and said, "No, I know this is not my work, but my poor missus is i' th' factory; she has to leave by half-past five and works till eight at night, and then she is so knocked up that she cannot do aught when she gets home, so I have to do everything for her what I can, for I have no work, nor had any for more than three years and I shall never have any more work while I live"; and then he wept a big tear. . . . Jack again said, "There is work enough for women folks and childer hereabout but none for men."[52]

At the end of this tale, Engels waxes as indignant as Jack's mate Joe had been at this "insane state of things—this condition which unsexes the man and takes from the woman all womanliness, without being able to bestow upon the man true womanliness, or the woman true manliness—this condition which degrades, in the most shameful way, both sexes and through them, Humanity . . ."[53]

But Engels is too penetrating a thinker to abandon this train of thought at the limit of his own offended bourgeois-humanitarian morality. Momentarily transcending the limits of his time and culture, he asks himself an eminently feminist question: "If this complete reversal of traditional sex roles was degrading to men, as it certainly was to poor Jack, then was not the traditional pattern equally degrading to women?"

He answers:

> We must admit that human society has hitherto sought salvation in a false direction; we must admit that so total a reversal of the position of the sexes can have come to pass only because the sexes have been placed in a false position from the beginning. If the reign of the wife over the husband, as inevitably brought about by the factory system, is inhuman, the pristine rule of the husband over the wife must have been inhuman too. If the wife can now base her supremacy upon the fact that she supplies the greater part, nay, the whole of the common possession, the necessary inference is that this community of possession is no true and rational one, since one member of the family boast offensively of contributing the greater share. If the family of our present society is being thus dissolved, this dissolution merely shows that, at bottom, the binding tie of this family was not family affection, but private interest lurking under the cloak of a pretended community of possessions.[54]

Engels was wrong here in projecting the preference of factory employers for female labour as a dominant trend of the future, but he nevertheless achieves, through inverting the sex roles, a remarkable insight into the reign of the husband over the wife in a situation where he is the sole or primary breadwinner. The breadwinner's claim "to supply the greater part, nay, the whole of the common possession," permits him to "boast offensively of contributing the greater share." This is precisely the material basis of "the private interest lurking under the cloak of a pretended community of possessions"–of what I have termed "breadwinner power" in the working-class family.

In *Origin of the Family*, Engels confines this insight strictly to the propertied classes.

> The modern, individual family is based on the open or disguised domestic enslavement of the woman; and modern society is a mass composed solely of individual families as its molecules. Today, in the great majority of cases, the man has to be the earner, the breadwinner of the family, at least among the propertied classes, and this gives him a dominating position which requires no special legal privileges. In the family, he is the bourgeois and the wife represents the proletariat.[55]

As regards the proletariat, however, he rejects this analysis. He assumes that the general entry of working-class women into wage labour rules out the consolidation of a situation of primary breadwinners:

> Since large-scale industry has transferred the woman from the house to the labour market and the factory, and makes her, often enough, the breadwinner of the family, the last remnants of male domination in the proletarian home have lost all foundation—except perhaps for some of that brutality towards women which became firmly rooted with the establishment of monogamy.[56]

With the advantage of historical hindsight, it is clear that Engels and Marx were wrong on this. The patriarchal form of the working-class family, based upon the male prerogatives of the primary breadwinner role, was eventually stabilized in the latter part of the nineteenth and the early part of the twentieth centuries in Western Europe and North America.

The specific timing and modalities of this consolidation varied, of course, from one country to another. But at the risk of some overgeneralization, we can identify the following confluence of forces prevailing in the class struggle to bring about this stability.

The more far-sighted sections of the bourgeoisie, particularly those who were not industrialists, became acutely conscious of the volatile instability of the "lower orders," resulting from the unfettered and chaotic exploitation of the industrial proletariat and the mass unemployment of adult males. Marx notes the beginnings of these concerns, raised by liberal philanthropists in the ruling class, in the struggle over the English Factory Acts at mid-century.[57] This impulse was given concrete and practical direction by the burgeoning ranks of the social science professionals—doctors, social workers, educators, public health officers, etc., who were located in the state apparatus and in the growing middle-class professional strata.[58]

And, from below, the organized labour movement was fast becoming a force to be reckoned with, exerting considerable pressure for legislative reforms to bring the exploitation of labour in industry under control. The industrial capitalists, for their part, had always resisted these encroachments on the sacred terrain of their private property, and they continued to do so. But they did so with less tenacity than before because the hump of the primitive accumulation of capital by labour extensive (absolute surplus value) means was now on the verge of being surmounted. In the 1860s in England, as Marx recounts, the industrialists responded to the Factory Acts by accelerating their conversion to capital intensive production methods (relative surplus value) and they did so without slackening the pace of capital accumulation.[59]

The legislative results of this conjunction of class forces varied from one country to another. Generally, they included the following: (a) legislation curbing child labour and limiting adult female labour; a limit to the normal working day (twelve, later ten and then eight hours); minimal health standards and working conditions in industry; (b) a rationalization of welfare provisions placed under full state control, designed to buttress the family, regulate the poor and continually reconstitute a competitive reserve army of labour; and (c) the provision of compulsory universal public schooling.

The consolidation of a stable, patriarchal family unit in the ranks of the proletariat (or, more precisely, in its upper half) was brought about by these types of political initiatives in the developed capitalist countries. They dovetailed well with the economic crystallization of a sexual division of labour in the better organized ranks of the industrial proletariat—wherein husbands became primary breadwinners, regularly employed, "good providers" to their families; and their wives became predominantly homemakers, "good mates" to their husbands, "good mothers" to their children, working outside the home only occasionally and rarely through their child-bearing years.

There were substantial material gains made by the working class in this period of reversion to a predominant single wage, in comparison with the chaotic and brutal conditions of the working class in the earlier period of the industrial revolution. And, it was surely a relief to those married women who could afford it, not to have to try to combine their family household duties with long and exhausting hours of unsafe factory work or poorly-paid domestic service.

But overall, and in the long run, the labour movement's victory in the fight for a single "living" family wage must be considered to be a Pyrrhic one by socialists concerned with the unification of the proletariat's ranks in life and struggle.[60] In the first place, the single family wage only became a viable proposition for the best organized, highest paid sections of the working class. Among these strata it entrenched the primacy of women's core domestic role and celebrated it as a natural and decent arrangement. It brought the sexual division of labour in this strata of the working class into formal symmetry with middle and upper-class households, laying the groundwork for a powerful conservative ideological bloc in favour of "preserving normal family life," against the poor strata of the working class who could not maintain it. For a large minority of women–single, divorced or deserted or whose husbands were unemployed, sick or at the bottom of the pay scale–their abstention from the labour market for a lengthy period was economically untenable. There was something vaguely "indecent" about these "working women," particularly those who were married.

The single-wage family system has collapsed in the second half of the twentieth century. The proletarian compulsion to sell one's labour power at the best price available has now pushed masses of married women onto the labour market, making "working women" the norm for the working class as a whole, rather than the practice of a suspect minority.

In the process, however, the contradiction of the double day of labour has become manifest. The problems of combining full-time wage work with domestic responsibilities are creating acute dilemmas for masses of women. Swelling numbers are opting to "resolve" this contradiction by delaying, reducing or curtailing altogether the demands of stay-at-home motherhood. At the same time, they are beginning to demand wage rates on a par with men in order to secure their economic independence out from under the subsidies of their husbands' pay cheques.

The structural primacy of women's domestic role is thus coming under attack by women themselves. Forced to choose, increasing numbers are opting to minimize the demands of motherhood. Falling birth rates (now at or below the replacement level), rising divorce rates, the growth of single parenthood—all of these indicators register the demographic dimensions of this change in the sexual division of labour. The anchors of this division, as I have analyzed them, were consolidated in the first half of the twentieth century, in the core role couplet of housewife/mother and husband/breadwinner. Both are now crumbling; not rapidly, for there are few attractive alternative models in sight, but slowly and irreversibly just the same. The implication of these changes for the future lies well beyond the scope of this paper. Suffice it to say that I think they will be both protracted and revolutionary.

Proletarianization and the Domestic Revolution

House cleaning, clothes washing, cooking, infant and husband care—these domestic tasks certainly did not originate with capitalism. They were typically women's work long before the bourgeois revolution, as they have continued to be afterward. This has given the whole context in which women do housework an appearance of continuity in the transition from the late feudal to the capitalist epoch. This, I will argue, is highly deceptive.

Among the feminist historians of women's work experience, a continuity thesis is widely held. Thus, Theresa McBride writes:

> Industrialization did not immediately disrupt the pattern of the family working together as a unit of production. Clearly, the family economy, to which all members contributed their earnings, remained as strong as ever and women, whether as wife or daughter, continued to assume a major part of the family's economic responsibilities.[61]

Mary McDougall echoes this appreciation:

> The one generalization we can safely make is that the powerfully corrosive and creative forces of industrialization had surprisingly little impact on most women's work and lives. Fundamental changes in the mode of production created more outside employment, but only for a minority, or more correctly, for young women.[62]

This perception misses the forest for the trees. In focussing on the *immediate* period of the industrial revolution and the short-term effects upon women's labour within that conjuncture, McBride and McDougall ignore the delayed impact of the industrial revolution on women's labour experience and the *revolutionary* transformation it eventually engendered in the material foundation of the household unit.

These authors note, of course, that the industrial revolution removed commodity goods production from the household sphere. I grant that this did not happen all at once, but very unevenly over a century and a half. Yet it is profoundly mistaken to perceive the household unit as a half-emptied shell still standing intact on its pre-capitalist foundations.[63] For the revolution in the mode of production did not merely "remove" certain functions from the household sphere; it *revolutionized* the material basis of the household form itself. Just as the proletariat was a new labouring class in world history with a new and distinct relation to production, so was its characteristic mode of subsistence new and distinct, once the bourgeois revolution had worked its way through this backward sphere of the old economy.

Compared to the transformation in industry, the revolution in the private household sphere was gradual. But the pace of change is not the decisive distinction between evolution and revolution. Far more critical is the fact that the bourgeois revolution *ended* a prior set of household relations within which most women had worked, and, after an immense period of protracted transition (which witnessed a bewildering array of hybrid forms, combining elements of the old with the new), a new household form emerged.

Through the revolution in the mode of production, the circumstances in which women performed their domestic labour were altered profoundly. Five facets of the "domestic revolution" stand out.

1. *The Sexual Division of Labour.* The process of capitalist industrialization struck working men and women, in their vast majorities, very differently. It increased the divergence of their work experience in both a locational and a social-relational sense.

The work team within which most men and women laboured diverged dramatically as the spread of the capitalist mode of production divorced goods production from household consumption. Within the pre-capitalist family household men and women had quite distinct tasks but, nevertheless, they worked together in the same unit and overlapped and shared a number of tasks. This ended with the industrial revolution. The bulk of men went from labouring in family-based small groups to large-scale production units based on an elaborate division of labour where team members were not selected on a kin or friendship basis by the workers themselves, but according to an impersonal market mechanism and the ultimate decision of the employer.

Most working women proceeded from the same starting point in the opposite direction: from small kin units to even smaller kin units, with practically no division of labour and increasingly solitary working conditions. Here, they were servicing men and children who were less and less working alongside them in the household. This change had a profound effect upon the relations between the sexes within the labouring classes.

2. *Changes in the Nature and Status of Domestic Labour.* With the removal of goods production from the home (both for use and for sale) the residual tasks of housekeeping and family care ceased to be embedded in a larger household economy and now emerged as a distinct and separate task set in a peripheral position in relation to the mainstream of the economy.

The deepening privatization of the household was accompanied by the obfuscation of its labour process. The rise of wage labour as the general and predominant form of labour in society increasingly cast unpaid domestic labour into the shadows. It tended to disappear as "real" work. This constituted a profound alteration in the socially recognized *status* of this work vis à vis other forms of labour.

The division of labour within the firm and departments of the state bureaucracy has undergone a tremendous fragmentation and specialization. In the same period, domestic labour has remained the generalist labour *par excellence*. This difference imbues domestic labour with a curiously static appearance—as if its composite task mix had not changed significantly in the last century. This is deceptive. The impact of electricity and machine appliances on the household maintenance component of women's work in the home has been considerable, and the tasks of cooking, cleaning, washing, etc. have been shortened and eased.

But at the same time, the slack has been taken up through a tremendous intensification of the demands of family members for personal servicing. These are precisely the components of women's work in the home that are least recognized as work. Their intensification does not appear to have added much to women's domestic burden, and, consequently, housework is widely considered to be easier today than it was a century ago. Time budget studies demonstrate, however, that the hours women work in the home have not been reduced significantly in the twentieth century and may well have increased. This is often falsely attributed to the fact that housewives "fill the time available." The "time fillers" are escalating attention to the needs of children and husbands, precisely that dimension of women's work which is most heavily laden with the mystification of being "a labour of love."

3. *The Transformation of the Household into a Leisure-Time Unit.* The removal of all other work from the household leaves the residual labour of the housewife at the centre of a leisure-time unit. Wage labour, under capitalist-time discipline, has

become sharply demarcated from leisure time for male workers. The entire rhythm and ordering of their lives becomes structured around this distinction. In one part of the day they must grit their teeth, defer gratification and work for another. When quitting time arrives, they can stop work and live for themselves. This pattern and all the psychic structures it reinforces is inimical to men's reciprocal participation in housework in their "leisure time."[64]

Domestic labour involves no such work/leisure distinction and the housewife consequently can afford to make none. She works around the clock, involved in a seemingly endless succession of small tasks, replete with interruptions and breaks. And insofar as the vast majority of women, including those who work for wages outside the household, perform domestic labour on a daily basis, they are subject to this peculiarly embedded, undifferentiated work/leisure experience where "a woman's work is never done." This profound difference between the work experience of men and women only comes into sharp counterposition through the protracted process of proletarianization.

One way, of course, of viewing this change is to point out that women's domestic labour has changed less than any other labour in the transition to capitalism, which is quite true. This is the line of argument of a continuity thesis. My inclination is to situate women's domestic labour in relation to men's wage labour and to the changing social relations of men and women as workers. From this vantage point, the fact that women's work experience is still uniquely embedded in their leisure time, while men's has been sharply separated, constitutes a facet of the revolution in the social relations of women's work and in the sexual division of labour.

4. *The Double Day of Labour.* This is, as I showed earlier, a by-product of the development of the capitalist mode of production. On this ground alone, I would argue that the conditions of women's work have been revolutionized. In the pre-capitalist household economy, women were able to combine productive labour with infant care right through their child-

bearing years. Gradually, with the development of capitalism, this became more and more difficult. It was not only the locational separation of industry from the household which complicated the combination of child care and goods production, it was the subsequent development of both spheres which rendered their combination almost impossible. There were several factors at work here:

(a) The working day in the factory became increasingly regimented, as costly machinery and semi-automated production lines commanded the pace of industrial work. The former porosity of the labour process, wherein interruptions and breaks were liberally interspersed with intensive work time, was steadily filled in and supervised. The capitalist labour process mitigated against short-shift scheduling and flexible work team self-organization which could have permitted women caring for infants to continue their participation in industrial work.

(b) With the growth of the cities, residential and industrial areas were regionally segmented so that it became more and more difficult to work for wages close to one's home. Rising transport costs and travel time thus accentuated the original separation of households from industry, complicating the double shift for women.

(c) On the home front, married women were progressively losing their former child-minding assistants—older daughters, their own mothers, aunts, live-in domestics and neighbours. Each household was thrown back on its own resources. The deepening isolation of the nuclear family unit gradually eroded informal neighbourhood and extended kin networks as reliable bases for easing the domestic burden of women in their childbearing and infant-rearing years.[65]

(d) Increasing reliance on wage income to sustain the entire family went hand-in-hand with the commoditization of the means of subsistence. The purchase of commodities in mass retail outlets and their private consumption is an anonymous, isolated, each-household-unto-itself affair.

> The private appropriation of the wage, private commodity purchase, atomized household—the deepening of all of these forms—cuts sharply against cooperative interhousehold labour and resource sharing activities in the residential neighbourhoods of the major urban centres. The deepening privatization of each household thus isolated housewives, pinning them down in their homes in solitary child-minding. This isolation became an important aspect of women's oppression in the twentieth century.

All of the foregoing factors have exacerbated the relation of households to industry and complicated the participation of married women in wage work, particularly in their prime childbearing years. This has become a central contradiction tending to subvert the stable maintenance of the sexual division of labour in the proletarian family household in the latter half of the twentieth century.

5. *The Form of Patriarchy*. Feminists have insisted on emphasizing the perpetuation of patriarchal domination and women's subordination within the family in the bourgeois epoch among *all* social classes. This point is well taken, correcting the erroneous prognostications of Marx and Engels discussed earlier.

The argument concerning the enduring nature of patriarchy from pre-capitalist to fully capitalist societies often obscures, however, the revolution which has occurred *in the way* in which patriarchal domination is sustained within the family household of the working class. It also ignores the class difference in the material basis of this relation of dominance between working-class househeads, who only possess property in their means of subsistence, and those above them, who own property in the means of production.

Most of the pre-capitalist bases of patriarchy were lost when worker/proprietor households lost their means of production. The inheritance prerogative was crippled in the working class and appears today (in the transfer of the male surname through marriage) as a pale reflection of its former patrilineal self. The *direct* supervision of the artisanal master over the joint production of his family was eclipsed as proletarian men were forced to absent themselves from the household for long hours every day to work. Monogamous conjugal rights and parental custodial rights were both continued through marriage, but they have been diluted and relativized. Arising to take the place, in effect, of all of these lost or weakened patriarchal prerogatives has been the new power of the primary breadwinner.

What is the nature of this power? That famous misogynist, J.J. Rousseau, accurately invoked its phenomenal form when he wrote in *Emile*: "Woman, honour your master. He it is who works for you. He it is who gives you bread to eat. This is he!" But what is the material basis of breadwinner power?

In *Capital*, Marx blew one half of the wage form's fetishistic cover—the way it provoked in common sense the mental confusion of labour with labour power, disguising in the process the source of profit in the surplus labour time the worker laboured for free in production. But he failed to uncover the other half of the wage's deception—the disappearance of domestic labour, the forgotten half of the double day of labour.

The wage appears as the payment of the person who works outside the household; it is her/his by legal right and perhaps, more importantly, by common sense; for it is "earned" in wage labour. The double labour condition of the proletariat thus disappears and a single labour is credited monetarily. The payment which will go to replenish the entire household's labour power comes first to a single member, who then, by virtue of the personal form of its appropriation, is able to preside with personal authority over its distribution in the household and its expenditure by other family members.

It is not only the wage, but the commodity labour power which is fetishized in this exchange. For the wage labourer appears independently in the labour market in search of an employer, apparently under her/his own steam and selling her/his own capacity to labour. The socially necessary preparatory labour conducted in the privacy of her/his household disappears in the process.

Domestic labour, overwhelmingly women's labour, is unwaged; lacking the wage as a signifier of work, it becomes insignificant. It does not appear as "real" work. It is not "worth" anything monetarily. It is a "labour of love," with all the attendant mystification that this involved.

The fetishism of the commodity labour power exhibits all of the features of commodity fetishism: a (household) production relation is obscured behind a (labour) market exchange; a finished commodity stands in for the labour process of its creation, its independent appearance is naturalized and legitimated; paid and unpaid labour are confounded; the commodity form becomes invested with the alienated social power of the atomized private producers who stand in its shadow. In this way the value logic of a commodity being exchanged is enforced upon all those (household members) who are dependent upon its sale in order to live. In a situation where male proletarians are the primary breadwinners, the fetishism of the wage and the commodity labour power is turned to patriarchal advantage in the private households of the working class.

In sum, the prerogatives that accrue to the primary breadwinner, by virtue of his personal appropriation of the bulk of the family's income, are basically threefold.

1. He holds an ownership claim over durable and saleable household property purchased with "his" pay cheque. This includes the right to uproot the family household and move it to a new location in order to remain conveniently close to the site of one's employment (which has changed, more and more frequently, in the twentieth century).

2. He has ultimate authority over the wage's distribution and expenditure by family members who remain dependent upon him and his wage in order to live. While the law recognizes the breadwinner's obligation to provide for his dependents, it does not cease to regard him as the owner of his

income, and, as the head of the household, the final arbiter of its proper expenditure.

3. He has absolution from domestic labour on the grounds that he has already discharged his obligation to his wife and children by bringing home his pay cheque. Professing thus to have "done his part," the primary breadwinner is entitled to treat the household as his leisure-time centre for rest and relaxation. And, he has a right to require his wife to serve him in the household as the reciprocal discharge of her obligation to him. Through this service relation, however discreetly it is done, he monitors and supervises the performance of her domestic tasks.

Thus, the double fetishism of the commodity labour power and the wage furnishes a powerful basis for petty male dominance in the proletarian household; furthermore, the enforced dependency of most working-class women upon the wage of their husband becomes a major factor in undermining their capacity to realize the full value of their own labour power on the market.

Taken together, the five changes outlined above constitute a full-blown revolution in the subsistence arrangements of the working class. Once we study the proletariat's birth and development as a class from the standpoint of its reproduction apart from capital, as well as from the more traditional angle of its immediate relations with capital in production, then the full significance of the domestic revolution may be appreciated.

We see a different side of the proletariat's life and struggle when we venture backstage to observe the preparation of the actors for the impending industrial drama. We note the stagehands, labouring busily–repairing a costume here and cueing an actor's entry over there. We see what the audience out front cannot see and was never intended to see. From here, behind the curtain, the play unfolds a little differently, and we notice things we did not see before. Here I merely want to suggest how the "backstage view" of the proletariat's drama with capital will alter our perception of this class, in two important ways.

First, the formation of the modern proletariat can now be seen as a much more protracted, uneven and delayed process than it looked from out front, where the growth of the factory system appeared to produce this class with one immense heave of history. Some of the abbreviated timetables which Marxists mistakenly projected for capitalism's demise in the developed countries of Europe and America are traceable, in part, to this misperception. Today, in "late capitalism," it is earlier than we had supposed. The whole process of industrialization, once we bear in mind the industrialization of the household, is much more drawn out and incomplete than it would otherwise appear.

Secondly, Marx anticipated that the proletariat's ranks would become increasingly homogenous and unified as capitalism developed. The socialization and abstraction of its labour, coupled with the swelling of its ranks (with the extinction of former petit-bourgeois pursuits), pointed in this direction. These estimates were not wrong; they were one-sided. The divisions of the proletariat's ranks were not adequately addressed within the tradition of classical Marxism. If we appreciate the bi-locationality of the proletariat, its household property, its sexual division of labour, its petty male breadwinner hierarchy (not to mention its ethnic, racial, national and occupational divisions), then we can appreciate that the strategic processes of forging proletarian unity are more difficult and complex than classical Marxists generally conceived them to be. How *can* the proletariat's ranks be unified in struggle to win its collective emancipation from the yoke of capital? This is the question I now turn to, in the concluding section of this article.

Conclusion

In the past few decades the single-wage family model has gradually broken down in all of the developed capitalist countries. Married women, in greater numbers, have obtained wage work and contribute more substantially to their household's monetary income. This has weakened the material basis of patriarchal breadwinner power in the working-class family. Women are in a much stronger position today than they were two decades ago to demand that their husbands share domestic duties. Their economic dependency, while still considerable, is less than it once was. If marriage and co-habitation with their husbands becomes intolerable, they are in a better position today than they formerly were to separate, although this is still far from easy. The change is not only economic, of course; the presence and activities of the women's liberation movement have altered the perception of genuine alternatives to the old, restrictive roles of homemaker and wife/mother.

Full equality between the sexes in the working class is clearly utopian under capitalism. Systematic discrimination against women in the labour market is a cornerstone of the overall exploitation of labour by capital. Nor can the working class be insulated from the patriarchal institutions and practices of the ruling class and the state as long as it remains in a subordinate position in society and does not take charge of its own social relations and historic destiny.

But there is room, under capitalism, for a reduction in inequality, an evening up between the sexes in the working class, precisely because the material foundations of patriarchal authority are less entrenched in the proletariat than they are in the bourgeois classes. Take, for example, the interplay between the socialization and the equalization of domestic labour. As more and more married women work for wages and are influenced by the women's liberation movement, they are increasingly demanding quality child care services to ease the burden of the double day of labour. As men find themselves increasingly responsible for the care of children, they begin to become acquainted with the double day of labour themselves, and recognize their own need for child care provision. There is a growing material basis for unity here, which provides the basis for confronting and diminishing the sexist resistance of working-class men.

On the question of equal pay for work of equal value, there is reasonable grounds for guarded optimism as well. The rationale of a living wage for a family of four is breaking down because it no longer reflects reality, even among the bastions of the unionized, industrial proletariat. The initial effect of this erosion is to weaken the legitimacy of the wage demands of these workers. Employers point out that their employees are normally no longer the sole family breadwinners and will not be paid as if they were. But the long-term effect of this situation cuts in the opposite direction. Working-class men begin to have a material stake in the wage rates of their wives, just as wives have always had in the pay of their husbands. The question of organizing women workers in banks and offices, of hiring women in high-wage, exclusively male sectors are both being posed. As the relatively privileged, sectional interest of the organized male bastions of the proletariat erodes, we see ideological evidence of a sexist backlash, combined with the partial reconciliation of formerly antagonized material interests, and the emergence of a small layer of male worker-militants who begin to see the class logic of fighting for women's demands. I do not wish to present this latter tendency in a euphoric fashion, but it would be a serious error to overlook it altogether.

These changes, while they are triggered by the economic shifts I have discussed, will not be realized spontaneously by women's mass entry into socialized production (which, in any case, is grinding to a halt in the present recession). Any residue of complacency on this score, based on a simplistic reading of Engels' *Origin of the Family*, should be firmly repudiated. The relative equalization of women's position within the working class can only be achieved in conscious struggle—led by the women's liberation movement and taken up in the heart of the organized labour movement. The women's movement is the indispensable spearhead of the self-organization of masses of working-class women, acting on the basis of their own needs and with their own demands for justice and equality in all spheres. It has been the pressure of the women's movement, initially outside and now, increasingly, inside the trade unions, that has begun to move the labour movement into action on issues of direct concern to working-class women. Equal pay for work of equal value, affirmative action, the provision of quality child care—these demands now get a hearing in the trade unions and often formal convention resolutions of support. With persistence and audacious initiative, they can become demands that the unions actually fight for in the Eighties.

Gains on these fronts will be of immediate benefit to masses of women and will increase their self-confidence in their own capacities to win such demands through struggle. Such struggles have a further significance: they are part of the process of unifying the working class, of reconciling its interests, a process which can only take place when the leading cadre of its most oppressed sectors come to the fore as central catalysts of the proletariat's struggle as a whole.

Feminists are often reminded by "orthodox" Marxists that women's social emancipation can only come about through socialist revolution. True enough. But this is a two-edged sword. The fatal weakness of the proletariat—the reason it has failed thus far to carry through a successful socialist revolution in the bourgeois democratic states—is intimately bound up with the oppressive divisions that capitalism reproduces in its ranks, too often with the acquiescence (conscious or unconscious) of the labour movement and the left. The sexual hierarchy of men over women is a central division within the working class. Only when class conscious activists of the workers' movement fight to unify its ranks on an up-from-under basis, by actively supporting women's demands, will the working class be able to become a class for itself, a universal class capable of taking charge of its own historic destiny.

NOTES

1. For their constructive comments and criticisms of various drafts of both my articles in this book, I am grateful to Robin Blackburn, Varda Burstyn, Susan Colley, Jim Dickinson, Susan Himmelweit, Michael Kaufman, David Livingstone, Branka Magas, Susan Mann, Simon Mohun, Maxine Molyneux, Mary O'Brien, Alison Prentice and Paul Willis. Full credit is due to the Women's Press for their original interest in this project, and their patient forebearance with the long process of its completion. I am especially grateful to Bonnie Fox, from the Press collective, for the long hours she spent patiently reading various drafts and forcing me to clarify my arguments, and to Jane Springer for her thorough editing. Meg Luxton (*More Than a Labour of Love: Three Generations of Women's Work in the Home,* The Women's Press, 1980) has been an invaluable source of support, insight and critical reflection at every stage in the development of these articles. Since my debt to her would not be adequately reflected through a smattering of footnote credits, I will limit myself to noting, in a few places, where her study has directly contributed to my own thinking.
2. Karl Marx, *Capital,* Vol. I (Moscow: Progress Publishers, 1954), p. 536.
3. Frederick Engels, *The Condition of the Working Class in England* (London: Panther Books, 1969).
4. Marx, *Capital,* Vol. I, p. 611.
5. The primary focus of Marxist feminist analytical efforts in the past decade has been on clarifying the nature of women's position and labour in the family household. The English-language literature on "the domestic labour debate" is extensive, as the Bibliography at the end of this volume demonstrates.
6. While the particular formulations of the mode of production in this section are my own, the Marxist feminist concern to reopen this pivotal concept of Marxist political economy to the processes of producing human life runs through the entire domestic labour debate. Already in 1973, for example, Susan Himmelweit "redefines the concept of the mode of production to include not only the relations and forces involved in the production of use values, but also those involved in the reproduction of the species. The capitalist mode comprises both commodity production and the production of people—hence a full analysis requires consideration of both, since they are interdependent and mutually influential." Discussion Paper No. 33, Department of Economics, Birkbeck College, University of London, London, England.

7. Karl Marx, *Capital,* Vol. II (Moscow: Progress Publishers, 1956), p. 398.

8. Ibid., p. 396.

9. Karl Marx and Frederick Engels, *The German Ideology* (New York: International Publishers, 1970), p. 50.

10. Frederick Engels, *The Origin of the Family, Private Property and the State* (New York: Pathfinder Press, 1972), pp. 25-26.

11. Labour power, as a productive force, is uniquely embedded in human beings. It waxes and wanes, over the course of their lifetime, according *roughly* with the pattern of their physiological maturation. Consequently, the social process of labour power's production has often suffered a grave naturalization within historical materialist studies. The distinct tasks of labour power's production, which equip the producers in a particular society to wield and develop the productive forces at hand, are often taken for granted, as if their accomplishment were a mere byproduct of human consumption based on survival instincts. Beginning from an implicit premise that human labour power is naturally malleable, it is assumed that the mere physiological reproduction of the human species somehow "takes care of" the production of its labour power, in forms adequate to the various socioeconomic and political tasks at hand. We are reminded of Marx's comment that: "The maintenance and reproduction of the working class is, and must ever be, a necessary condition to the reproduction of capital. But the capitalist may safely leave its fulfilment to the labourer's instincts of self-preservation and of propagation" (*Capital,* Vol. I, p. 537).

    This is a naturalist fallacy. The observed adaptability of the proletariat to various conditions of production is a social accomplishment, by no means reducible to the fulfilment of needs based on survival and propagation instincts. Marx's inclusion of a cultural component in the formation of the value of labour power, above and beyond the physiological minimum necessary for survival, cuts in the exact opposite direction—against the natural price theory of wages held by most classical political economists.

12. See Mary O'Brien, "The Dialectics of Reproduction," *Women's Studies International Quarterly,* Vol. I (1978), pp. 233-39, for a trenchant critique of the historical materialist tradition on this score and a tantalizing but cryptic sketch of a feminist alternative. Routledge and Kegan Paul will soon publish a more elaborate version of her thesis, provisionally entitled, *The Politics of Reproduction.*

For a mind-stretching approach to the same ground from a very different direction, see Gad Horowitz, *Repression: Basic and Surplus Repression in Psychoanalytic Theory; Freud, Reich and Marcuse* (Toronto: University of Toronto Press, 1977).

13. Several Marxists working within the field of anthropology have recently insisted on the importance of conceptualizing production from the standpoint of reproduction in studying pre-capitalist societies. J. Friedman, in *Critique of Anthropology*, Vol. 2, No. 7 (1976), p. 15, asserts that reproduction and not production was Marx's basic analytical starting point. C. Messailloux, in *Femmes, Greniers, et Capitaux* (Paris: Maspero, 1975), is more sanguine and undoubtedly more correct when he maintains that historical materialism, from Marx on, has posed the problem of reproduction, but has inadequately incorporated it within its general framework.

14. See Karl Marx, *Capital*, Vol. III (Moscow: Progress Publishers, 1959), pp. 791-92.

15. It is a cardinal principle of historical materialism that each mode of production constitutes an historically unique ensemble of forces and relations of production. But this does not imply that each and every element in a given ensemble is unique to that mode. Money and rent, to take only two examples mentioned by Marx, are certainly found in several modes, and in several historical epochs; but with a different position and significance in each case. The same principle applies to the subsistence elements I discuss here. Elements may well be common to two or more modes, but their combination will be historically unique in each case.

16. Pure modes of production exist nowhere in history, of course. We are dealing at an historically determinant level of abstraction, beneath which it is necessary to construct mediating categories that approach the concrete level of particular social formations in their historical development.

17. If "labour" is taken to include both material goods and the production of human life itself, then "the division of labour" and "labour force" must be symmetrically reworked. The division *between* domestic and industrial labour thus becomes a central cleavage in the entire structuration of the division of labour in capitalist societies. And "labour force" must no longer be equated with the waged labour force. The domestic labour force is not only an immense reservoir, potentially engageable as wage labour; it is also a massive labour force *presently engaged*, whose labour can be

invisibly intensified in defence of the living standards of the proletariat, during periods when real wages are falling.

18. Ernest Mandel offers a very expansive definition of the relations of production in *Late Capitalism* (London: New Left Books, 1975), pp. 562-63, explicitly rejecting their confinement to the interior relations of the predominant unit of production. He includes "the particular form of the reconstitution of social labour," which certainly incorporates subsistence relations within the larger ensemble of relations of production.

19. Both the strengths and the pitfalls of this theorization of reproduction are evident in the collected essays of *Feminism and Materialism,* Annette Kuhn and AnnMarie Wolpe, eds. (London: Routledge and Kegan Paul, 1978). See especially "Patriarchy and Relations of Production," by R. McDonough and B. Harrison, pp. 11-41.

20. Marx, *Capital,* Vol. I, p. 537.

21. Once we establish the bi-locationality of the proletariat, we can clarify the positions of married women within this class without simply deriving them from their husbands' occupations. Because the double day of labour is part and parcel of the proletarian condition, we can locate working-class women in their main concentrations in both spheres and investigate the relation between them. (That is, what is the relation between women's ghettoization in certain sectors of the paid labour force and the primacy of their domestic responsibilities?)

    The difficulties of "fitting" women into a class analysis often stem from idealist treatments of social classes as pure types. A social class is not a "position" in any singular sense; it is a living ensemble of people, internally organized and stratified, whose unity, or common interest is based, not upon the absence of antagonistic intra-class relations, but upon the *external* threat posed by another class. When class societies go into deep crisis, they characteristically come apart and polarize along class lines. During these conjunctures, class unity becomes an *overriding* concern for the bulk of a class' members, despite their particular group interests, because they share a common destiny and a vital interest in ensuring that the crisis is resolved to their class' advantage. The common destiny shared by the members of a class does not imply benevolent relations between its strata, nor does it suggest that they share a common fate forever. It merely means that they have been cast in the same boat in the particular society in which they live, and, like it or not, it is in their interest to recognize this fact.

22. On the character of this incomprehension, see Jacqueline Heinen's "Kollontai and the History of Women's Oppression," *New Left Review,* 110 (July-Aug. 1978), pp. 43-64.

23. This distinction between form-limits and predominant or typical forms, which will be clarified in Section VII, is of critical methodological importance. It distinguishes different levels of analysis, in correspondence with and respect for distinct levels of determination within capitalist social formations.

24. The reader may find this "she/he" terminology awkward, but I make no apologies for it. I have come to appreciate its constant jarring impact as a positive virtue. It does not permit us to forget, even for a moment, that the female sex cannot easily be represented in mixed gender social categories such as class. Most (male) authors, when not specifically addressing gender relations, prefer to revert to masculine collective nouns and pronouns on the grounds that the fault lies with the English (French, German, etc.) language, and their usage is obviously meant to include women. I find this position to be unconvincing and complacent. Everyday language deters the expression of many (subversive) ideas; why should we passively accept this state of affairs? The problem is much more than a semantic one. The path-of-least-resistance usage of masculine collective nouns and pronouns obscures theoretical deficiencies reflected in the absence of women's reality within categories (such as class) that supposedly reflect mixed-gender phenomena. Such usages thus serve to inhibit critical reflection upon these deficiencies.

25. On the relation between capital's abstraction and the abstraction of labour, see Marx, *Capital,* Vol. III, p. 195.

26. Recognizing this contradiction, Marx wrote: The capitalistic mode of production (essentially the production of surplus-value, the absorption of surplus-labour), produces thus, with the extension of the working-day, not only the deterioration of human labour-power by robbing it of its normal, moral and physical, conditions of development and function. It produces also the premature exhaustion and death of this labour-power itself. It extends the labourer's time of production . . . by shortening his actual lifetime.

    But the value of the labour-power includes the value of the commodities necessary for the reproduction of the worker, or for the keeping up of the working-class. If then the unnatural extension of the working-day, that capital necessarily strives after in its unmeasured passion for self-expansion, shortens the length of life of the individual labourer, and therefore the duration of his labour-power, the forces used up have to be replaced at a more rapid rate and the sum of the expenses for the reproduction of labour-power will be greater; just as in a machine the part of its value to be reproduced every day is greater the more rapidly the machine is worn out. It would seem therefore that the interest of capital itself points in the direction of a normal working-day (Marx, *Capital*, Vol. I, p. 253).

27. Marx, *Capital*, Vol. I, p. 166.

28. Ibid., p. 165-66.

29. Ibid., p. 168.

30. Marx and Engels often discuss the working-class family, quite correctly, as a variant of the bourgeois family. This homology must surely be founded upon the similarity in their *property form* and *division of labour*. Both are private property household units based upon a sexual division of labour wherein men go out to work and women are primarily responsible for child care and household management. It is men, characteristically, who are the "heads" of the household and own its substantial property. This is the material basis for a vertical inter-class ideological appeal fostered by bourgeois men, directed towards their "brothers" in the lower classes, against women.

But the class *difference* between the bourgeois and the proletarian family is profound and should not be obscured. Whereas the family form of the bourgeoisie seals the *connection* between their private property in subsistence and production (through inheritance), the working-class family realizes their *disconnection*. In the very act of living and consuming its means of subsistence, the proletariat "annihilates," to use Marx's term, its money wealth and continuously eliminates its capacity to secure ownership in the means of production. The children of the proletariat thus "inherit" this class' poverty in the means of production. This is why they are destined to become another generation of proletarians.

This is hardly the situation of the bourgeois family. The bourgeoisie, like the proletariat, is necessarily constituted as a class at two locations—in this case, the point of production and the point of private (yet conspicuous) consumption. The ownership form of capital joins these two locations. Capitalist wealth, even in its most modern form, is still owned by individual members and families of the capitalist class. Fifty odd years after A.A. Berle and G.C. Means wrote *The Modern Corporation and Private Property* (New York: Macmillan, 1932), the great concentrations of capitalist wealth and power are still in the hands of the family dynasties: the Rockefellers, the Melons, the Taylors, the Bronfmans, etc. Inheritance seals the connection between the personal possession of wealth and ownership and control of the means of production in the form of capital. Herein lies a link between patriarchal power and the capitalist property form. The active transmission of capitalist power through inheritance is almost exclusively patrilineal. The wives and daughters of the bourgeoisie become coupon clippers and figureheads on company boards. They rarely step in and run businesses when their husbands and fathers die, as sons, it is fervently hoped, will be prepared and eager to do.

31. E.A. Wrigley, *Population and History* (New York: World University Library, 1969), p. 173.

32. Ibid., p. 173.

33. On this generally neglected aspect of the struggle for women's reproductive freedom, see *Feminist Studies,* Vol. 5 No. 2 (Summer 1979), where the reproductive hazards of different work place environments and labour processes are featured.

34. Marx, *Capital,* Vol. I, p. 538.

35. While men and single working-class women are widely understood to have no choice but to seek employment, it is broadly held that married women "prefer" or "choose" to seek employment. The income they receive is thus considered "discretionary income." Here we have a very neat construct: optional work for optional pay. It effectively obscures the proletarian compulsion operating upon married women with primary domestic responsibilities to enter the labour market, who thereby undertake a second shift on top of their domestic burden.

36. This prerogative can normally be exercised only within the bounds of a single state. There has never been, in the history of capitalism, anything remotely approaching a free international market in the commodity labour power.

37. The statement that the proletariat has nothing to sell but its labour power must be qualified. It has nothing to sell *which can by itself replace its compulsion to sell labour power.* Particularly among the upper layers of the proletariat, many of the consumer durables it purchases with the wage are resaleable. Houses certainly are. Thus, while the use value of the vast majority of the commodities it purchases are the essential concern of the proletariat, its upper layers, in particular, do develop an exchange value orientation to their private possessions which can often have a very conservative

effect on their consciousness. The concern with property values in white working-class neighbourhoods in the United States is perhaps the clearest example of the divisive complications of this phenomenon in forging proletarian unity.

38. On the state management of the reserve army of the unemployed, see Suzanne de Brunhoff, *The State, Capital and Economic Policy*, trans. M. Sonenscher (London: Pluto Press, 1978), and F.F. Piven and R.A. Cloward, *Regulating the Poor: The Functions of Public Welfare* (New York: Random House, 1971).

39. The rental of housing accommodation, increasingly the norm for working-class households as the purchase price of housing soars, is a purer expression of the characteristic proletarian condition than is home-ownership. The tenuousness of this form of private possession accords with the insecurity endemic to the proletarian condition; furthermore, it pits the worker tenant, once again, against a capitalist (this time a landlord) with whom she or he must strike a contract. The imbalance of their respective powers, despite the formal contractual equality, is reminiscent of her/his other contract with capital. Tenancy, tenant unions and rent strikes thus reinforce the proletarian condition, in symmetry with employment, trade unions and industrial strikes.

40. Rayna Rapp elucidates this vital family/household distinction in an article she co-authors with Ellen Ross and Renate Bridenthal, "Examining Family History," in *Feminist Studies*, Vol. 5, No. 1 (Spring 1979), pp. 174-200. See especially "Household and Family," pp. 175-81.

41. It may seem ironic that I warn of this danger since I have made strong arguments against the reduction of the mode of production concept to the immediate on-site forces and relations of private capitalist production. I have been attempting to elaborate the subsistence structures of this mode and, thus, to enlarge the explanatory field of its concept. But there are conceptual limits here that must be respected. We must stop where the capitalist mode of production stops—in defining the boundaries of the private household sphere but leaving its content relatively open to various arrangements, patriarchal and non-patriarchal.

42. It should be noted here that the same charge can and has been levelled against Marxism for remaining conceptually blind to racism in its mode of production concept.

43. Karl Marx, *Grundrisse, Foundations of the Critique of Political Economy*, trans. Martin Nicolaus (New York: Vintage Books, 1973), p. 101.

44. For a useful survey of the various meanings given to patriarchy in feminist analyses, see Veronica Beechey, "On Patriarchy," *Feminist Review,* No. 3 (1979), pp. 66-82.

45. Karl Marx and Frederick Engels, "Manifesto of the Communist Party" in *The Revolutions of 1848,* David Fernbach, ed. (New York: Vintage Books, 1974), p. 77.

46. Engels, *Origin of the Family,* p. 80.

47. Ibid., pp. 79, 80.

48. A note on marriage forms. In rough correspondence with this contrast in family household forms there is a before/after norm in marriage forms that should be briefly discussed here. Marriage timing and mate selection, which formerly rested firmly in the hands of parents and guardians, shifted gradually to a situation of individual free choice ("free" in a market sense) which could be exercised from late adolescence on. The shift was closely linked to the extension of opportunities for adolescents to become full proletarians, "making it on their own"; and this, in turn, to the extension of an impersonal and extra-local labour market. If the marriage contract came increasingly to resemble commercial and employment contracts in the manner of its engagement, it nevertheless remained, until well into the second half of the twentieth century, firmly pre-capitalist in the manner of its severance. While workers and employers were legally free to "divorce" one another without subsequent obligation, this was not the case for husbands and wives. Thus, the bonds of "sacred matrimony" involve a peculiar form of bondage—voluntarily entered, but binding for life thereafter. The specific aspects of patriarchal authority in the modern family, which are clearly pre-capitalist, are intimately related to the indissolubility of marriage. These include conjugal rights of monogamy—exclusive rights of sexual possession and the obligation of sexual fidelity (rendered manifestly one-sided by the sexual double standard); the right to "possess" one's wife sexually against her will, that is, to rape her—and custodial rights of parents over their children, especially when residing under the same roof—including the right to physically punish children for disobeying parental authority.

In the case of conjugal and custodial prerogatives, the right of the abused individual to dissolve the contract by leaving the household would undermine patriarchal authority. The assertion of this right for women, however, is hampered by being closely associated with the formally reciprocal right of primary breadwinners to desert without subsequent financial obligation. As long as women's low wages, limited employment opportunities and lack of child care curtail their own capacity for proletarian independence, the removal of subsequent legal obligation, in cases of unilateral separation, cannot, unfortunately, be considered progress in women's civil liberties.

However, as marriages gradually secularize and divorce becomes easier to obtain, conjugal and custodial prerogatives are being eroded through contestation in the courts and ensuing legislative changes in family law. The right to rape one's wife and to physically punish children are both now under attack. In all these ways, the legal institution of marriage is gradually being brought into alignment with the rationale of the bourgeois revolution, where individual freedom was equated with the solubility of voluntarily entered contracts.

49. Marx, *Capital*, Vol. I, p. 459.

50. Engels, *Condition of the Working Class*, pp. 171-72.

51. Ibid., p. 173.

52. Ibid.

53. Ibid., p. 174.

54. Ibid., pp. 174-75.

55. Engels, *Origin of the Family*, pp. 81-82.

56. Ibid., p. 80.

57. It is important to realize that an impulse within the bourgeoisie towards a managerial rationalization of capitalism to curb the system's more anarchic features does not begin with Keynesianism in the Depression, but originates in the nineteenth century.

58. See Barbara Ehrenreich and Deirdre English, *For Her Own Good: 150 Years of the Experts' Advice to Women* (Garden City, N.Y.: Anchor Press, 1978). The authors' thesis is that the rise of "the Woman Question" and the experts' concern to exercise remote control over women in their households arose because the tight patriarchal control of women by their fathers and husbands in the pre-capitalist household had been lost in the bourgeois revolution.

59. Cf. Marx, *Capital*, Vol. I, pp. 442ff.

60. An excellent paper making this case was presented at the Conference of Socialist Economists, 1979, by Michelle Barrett and Mary McIntosh, entitled, "The Family Wage: Some Problems for Socialists and Feminists." It can be obtained by writing to them at 65 Manor Road, London, N. 16, England. The opposite (positive) appreciation of the labour movement's struggle for a single family wage has been well argued by Jane Humphries in two articles:

"Class Struggle and the Persistence of the Working Class Family," *Cambridge Journal of Economics,* Vol. 2, No. 3 (1977) and "The Working Class Family, Women's Liberation, and the Class Struggle: The Case of Nineteenth Century British History," *The Review of Radical Political Economics,* Vol. 2, No. 3 (Fall 1977), pp. 25-41.

61. Theresa McBride, "The Long Road Home: Women's Work and Industrialization," in Renate Bridenthal and Claudia Koonz, eds., *Becoming Visible* (Boston: Houghton Mifflin, 1977), p. 286.

62. Mary Lynn McDougall, "Working Class Women During the Industrial Revolution, 1780–1914," ibid., p. 275.

63. This position was advanced by Margaret Benston, "The Political Economy of Women's Liberation," *Monthly Review,* Vol. 21, No. 4 (Sept. 1969), pp. 13-27.

64. See Meg Luxton's study of three generations of women's housework in Flin Flon, op. cit. In this single industry town, where men work for "the Company" and women work almost exclusively as housewives, the contrast between industrial-male and domestic-female labour takes a particularly stark form. The author chose Flin Flon as her social laboratory precisely in order to investigate women's domestic work in the context of a "pure," typically capitalist, sexual division of labour.

65. This is a change which Peter Laslett, in his exclusive preoccupation with nuclear co-residence patterns, misses completely. At pains to dispel the myth of the pre-capitalist extended family household, he downplays the significance of the gradual loss of reliable extended family support between households, which has been a byproduct of capitalist development. See *Household and Family in Past Times,* Peter Laslett, ed. (Cambridge: Cambridge University Press, 1972). See especially Laslett's "Introduction: the history of the family," pp. 1-90.

CAPITAL, THE STATE AND THE ORIGINS OF THE WORKING-CLASS HOUSEHOLD

Bruce Curtis

The main thrust of Bruce Curtis' article is the argument that the household and domestic labour, as they exist under capitalism, must be seen to originate in a process of class conflict. To make this argument, Curtis first criticizes the tendency of contributors to the debate on domestic labour to locate the origins of domestic labour in the functional needs of the capitalist system. Curtis attempts to demonstrate that a functional analysis of domestic labour is not only ahistorical, but it leads to peculiar political conclusions.

The article concludes with an historical sketch that locates the development of domestic labour under capitalism in a process of class conflict and refutes the contention that women's oppression is a result of an alliance among men of all social classes. More specifically, it provides a striking contrast to the argument that the sexual segregation in the labour market is a consequence of the sexism of male workers. Curtis highlights the role of the state in the origins of a domestic sphere and of domestic labour and suggests that working-class men and women share a common political position with respect to the state.

A characteristic feature of capitalist development is the *unevenness* with which different branches of production have come to be organized along strictly capitalist lines. Some branches of production have shown themselves to be remarkably resistant, if not immune, to the large-scale employment of wage labour by capital. This phenomenon has attracted a considerable amount of attention with respect to differences in capitalist development in different nations. The uneven development of town and country has also long been a concern of socialist writers. A third form of uneven development has only recently reappeared as a serious political and scholarly concern—this is the uneven development of economy and household.

In its major branches, industrial capitalist production is based upon the employment of wage labourers in large enterprises where the labour process demands cooperation among the labourers. Participation in industrial capitalist production places the working class in a situation in which a consciousness of common class interests can emerge. At the same time this participation provides a practical training in the management of social production. Yet the development of industrial capitalism has involved the emergence of privatized, isolated and technically backwards production in the working-class household. The directly social production of commodities in capitalist industry has involved the private reproduction of the working class in the household. This social difference in the conditions of production in household and industry coincides with and to some extent at least causes a division within the working class between men and women. Men predominate in industrial employment while women predominate in the household labour force. Married women who work in industry generally face the double burden of wage labour and unpaid domestic labour.

The current debate over domestic labour addresses the phenomenon of uneven development. Participants in the debate have drawn our attention to the existence of a large unpaid working population and a massive labour reserve in the household. They have attempted to understand the process of uneven development by focussing chiefly on two questions. One of these questions is that of the relationship between domestic labour in the working-class household and productive labour in capitalist industry. How is the work that the housewife does related to the work the wage labourer does? How is the housewife related to her husband's capitalist employer? More generally, how are housewives in the working class related to the capitalist class?

The second question central to the domestic labour debate concerns the origins and causes of the separation between economy and household. This question really contains two parts: first, what are the origins of the private household production of the elements of working-class subsistence? How does it come about that the household and industry develop along different lines? How is the uneven development of household and industry reproduced over time? Second, how does it come about that this private household production is carried on in the vast majority of cases by women? How does domestic labour become women's work, and how is this feminization of domestic labour maintained and reproduced over time?

A failure to separate these questions analytically characterizes many contributions to the debate over domestic labour. These questions are clearly related, but an answer to one of them is not automatically an answer to all of them. A large number of contributors to the domestic labour debate, for example, have focussed primarily upon the relationship between domestic labour and capitalist production. They have approached this relationship largely through an examination of the consequences of domestic labour for capitalists and for capitalist relations of production in general. Then, without any serious historical investigation, they have argued that the current functions of domestic labour and its current social consequences were the forces that led to its initial organization. In place of historical investigations of the social conditions under which the separation of household and industry developed, we find a few stock phrases about the splitting of the working household into two spheres. The struggles that have surrounded the development of a family life in the working class are obscured in these accounts and we are left with mechanical conceptions of historical development. This is well exemplified by the work of Mariarosa Dalla Costa, who writes:

> Capital established the family as the nuclear family and subordinated within it the woman to the man, as the person who, not directly participating in social production, does not present herself independently on the labor market.[1]

The central concern of this article is to demonstrate that the organization of the working-class family and household production under capitalism must be understood as a product of class struggle rather than simply as a product of the sexist tendencies of capitalists and male workers. This article will demonstrate that the current consequences of the privatization of the household were not the aims that guided the participants in the struggle for a working-class household and family life. This will become clear from an examination of the emergence of the working-class household in nineteenth-century England. First, however, it is useful to consider the attempts that have been made in the domestic labour debate to explain the existence and reproduction of domestic labour as a social phenomenon over time. Two major lines of argument commonly appear: domestic labour is seen to exist because it is profitable for capital, and/or because it performs functions necessary for the operation of the capitalist economy.

Domestic Labour and Profit

Dalla Costa maintains that housewives are merely wage labourers without a pay packet.[2] Parallel to the factory in industry proper where men work for wages is the "social factory," where housewives produce the commodity labour power for no wage. In this view housewives are directly productive workers for capital. They produce by domestic labour necessary social services at no cost to capitalists; hence their labour is a direct source of accumulation of capital. This is the reason for the existence of domestic labour, according to Dalla Costa.

> The rule of capital through the wage compels every ablebodied person to function, under the law of division of labor, and to function in ways that are if not immediately, then ultimately profitable to the expansion and extension of the rule of capital.[3]

Other contributors to the debate who do not share Dalla Costa's view that domestic labour is directly productive labour argue that it is beneficial to the owners of the means of production, pointing to the benefits that capitalists derive from domestic labour as a cause of its existence. Thus Seccombe remarks in passing,

> Although Capital accumulates from the appropriation of the use value of both [domestic and industrial] labours, it is only in production "proper" that a wage is paid.[4]

While Seccombe suggests that domestic labour is a source of capitalist accumulation, Margaret Benston asserts that the profitability of domestic labour leads capitalists to promote its existence.

> The need to keep women in the home arises from two major aspects of the present system. First, the amount of unpaid labour performed by women is very large and very profitable to those who own the means of production. To pay women for their work, even at minimum wage scales, would imply a massive redistribution of wealth.[5]

Other writers have taken up and extended Benston's claim that the payment of women for housework would entail an enormous redistribution of wealth. Jean Gardiner argues that it is the necessity of redistribution of wealth which prevents the abolition of domestic labour.[6]

A significant number of contributors to the domestic labour debate see domestic labour as a source of profit for capitalists, and suggest that this characteristic of domestic labour is the basis of its continuing existence. These arguments are misleading and erroneous.

Is domestic labour a directly productive labour in the Marxist sense, as Dalla Costa suggests? According to Marx, a productive labourer under capitalism is one who directly exchanges her labour power for a wage and works in a production process that produces commodities containing surplus labour. He writes,

> Capitalist production is not merely the production of commodities, it is essentially the production of surplus-value. The labourer produces, not for himself, but for capital. It no longer suffices, therefore, that he should simply produce. He must produce surplus-value. That labourer alone is productive, who produces surplus-value for the capitalist, and thus works for the self-expansion of capital. If we may take an example from outside the sphere of production of material objects, a schoolmaster is a productive labourer, when, in addition to belabouring the heads of his scholars, he works like a horse to enrich the school proprietor. That the latter has laid out his capital in a teaching factory, instead of in a sausage factory, does not alter the relation. Hence the notion of a productive labourer implies not merely a relation between work and useful effect, between labourer and product of labour, but also a specific, social relation of production, a relation that has sprung up historically and stamps the labourer as the direct means of creating surplus-value.[7]

In considering the question of productive and unproductive labour we are not making a judgment about the social necessity of a function or occupation. The question concerns the way in which occupations or branches of production are *organized.* Many socially necessary functions are not organized by capitalist industry—municipal garbage collection, education and social work, to name a few. To suggest that these occupations and functions are not productive in the sense of capitalist accumulation is not to say that they are not useful or necessary. Making the distinction between productive and unproductive labour under capitalism rather permits us to trace capitalist exploitation to its source and to distinguish those classes in society that are directly subjected to its full force from those subjected to it indirectly or not at all. It is the relation between capital and productive labour that forms the key contradiction in capitalist society, and it is in terms of this relationship that we seek to understand the social conditions of other classes and sections of classes in capitalist society.

The housewife does not qualify as a productive labourer in the Marxist sense. She does not exchange her labour power for a wage in the course of her function as a housewife. Her products—child care, meals, clean houses and clothes, sexual satisfactions and so forth—are not exchanged at a stable rate for the products of other workers, and hence are not commodities. She is supported out of her husband's wage, or, less commonly, out of state revenue (in the form of welfare payments, e.g.). Her relation to capital is indirect and quite different from that of her husband. That is not to say the housewife does not perform useful labour, or even labour indispensable to the household. Clearly she does. Dalla Costa, however, confuses a conventional notion of productive labour as "doing something useful" with the Marxist conception of the productive worker.

Is domestic labour indirectly productive for capital? Does it increase the production of surplus value by making workers more tractable, or by providing an outlet for the release of tensions built up in the work place? In part this is also Dalla Costa's argument: the domination of husbands over their wives is compensation offered to them by capital for the exploitation they suffer at work. Husbands find satisfaction in this and hence capital can exploit them more fully at work.[8] There is no clear body of evidence to support this position. While the literature of working-class life contains instances of workers restraining their antagonism to industrial discipline for the sake of their dependent wives and children, we can equally see that the necessity of supporting dependents can lead to demands for higher wages, and that the housewife herself may push for these demands.[9] In any case there is no ground upon which we can argue that the indirectly productive nature of domestic labour is responsible for its existence.

Dalla Costa argues that domestic labour is productive labour for capital. She maintains that without this argument, housewives are not considered part of the working class and the oppression of women is not addressed by socialist political practice. She writes,

> If we fail to grasp completely that precisely this family is the very pillar of the capitalist organization of work, if we make the mistake of regarding it only as a superstructure, dependent for change only on the stages of the struggle in the factories, then we will be moving in a limping revolution that will always perpetuate and aggravate *a basic contradiction in the class struggle, and a contradiction which*

> *is functional to capitalist development.* We would, in other words, be perpetuating the error of considering ourselves as producers of use values only, of considering housewives external to the working class. As long as housewives are considered external to the class, the class struggle at every moment and any point is impeded, frustrated, and unable to find full scope for its action.[10]

From the position that housewives are indeed productive workers for capital Dalla Costa moves on to argue that housewives' refusal of work itself can be a revolutionary activity. This is a difficult and in some ways curious position. It stems from a reading of Marx's analysis of the process of the reproduction of capital.[11] Marx argues that, seen from one aspect, the consumption of the working class is simply the reproduction of labour power for capital. By consuming the means of subsistence purchased out of the wage, the working class continually provides capital with a fresh source of labour power and continually recreates the possibility of capitalist exploitation. In this sense, the workers' independence from capital in the sphere of private or domestic life is largely a fiction.

> From a social point of view, therefore, the working-class, even when not directly engaged in the labour-process, is just as much an appendage of capital as the ordinary instruments of labour. Even its individual consumption is, within certain limits, a mere factor in the process of production. That process, however, takes good care to prevent these self-conscious instruments from leaving it in the lurch, for it removes their product, as fast as it is made, from their pole to the opposite pole of capital. Individual consumption provides, on the one hand, the means for their maintenance and reproduction: on the other hand, it secures by the annihilation of the necessaries of life, the continued re-appearance of the workman in the labour-market. . . . The appearance of independence is kept up by means of a constant change of employers, and by the fictio juris of a contract.[12]

Dalla Costa interprets Marx to say that the consumption of the working class itself is a form of productive labour for capital. Not only then are women in the household productive workers, but the refusal of housework would prohibit the reproduction of labour power and hence the reproduction of capitalist exploitation.

Two difficulties with this approach are immediately obvious. In the first place, Dalla Costa does not address the question of working-class consciousness. She reproduces a mechanical notion of capital and social relations that leaves no place for political practice to emerge out of the consciousness of the participants in capitalist class relations. Yet at the same time, she argues that it is *possible* as well as revolutionary to organize housewives, who exist in a condition of social isolation, into a movement of opposition to work. In the second place, Dalla Costa seems to lose sight of the fact that the working class is a propertyless class. The consumption of the working class is dependent upon its production of surplus value for capital. Capital possesses a monopoly over the means of production and subsistence. The working class as a whole cannot bring about a social revolution by refusing to produce, because without producing it cannot consume. Revolutionary political practice necessarily involves the management of production and the appropriation of the means of production and subsistence by the working class itself.

Dalla Costa's position is also problematic in that it seeks an independent class position for the domestic worker. In doing this, it obscures the dependent condition of the domestic worker, precludes the possibility of cooperation within the household and mystifies the source of the barbarism to which the domestic worker is subject. If the housewife is not at the same time a wage labourer in industry (as perhaps one-half of housewives in Canada are), she is completely dependent upon her husband's wage for her subsistence. Her social position is different from that of her husband, but it has things in common with his as well. She leads a working-class life, dependent upon the wage and subject to the rhythms of capitalist production, but her dependency and isolation separate her position from his. In the case of the married woman who is a wage labourer as well as a domestic labourer, the social position of husband and wife is closer. The latter's position is differentiated from that of her husband by the fact that she performs domestic labour in the household in addition to wage labour in industry, as well as by the nature of her participation in industry, where she is segregated into low-paid and low-skilled occupations.[13] We can capture the commonality as well as the difference between the social position of the male wage labourer in industry and the female domestic worker in the household by regarding women as a fraction of the working class. In other words, women must be seen as a section of the working class which shares the general interest of the class, but which has an interest in the abolition of its dependency and isolation that in the short run will differentiate its political interest from that of other sections of the class.

Dalla Costa presents an analogy between the foreman in industry and the working-class husband in the "social factory," the household. But is the source of the barbarity to which many housewives are subjected to be found in the figure of the working-class husband? The husband is clearly an immediate participant in the physical and psychological violence to which housewives are prey. He participates in physical fights, joins her in distorted sexual activity and creates many of the practical tasks which tie her to the household. But surely the ultimate source of this barbarity is capitalist exploitation! It is capitalist exploitation that creates the social conditions for the separation of household and industry and for the isolation of women in the former. It is capitalist exploitation that subjects workers to mechanical, meaningless and repetitive daily activity. It is the conditions of exploitation in work and in the political arena that reappear as violence and domination in intimate relations. It is the state and capital that are responsible for the continuing existence of the working-class household and the private reproduction of labour power.

Insofar as Dalla Costa's analysis does not capture the ultimately congruent class interests of working-class women and men it must be viewed cautiously. The refusal of housework as a political tactic, apart from the practical difficulties of organizing isolated housewives, is dubious. It can by itself be expected to exacerbate rather than to eliminate fractional antagonisms between working-class men and women. The refusal of housework must be joined to a systematic attempt to socialize the household and to eliminate the uneven development of economy and household that serves to legitimate differences in the social position of women and men.

To return to the question of domestic labour as a source of profit, it must be pointed out that while the domestic labourer's wageless condition creates the impression that the products of domestic labour cost capital nothing, this is in fact not the case. The housewife is supported out of her husband's wage or out of the revenue of the state. Her labour and her existence constitute *costs* to capitalists that are paid in the form of higher wages to workers or higher taxes to the state. The wage must be higher if it is to support a family than to support an individual. At the same time, the amount of surplus value capital can extract by employing a male adult worker and paying him a family wage is clearly less than that which could be extracted if each family member were forced to work for an individual wage in a capitalist enterprise.

If we consider this question more abstractly, in terms of the working class as a whole, we can see, following Marx, that the working day for the productively employed working class can be divided into two parts. During one part of the day, which Marx called the sphere of necessary labour, the workers produce an amount of value necessary to reproduce themselves under prevalent social conditions. The sphere of necessary labour produces the sum of value that workers receive in the form of the wage and constitutes a fund for the daily maintenance of the employed workers and for the support of dependent sections of the working class. Various mechanisms exist for the transfer and redistribution of this value to dependent sections of the class, including state transfer payments and the private redistribution of the wage in the household.

During a second part of the working day, the working class creates a value that is appropriated by the capitalist class without any equivalent returned to the workers. This is called surplus value and the part of the working day during which it is produced is the sphere of surplus labour. Surplus labour creates a fund for the extension and expansion of production, for the replacement of obsolete and worn-out machinery, for the support of the state apparatus and for the personal consumption of the capitalist class.

These two spheres are antagonistic. The larger the sphere of necessary labour, the smaller the sphere of surplus labour, and vice versa. The larger the number of productive workers relative to the number of workers' dependents, the larger the sphere of surplus labour relative to the sphere of necessary labour. In short, if we consider the question of domestic labour purely from the perspective of the economic interests of capital, the transformation of domestic production into a branch of capitalist industry proper and the transformation of housewives into wage workers would be most congenial to capital. We can explain neither the existence nor the origins of domestic labour by simply considering the economic interests of capital.

If domestic labour's existence is not directly in the economic interests of capital, why has it not been abolished? In part, the answer to this question lies in the nature of some household activities such as child care, which present technical difficulties to the large-scale investment of capital. These difficulties are discussed at length in the article in this volume by Mann and Blumenfeld. In addition to the difficulties presented by the conditions necessary for capitalist investment, there are serious political obstacles to the socialization of domestic production under capitalism. The privatization of the reproduction of labour power and the sexual divisions within the working class which result are serious barriers to the emergence of a revolutionary class consciousness.[14]

Because the housewife is already supported out of the wage, it is *technically* possible to pay her for her domestic labour without any redistribution of wealth between labour and capital. Technically all this would require is some formal regulation of the currently private and unregulated redistribution of the wage in the household. Such a redistribution might well demonstrate to workers and to housewives the miniscule amount of value contained in the wage, but it is analytically incorrect to see capitalists engineering the maintenance of domestic labour out of a reluctance to pay housewives for their work.

The housewife, like the wage worker, is supported out of the sphere of necessary labour which occurs at the expense of surplus labour for capital. At one level, the housewife receives precisely what the wage labourer does: she is reproduced from day to day and from generation to generation just as he is. At another level, however, we can see that the domestic worker is reproduced under conditions of *domestic slavery.*[15] She exists in a condition of dependence upon a particular man. She is incarcerated in an isolated, technically backwards and stagnant social unit. Her domestic condition structures to a large degree the conditions of her labour force participation. It is this condition of domestic slavery that a demand of pay for housewives does not address.

To some extent, domestic labourers constitute an industrial reserve army of labour, that section of the working class which is unemployed or irregularly employed. The reserve army serves to meet the demand for labour power occasioned during periods of intense capital investment and provides a pool of cheap labour power for this purpose. The continual or irregular unemployment of sections of the working class is an important element in "proletarian insecurity," which suppresses wages and which may discipline workers in the work place.[16] It is both a product and a precondition of capitalist production. As Marx explains,

> But if a surplus labouring population is a necessary product of accumulation or of the development of wealth on a capitalist basis, this surplus-population becomes, conversely, the lever of capitalistic accumulation, nay, a condition of existence of the capitalist mode of production. It forms a disposable industrial reserve army, that belongs to capital quite as absolutely as if the latter had bred it at its own cost. Independently of the limits of the actual increase of population, it creates, for the changing needs of the self-expansion of capital, a mass of human material always ready for exploitation.[17]

Housewives constitute one form of the industrial reserve army. In periods of high labour demand they are recruited for capitalist industry, although their participation tends to be restricted to certain sectors of the labour market.[18] While unemployed they are dependent upon the wages of their husbands. Their condition as housewives structures their participation in production in capitalist industries. It disciplines them in relations of subordination and dependence and may reduce their ability to unite with other workers in pursuit of common aims.

The household contains one of the major forms of the industrial reserve army of labour. Can we argue that household labour exists because it serves as a means of supporting an industrial reserve army? While it is clear that domestic labour is one form the industrial reserve army takes at this period of capitalist development, we can make no statements about household labour until we understand the social processes whereby the reserve army comes to consist of female domestic workers in private households. There is nothing peculiar to the processes of domestic labour that stamps it as the sphere of an industrial reserve army, any more than there is anything that stamps domestic labour as women's work. We cannot understand women's domestic labour nor the relations between working-class men and women by looking only at the current functions of domestic labour and the working-class household. If we approach domestic labour in this fashion, mechanically and ahistorically, we are led to envision (as Dalla Costa does), a class alliance between working-class men and male capitalists to oppress women.

Women's domestic slavery is reproduced by the state, the bourgeois press and by the occupational segregation of women. It results in antagonistic relations between working-class men and women as well as in the privatization of the antagonisms that surround wage labour in capitalist industry. Is there evidence here to suggest that these consequences were anticipated by capital and working-class men and guided the initial organization of household labour? I will argue in the third section of this paper that this is not the case.

Domestic Labour as Necessary Labour

If a capitalist economy is to function, the labour force must be continually reproduced. Workers must be maintained from day to day at a given social standard and the next generation of workers must be created. Workers must be equipped with the skills and dispositions demanded of them by capitalist production. Labour power is partly reproduced in the working-class household through the labour of the housewife so we can say that domestic labour performs functions that are necessary, to some extent, for the operation of the capitalist economy. But does this explain the existence of domestic labour? Consider the analagous case of the existence of labour in the capitalist form of labour power. The existence of labour as a commodity, labour power, which the capitalist class can purchase on the commodity market and exploit in the labour process is a necessary condition for the capitalist mode of production. Does labour then exist as labour power because it is necessary for capitalist production? No. According to Marx, labour exists as labour power because of certain historically specific social conditions: the separation of the worker from the means of production and the monopolization of the means of production and subsistence by the capitalist class.[19] Labour exists as labour power only so long as these social conditions obtain. Similarly, domestic labour exists as a private labour of women only so long as the separation between household and industry and occupational segregation continue to exist. We may understand the *continued* existence of labour power or of domestic labour in terms of the social consequences of these forms. However, their current social consequences do not explain their origins.

The tendency to seek the causes of the existence of domestic labour in the necessity of its functions for the capitalist economy is closely tied to the value controversy. This controversy, which is a difficult and confusing one, concerns the social form in which the products of domestic labour exist. The central question is whether or not the housewife produces a commodity. If she is a commodity producer, then we should be able to analyze her social position and to explain the distribution of labour power between the household and capitalist industry in terms of value theory.

The champion of the position that domestic labour creates value is Seccombe, who argues that "only value as a category can express the relation of separated private labours to the total social labour in a society of generalized commodity production."[20] If we do not approach domestic labour by means of value analysis, Seccombe asserts, inevitably we will "tend to fall back into a dualistic conception where the household appears outside the economy, completely impervious to its laws of motion."[21]

Value is a social form in which the products of human labour exist at particular periods of human history.[22] When the products of human labour are exchanged in a regular manner, the different labours that produced those products are practically equated and are reduced to one common social standard. As Marx shows, what diverse labours have in common is that they are all the expenditure of a general human capacity to labour. Commodities exchange, in general, in proportions regulated by the quantities of this general human capacity to labour which they require for their production. Value then, comes to exist when the products of human labour are regularly exchanged and equated in the market. The labour of any commodity producer is brought into a relation in this manner with the labour of all other commodity producers.[23] Value-creating labour is universal, abstract and homogeneous human labour. It is human labour in general and it acquires this abstract character through the practical equation of concrete labours in the process of exchange.

Value-creating labour creates commodities. Under capitalism, however, the dominant form of production is the production of commodities by means of the employment of wage labour. Production in this mode of production is primarily the production of commodities which embody unpaid labour, that is, which contain surplus value.

Seccombe does not maintain, as does Dalla Costa, that housewives produce surplus value. For Seccombe domestic production is an instance of simple commodity production. As such, we must understand it from the outset as a derivative form of production, dependent for its existence in the capitalist mode of production upon the structure of capitalist commodity production.[24]

Seccombe proceeds as follows: the family and domestic labour stand in an indirect relation to capital, mediated by the wage. Domestic labour is a necessary labour that produces the commodity labour power. The wage commands the working-class family's subsistence on the commodity market, but these commodities are not in a directly consumable form at the moment of purchase. They must be prepared for consumption and this preparation requires the expenditure of labour. The housewife performs this labour. She adds her labour to the commodities purchased with the wage. These commodities are then consumed by the worker. The worker sells his labour power for the wage, and in this exchange the labour of the housewife is practically equated to the labour of all other commodity producers. Hence it is value-creating labour. And hence, according to Seccombe, we can apply general laws of political economy to its analysis. However, there is a curious duality to the situation of the housewife: she creates value, and yet her labour "remains a privatized labour outside of the exercise of the law of value."[25]

As a number of commentators have demonstrated, Seccombe's position contradicts the assumptions of the theory upon which he formally bases it.[26] If the housewife's labour is indeed a derivative form, outside of the operation of the laws of value, and if the value created by the housewife is invisible, then the contention that the housewife creates value is at best a mystification.[27] Yet when Seccombe attempts to build upon this contention to explain the situation of the housewife, value creation does not appear in the analysis. If we argue that the value of labour power determines the level and conditions of domestic labour, or if we argue that the conditions of production in certain branches of capitalist industry determine the conditions of the domestic labourer, then the contention that domestic labour creates value is immaterial.[28] The position that domestic labour does not create value yields the same conclusions without the analytic confusion.

If the domestic worker actually produces value that is embodied in the commodity labour power, then the average value of labour power must be determined in part by her labour. This contradicts a fundamental proposition of the labour theory of value, that on the average, equivalents are exchanged in the market. The central contribution of Marxist theory to our understanding of capitalist production is the demonstration that the existence of profit and exploitation is compatible with the exchange of equivalents on the market. Marx shows that profit originates not in the sphere of exchange, but in the process of capitalist production. According to the laws of commodity production, the wage and labour power are equivalent values. The wage is the amount of value socially necessary for the reproduction of labour power, and on the average the working class sells its labour power for its value. In the sphere of production labour power is consumed in the creation not only of the value contained in the wage but also in the creation of a surplus value, which forms the profit of the capitalist class. Marx debunked the notion of the "apologetic" economists that profit arose from simple buying and selling.

The contention that the housewife creates value by adding her labour to the commodities purchased with the wage implies that labour power contains more value than the wage. If domestic labour creates value, then labour power contains the value embodied in the wage plus the value created by domestic labour. Labour power and the wage cease to be equivalents and the capitalist class would profit simply by buying labour power. Seccombe describes this as a "problem of bourgeois appearence occurring as a result of the phenomenal wage form."[29] He attempts to remove this difficulty by suggesting that the wage is actually divided into two parts. One part sustains the domestic worker and her substitutes, the other part the wage worker and his substitutes. Domestic labour creates an amount of value "equivalent to the 'production costs' of its own maintenance."[30]

This explanation simply concatenates the theoretical problems introduced by the assertion that domestic labour creates value. If Seccombe means that the value the domestic labourer produces is consumed in the household, then her product is not exchanged on the commodity market, is not equated with the products of other producers, and hence her labour is not value-creating labour. Furthermore, if Seccombe contends that domestic labour creates an amount of value equivalent to that which the housewife consumes, then value ceases to be a product of objectified labour time. In other words, if we take two housewives working under identical technical conditions for identical periods, they will produce different amounts of value depending upon how much of the wage they consume. In contradiction to the labour theory of value, which suggests that workers working for equal periods under identical technical conditions will produce equal amounts of value, Seccombe argues that they will produce different amounts of value if they are paid different amounts of money. In short, it is not possible to maintain that domestic labour creates value through the mechanism suggested by Seccombe. No one else to date has specified a mechanism in place of this to support the position that domestic labour creates value. Unless this can be done at the level of theory, there are no grounds for arguing that domestic labour creates value.

In his later work, Seccombe's contention that domestic labour creates value is immaterial to his analysis. In studying the effects of changes in the productivity of industrial labour in Department II (production of means of consumption), Seccombe argues that domestic labour is directly affected by the conditions of production in capitalist industry.[31] This analysis is promising, but in it domestic labour figures as a derivative labour, determined by changes in the value of the wage, or by increases in the productivity of labour engaged in producing means of consumption. In other words, when capital undertakes the mass production of domestic appliances, the conditions of domestic production change. According to Seccombe, the value of the wage determines domestic labour in this instance and the value supposedly created by domestic labour has no visible consequences.

Domestic labour cannot be seen as productive labour nor as a form of commodity production. Domestic labour takes place outside of the capitalist economy and the concepts used in Marxist theory to understand capitalist commodity production do not apply to it. The housewife reproduces labour power in part and maintains labour power on a day-to-day basis. This is a necessary kind of labour in the absence of other institutions that might maintain it. The fact that her labour is outside the sphere of capitalist production does not mean that the housewife is unaffected by the conditions of production in capitalist industry. She reproduces labour power and experiences the conditions of production in industry through sharing her husband's experience of the work place. Objectively, her labour is constrained by the worn-out condition of her husband after his labour power has been consumed, by the level of the wage and by the availability of domestic commodities.

The Origins of Domestic Labour

> With the advent of the capitalist mode of production . . . women were relegated to a condition of isolation, enclosed within the family cell, dependent in every aspect upon men. The new autonomy of the free wage slave was denied her, and she remained in a pre-capitalist stage of personal dependence.[32]

> With the advent of industrial capitalism, the general labour process was split into two discrete units; a domestic and an industrial unit.[33]

The tendency on the part of many contributors to the domestic labour debate to seek the basis of the existence of domestic labour in its functions and consequences is frequently projected onto the history of domestic labour as well. The separation of industry and household is taken as a given and largely mechanical outcome of the development of industrial capitalism. Women are supposedly left in the household in a condition of oppression while men venture out to find independence in wage labour. This state of affairs is commonly seen to be caused by capital. It is also commonly seen to be an outcome promoted by male workers at the expense of women and children.[34] The current situation of the housewife is likened to that of the housewife during the rise of industrial capitalism, and some writers go so far as to suggest that an interest in the oppression of women shared by male workers and capitalists *motivated* the organization of the domestic sphere. This analysis tends either to disregard or underestimate the significance of class differences in the process of historical development. It presents capital and male workers as sharing a common interest in the oppression of women. The exploitation of labour power by capital, which itself structures the oppression of working-class women, is replaced by a conception in which men in general oppress women in general. The historical specificity of women's oppression under capitalism vanishes.

Secondly, as an account of the development of the separation between household and industry, the view that the working household splits into an industrial and a domestic unit is in large measure factually incorrect. The working-class household is not a feudal remnant, nor a survival from some murky period of pre-capitalist production. On the contrary, it is a social institution that emerges through the struggle of the working class for a domestic life. This struggle for a domestic life is one in which working-class women as well as working-class men participated, and one which was opposed in general by capital. Those who argue that the domestic sphere emerges as a plot on the part of male workers and capitalists to oppress women and children are placed in the difficult position of arguing that the conditions of production in early capitalist industry were liberating for women and children. They must see the superexploitation to which women and children were subject as a form of social progress. It is absurd to suppose that the level of social independence that a contemporary working-class woman may enjoy through earning a wage could have characterized her sister in any capitalist nation in 1850.

The rise of capitalist industry, far from incarcerating women and children in the household in relations of dependence upon the wages of male industrial workers, tended to destroy pre-existing domestic relations. In the leading branches of capitalist industry in England in the late eighteenth and early nineteenth centuries, women and children formed the largest section of the wage labour force. Women and children were subjected to conditions of superexploitation in industry. The degradation and demoralization of the English workers as a whole which resulted led to struggles for the possibility of a domestic sphere.

In England before the development of industrial capitalism, the household, for most of the productive population, was patriarchal in its authority relations. Yet while women and children were subordinate members of this social unit, the contribution of all members was visible and socially recognized.[35] In the English case, the penetration of capital into social production did not initially destroy existing relations of production, but it set them on a capitalist basis. The division of labour within the household initially remained the same and the household was coterminously a unit of production and reproduction. What changed was the amount of time the household had to devote to producing commodities.

The cotton textile industry is a case in point. The domestic textile industry survived for several decades after the emergence of textile factories. In the households of textile producers, men wove and children span. Children were taught to spin as soon as they were able, and as they matured, boys were taught to weave. At first, the competition of the household industry with factory industry simply involved an increase in the amount of time household members had to devote to textile production to maintain the same income. Capital turned spinning into a branch of factory industry first. As a domestic occupation, spinning was more or less completely destroyed by 1800. To some extent, this led to the creation of a wage labour force drawn from female members of textile producing households. However, this wage labour force contained a high proportion of pauper children as well. The rise of spinning as a factory industry gave a temporary impetus to the domestic weaving industry. It increased the supply and reduced the price of yarn, thereby overcoming two of the major constraints of the domestic cloth industry. Handloom weaving flourished for at least two decades before capital penetrated the branch of weaving.

Initially, the penetration of capital into the branch of spinning probably tended to destroy the sex-based and age-based division of labour within the household. This tendency was likely intensified as domestic weaving came into competition with factory weaving. Far from cutting women and children off from social production, the competition between domestic and factory industry drew them more deeply into it. The decline of the conditions of domestic production under competition with factory industry forced all household members to weave, and to weave for more of the day. It tended to destroy the division of labour in the household between spinsters and weavers.

Before the dominance of industrial capitalist production, large numbers of English households were dependent for their reproduction upon the production of textiles. The transformation of this domestic industry into a factory industry led to the proletarianization of a large portion of the English population. The household producers were separated from their means of production and forced to seek employment in industry. To some extent, the household and its patriarchal authority relations were destroyed in this process. Proletarianization affected all members of the household. The household was not split into two units along age and sex lines by the mere fact of proletarianization. To some extent, whole families were hired together in industry under the "subcontracting" system, where the male household head acted as foreman over his wife and children.[36] Increasingly, however, women and children came to predominate in the factory labour force. In the textile industry, the leading edge of capitalist industrialization, women and children formed more than 75 percent of the wage labour force by 1838.[37] Male workers clustered in the relatively few skilled jobs while women and children formed the bulk of the unskilled labour force. In the mills around Preston, the heart of the Lancashire textile district, at mid-century women and children were almost exclusively employed.[38] Women and children also formed important sections of the wage labour force in such industries as silk production, printing, papermaking, pottery production and mining during the middle of the nineteenth century.[39]

Women and children came to predominate in the factory production of textiles and in other branches of industrial production in part for technical reasons. Increases in the productivity of labour occasioned by technical innovation, in combination with organizational innovations that separated planning from execution (i.e., mental from manual labour) facilitated the employment of unskilled women and children. More importantly, however, the subordination of women and children in the patriarchal household and in society at large made them more susceptible to factory discipline, less able and likely to form unions, and less susceptible to socialist agitation (in the words of the bourgeoisie, "obnoxious doctrines").

Women and children in particular were subjected to super-exploitation in industry. The prevailing conditions of production led to the demoralization and degradation of the workers and to the destruction of the economic and social conditions necessary for their reproduction. Utopian socialist Robert Owen regarded as the worst of the consequences of the "manufacturing system,"

> The employment of children before they possess sufficient strength for their work; before they can be initiated in their necessary domestic duties; and before they can acquire any fixed moral habits or knowledge that may render them useful, or not injurious, members of the community.[40]

Engels, writing two and a half decades later on the Manchester working class, remarked in a passage which bears quoting at length:

> Thus the social order makes family life almost impossible for the worker. In a comfortless, filthy house, hardly good enough for mere nightly shelter, ill-furnished, often neither rain-tight nor warm, a foul atmosphere filling rooms overcrowded with human beings, no domestic comfort is possible. The husband works the whole day through, perhaps the wife also and the elder children, all in different places; they meet night and morning only, all under perpetual temptation to drink; what family life is possible under such conditions? *Yet the working-man cannot escape from the family, must live in the family,* and the consequence is a perpetual succession of family troubles, domestic quarrels, most demoralising for parents and children alike. Neglect of all domestic duties, neglect of the children, especially, is only too common among the English working-people, and only too vigorously fostered by the existing institutions of society [emphasis added].[41]

Why did Engels and other socialists in England argue for the necessity of family life? Certainly not for sexist nor for sentimental reasons. This agitation for domestic life was part of the the agitation against social and political subordination of women. While they were trapped to some extent in contemporary conceptions of women's capabilities, socialist writers opposed women's domestic slavery and worked to achieve civil rights for women.[42] Some Chartist women at least shared these concerns both for political rights and for the existence of a domestic sphere.[43]

In general, we can see two major bases to the agitation of the workers' movement against the employment of women and children in industry. The first of these concerns the uneven development of capitalist industry and its consequences for the reproduction and political progress of the working class. The second concerns the particularity of the class struggle in England in the first half of the nineteenth century.

Capital destroyed the economic basis of the household for a large section of the working class when it destroyed the domestic textile industry. It forced all members of the household onto the labour market, and through its superexploitation of the labour power of women and children depressed the living standards of large sections of the class to a bare subsistence level (and at times below it). Workers were made more or less completely dependent upon the commodity market for the elements of their subsistence. Yet capital did not undertake the mass production of many items of working-class subsistence until the last quarter of the nineteenth century.[44] Capital destroyed the economic basis of the domestic production of elements of working-class subsistence while maintaining the necessity of domestic production for the reproduction of the class. This is the meaning of Engels' remark concerning the necessity yet impossibility of domestic life. Not only did the working class lose the possibility of domestic life through the industrial employment of all family members, but the domestic skills and traditions of the household were destroyed. The "improvident" worker was a necessary product of capitalist industry where "economy and judgment in the consumption and preparation of the means of subsistence" was destroyed.[45]

Important sections of the working class in England in the mid-nineteenth century could be reproduced under prevailing conditions of production only as a miserable, demoralized and brutalized rabble.[46] Workers struggled for the limitation of the working day and for political and economic emancipation from capitalist exploitation. This struggle was shaped by the ideology of the English bourgeoisie that opposed state intervention into the conditions of production.[47] An element in this ideology, which the English bourgeoisie successfully employed in its struggle for political power against the landed aristocracy, was the sanctity of the rights of "freeborn Englishmen." Supposedly in defence of the sacred right of free English workers to sell their labour power as they saw fit, the bourgeoisie refused to limit the conditions of exploitation in industry. The workers' movement was forced to fight the battle for the limitation of the working day on this terrain. The rights of "freeborn Englishmen" did not extend to women and children. It is for this reason, in large part, that the struggle to limit the working day became a struggle to limit the participation of women and children in industrial labour.

The struggle for a normal working day on the part of the English working class culminated in the Factory Acts of 1847 and 1850. The latter limited the working day for women and children in the leading branches of capitalist industry to ten and a half hours a day for the first five days of the week and to seven and a half hours on Saturdays. As a result:

> The manufacturers began by here and there discharging a part of, and in many cases half of, the young persons and women employed by them, and then, for the adult males, restoring the almost obsolete nightwork.[48]

The principle of the ten-hour day, and a tendency towards the removal of women and children from the industrial labour force appeared in

> those great branches of industry which form the most characteristic creation of the modern mode of production. Their wonderful development from 1853 to 1860, hand-in-hand with the physical and moral regeneration of the factory workers, struck the most purblind.[49]

Women and children tended to be separated from industrial employment through the agitation of the organized workers' movement and through the response of the British state to this agitation. They came to form an important segment of the industrial reserve army. However, this reserve army did not exist, in the 1860s and 1870s, in the form of dependent domestic workers supported by male wage earners. On the one hand, women continued to work in the marginal or "sweated" branches of capitalist production. On the other hand, and more importantly, the predominant form of the industrial reserve army during this period in England was domestic servitude. Working-class women, children and men as well, lived under conditions of domestic servitude in the households of the bourgeoisie and the petty bourgeoisie. The numbers of domestic servants increased enormously in the period from 1850 to 1870.

> [T]he extraordinary productiveness of modern industry, accompanied as it is by both a more extensive and a more intensive exploitation of labour-power in all other spheres of production, allows

> of the unproductive employment of a larger and larger part of the working-class, and the consequent reproduction, on a constantly extending scale, of the ancient domestic slaves under the name of a servant class, including men-servants, women-servants, lackeys, &c.[50]

Marx estimated that the section of the working class that existed in a condition of domestic servitude to the bourgeoisie and petty bourgeoisie was at least one-half the size of the working class employed in capitalist industry.[51]

In nineteenth-century England, there were no vaguely adequate social welfare policies, and unemployed workers were necessarily dependent upon the incomes of other people. The wage of most workers in the nineteenth century was not sufficiently high to support dependents. At the same time, the mass production of consumer goods was undeveloped. Private domestic labour was extremely arduous and necessary for the reproduction of the households of all classes. Working-class women and children especially entered into conditions of direct servitude in the households of the ruling and middle classes.

The numbers of domestic servants employed by the bourgeoisie and petty bourgeoisie declined after 1900, and again after the end of World War I. In the developed capitalist nations, the production of domestic appliances and consumer goods, as well as the penetration of electricity and telephones into households reduced the labour necessary for the reproduction of these households.[52] The trade union movement in the working class and the increasingly common appearance of domestic necessities on the commodity market created a situation in which the working-class household composed of a male wage earner and female and juvenile dependents was feasible. However, it is extremely unlikely that this form of domestic life was the most common in the working class in England. Married women and children continued to participate in non-domestic production although they were excluded from direct employment in the leading branches of capitalist industry.

Summary and Conclusion

What are the origins of women's domestic labour in the working-class family? Do men of all classes ally themselves in an effort to incarcerate women in the household? No clear justification for such an argument exists.

The structural conditions of the separation of household and industry are present in the capitalist economy. The uneven development of capitalism largely necessitates the private production of the elements of working-class subsistence. In the first place, the penetration of capital into certain branches of social production historically leads to the proletarianization of the population. The economic basis of the household as a coterminous unit of production and reproduction is destroyed. People are thrown onto the labour market and become dependent upon the commodity market for acquiring the means of subsistence. Yet capital, which destroyed the independent household by capitalizing one of the forms of production contained in it, does not penetrate all branches of production at the same rate. Such basic elements of the existence of the working class as food and clothing were not produced by capital on a mass basis until the twentieth century. Capital destroyed the economic basis of the domestic unit as it had existed, yet preserved the necessity of domestic labour for the reproduction of the working class.

While capital created the necessity for the private production of working-class subsistence, it also created an unemployed population which could exist as a household labour force. Increases in the productive powers of labour under capitalist conditions led to the creation of a large unproductive population.

Thus capital creates the conditions for the existence of domestic labour and a condition of mutual dependence between the wage worker and the domestic worker. As a member of the industrial reserve army the domestic worker depends for her subsistence upon the wage of her husband (or upon state revenue). The creation of an industrial reserve army forms the basis of the dependence of the domestic worker. In turn, the wage worker is dependent upon the domestic worker. He is unable to reproduce himself without her labour because of the uneven development of the capitalist economy. At the same time, largely because of his control over the wage and through his participation in social production, the wage worker is in a position to dominate the domestic worker.

The conditions for the existence of domestic labour in the working-class family are specific to the organization of capitalist production. The working-class family is a creation of capitalism; it is not a feudal remnant nor a survival from a previous era. The oppression of the domestic worker has a different form than the oppression of women in other historical periods. While an examination of the structural features of capitalism reveals the structural bases of domestic labour and the working-class family, it does not explain the sex-based division of labour between working-class men and women. How does the industrial reserve army come to be dominated by women and children? The age and sex of the industrial reserve army is specified by the state. As we have seen in the English case (and the leading capitalist nations are similar) the state directly fostered the removal of women and children from the industrial labour force. Specific enactments, more or less enforced, tended to structure patterns of labour force participation for women and children.

The state responded to an agitation on the part of organized workers in England for a normal working day by removing women and children from the industrial labour force. A reform in the conditions of labour in industry, particularly with respect to the superexploitation of the labour power of children and women would not have occurred without the agitation of the workers' movement. However, we cannot regard the removal of women and children from the industrial labour force in and of itself as the objective of the working class. The struggle for a normal working day and for the removal of women and children from the industrial labour force was part of a broad struggle on the part of the socialist workers' movement for political rights for women, for universal education under working-class control, for the abolition of women's domestic slavery and other similar social policies. The state did not respond to these demands.

Insofar as the agitation against the superexploitation of women and children included an agitation for the social and political liberation of women and children, the struggle of the workers' movement for the possibility of domestic life must be seen as a progressive one. It is true that the progressive character of this struggle was limited by the extent of the subordination and oppression of women with which it was forced to contend. The subordination of women and children in the household before the rise of the factory itself shaped the problem and its solution, by making women and children more susceptible to superexploitation and also by ensuring that men clustered in skilled industrial jobs. The progressive character of the movement is most obvious with respect to the condition of children. While it did not achieve the balance between wholesome labour and education which sections of the workers' movement sought, it did markedly improve the material condition of child workers. Certainly the same is true of many working-class women in terms of longevity, health and so on. The failure of the agitation for social equality of women obscures the progressive character of the struggle for a domestic life.

The separation of household and industry under capitalism and the sex-based division of labour which it involves forms the basis of the division of the working class along sex lines. This separation is a product of capitalism as a mode of production. It is reproduced by the state through the separation of women from industrial wage labour, and through the maintenance of the existence of labour power as a commodity. It is the state that reproduces labour power in the commodity form and that reproduces the oppression to which the unemployed domestic worker is subject. Working-class men and women share a common position of opposition to the capitalist state.

NOTES

1. Mariarosa Dalla Costa and Selma James, *The Power of Women and the Subversion of the Community* (Bristol: Falling Wall Press, 1973), p. 28.
2. Ibid., pp. 30-34.
3. Ibid., p. 26.
4. Wally Seccombe, "The Housewife and Her Labour Under Capitalism," *New Left Review*, 83 (Jan.-Feb., 1974), p. 4.
5. Margaret Benston, *The Political Economy of Women's Liberation* (Toronto: New Hogtown Press, 1973), pp. 9-10.
6. Jean Gardiner, "Women's Domestic Labour," *New Left Review*, 89 (Jan.-Feb., 1975), pp. 80-83.
7. Karl Marx, *Capital*, Vol. I (Moscow: Progress Publishers, 1954), p. 477.
8. Dalla Costa, *The Power of Women*, p. 31.
9. Studs Terkel, *Working* (New York: Avon Books, 1975), pp. 1-10.
10. Dalla Costa, *The Power of Women*, p. 33.
11. Marx, *Capital*, Vol. I, pp. 536-39.
12. Ibid., p. 538.
13. Patricia Connelly, *Last Hired, First Fired* (Toronto: The Women's Press, 1978), passim.
14. I agree that privatization has these consequences. I do not agree, however, that these consequences motivated the privatization of the reproduction of labour power.
15. Brian Simon, ed., *The Radical Tradition in Education in Britain* (London: Lawrence and Wishart, 1972), pp. 177-224. Simon reprints here a section of a work by the radical Ricardian, William Thompson, in which this concept is elaborated.
16. Suzanne de Brunhoff, *The State, Capital and Economic Policy* (London: Pluto Press, 1978), pp. 1-36.
17. Marx, *Capital*, Vol. I, p. 592.
18. Connelly, *Last Hired, First Fired.*
19. Marx, *Capital*, Vol. I, pp. 667-93.
20. Wally Seccombe, "Domestic Labour—A Reply to Critics," *New Left Review*, 94 (1975), p. 86.
21. Ibid., p. 87.

22. Marx, *Capital,* Vol. I, pp. 43-88; see also, Karl Marx, *A Contribution to the Critique of Political Economy* (New York: International Publishers, 1972), pp. 27-72.

23. Marx, *Capital,* Vol. I, pp. 43-88.

24. Insofar as Seccombe sees domestic labour from the outset as a derivative form of labour, the attempt to apply the concepts used by Marx to reveal the inner workings of capitalist production can at best apply to it indirectly.

25. Seccombe, "The Housewife," p. 9.

26. The best of these comments is Paul Smith, "Domestic Labour and Marx's Theory of Value," in *Feminism and Materialism: Women and Modes of Production,* Annette Kuhn and AnnMarie Wolpe, eds. (London: Routledge and Kegan Paul, 1978).

27. Smith, "Domestic Labour," pp. 202-203, shows that Seccombe's argument is not only mystified, but nonsensical.

28. Since it is immaterial to Seccombe's analysis whether or not the domestic worker creates value, we must discount his claim that we can locate the domestic worker in relation to the capitalist economy only through value analysis.

29. Seccombe, "The Housewife," p. 10.

30. Ibid.

31. Seccombe, "Domestic Labour," pp. 91-94.

32. Dalla Costa, *The Power of Women,* p. 27.

33. Seccombe, "The Housewife," p. 6.

34. This position appears very frequently in the current literature dealing with women's history in Canada. For example, see Leo Johnson, "The Political Economy of Ontario Women in the Nineteenth Century" in *Women at Work: Ontario, 1850–1930,* Janice Acton, et al., eds. (Toronto: The Women's Press, 1974), pp. 13-31. Connelly, in *Last Hired, First Fired,* pp. 37-41, summarizes this position and accepts that while capitalists played a central role in the division of the working class along sex lines, working-class men in unions were also responsible, and the division of the class in this way was in their (unspecified) interest.

35. This is well covered in Mildred L. Campbell, *The English Yeoman under Elizabeth and the Early Stuarts* (New Haven: Yale University Press, 1942), pp. 250-59. See also, Alice Clark, *Working Life of Women in the Seventeenth Century* (London: George Routledge and Sons, Ltd., 1919), pp. 5ff.

36. J.L. Hammond and Barbara Hammond, *The Rise of Modern Industry* (New York: Harper and Row, 1969), pp. 204-208.
37. E.J. Hobsbawm, *Industry and Empire* (Harmondsworth: Penguin Books, 1975), p. 38.
38. Michael Anderson, *Family Structure in Nineteenth Century Lancashire* (London: Cambridge University Press, 1971), p. 22.
39. A.H. Robson, *The Education of Children Engaged in Industry in England, 1833-1876* (London: Kegan Paul, Trench, Trubner and Co., 1931), p. 81.
40. Robert Owen, "On the Employment of Children in Manufactories," in *A New View of Society* (London: J.M. Dent and Sons, 1972), p. 131.
41. Friedrich Engels, *The Condition of the Working Class in England* (Moscow: Progress Publishers, 1973), p. 168.
42. Engels, *The Condition,* p. 182-86, argues that the reversal of roles in the working-class household consequent upon employment for women and unemployment for men makes it clear that male domination was a "false position from the beginning." See also Dorothy Thompson, *The Early Chartists* (London: Macmillan, 1971), pp. 115-27.
43. Thompson, *Early Chartists,* pp. 128-30.
44. Hobsbawm, *Industry,* p. 154ff.
45. Marx, *Capital,* Vol. I, p. 373.
46. Engels, *The Condition,* p. 153. Marx, in *Capital,* Vol. I, p. 372n, remarks on the report of Dr. Edward Smith, a factory inspector, concerning the consequences for working-class women and the working-class household of the cotton crisis of 1861-65. Only when they were unemployed did working-class women have an opportunity to breastfeed their babies and learn to cook.
47. See for example, G.D.H. Cole and Raymond Postgate, *The British Common People, 1746-1946* (New York: Barnes and Noble, 1961), p. 259.
48. Marx, *Capital,* Vol. I, p. 271.
49. Ibid., p. 279.
50. Ibid., p. 420.
51. Ibid.
52. With respect to Canada, see Genevieve Leslie, "Domestic Service in Canada, 1880-1920" in Acton et al., *Women at Work,* pp. 71-125.

DOMESTIC LABOUR: A METHODOLOGICAL DISCUSSION

Linda Briskin

In a fresh approach to the issue of women's domestic labour, Linda Briskin concentrates on determining the methodology that is most in accord with Marx's theory of capital. She focusses on the relationship between the laws governing the capitalist production of value and the historically determined social relations characteristic of capitalism. Certain contradictions are seen to arise out of this relationship. One of the key contradictions is the existence of forms of labour other than wage labour, such as domestic labour, which are nonetheless a necessary part of capitalism.

Briskin argues that the laws governing the production and reproduction of value do not apply to the household, and that the conceptual categories relevant to understanding capitalist commodity production do not, therefore, apply to domestic labour. These categories have been applied rather indiscriminately to domestic labour in the past, resulting in some confusion. Among the conclusions Briskin sees as confused are the ideas that domestic labour produces value (see SECCOMBE *and* BLUMENFELD *and* MANN*), and that it can affect the value of labour power and, ultimately, the amount of surplus value capital appropriates (see* FOX*).*

In developing the argument that domestic labour is not value production, and to distinguish between the abstraction of the theory of value and the historical reality of capitalism, Briskin describes domestic labour as a form of labour that emerges with the rise of capitalism and the development of the capitalist family form. She ends with an examination of the effect of the laws of capitalist production on the performance of domestic labour through a consideration of the industrial reserve army.

Introduction[1]

The re-emergence of the women's movement in the last ten years has led to a renaissance in Marxist theory on the "woman question"—particularly concern with the family and domestic labour. In the past, these issues have received little attention from Marxists: the family was traditionally viewed as outside the arena of class struggle and domestic labour was considered to be irrelevant to the sphere of production. Yet an investigation of the family and domestic labour is important not only for achieving a better understanding of women's oppression, but also for clarifying the strategic political questions facing the women's movement.

The key struggle facing feminists today is the building of an autonomous women's movement, which can both act independently in women's interests, and begin the arduous process of building links with other groups—such as the trade unions and the left—which are also concerned with a radical restructuring of the social order. To some extent the success of this task will depend upon a correct theoretical elaboration of women's role in capitalist society.

Making the distinction between exploitation and oppression is an important step in analyzing women's role under capitalism. Exploitation, rooted in the economic reality, is expressed in the class structure of capitalist society. Those who own only their ability to work are forced to sell their labour power for a wage, while those who own and control the means of production, the capitalist class, are able to appropriate the surplus that the working class produces. Exploitation faces all those who work for wages—both men and women.

Oppression, on the other hand, is a condition that takes many forms, including racism and sexism. Although forms of sexism have existed in all societies, the specific form that sexism takes is a function of the dominant social relations of the mode of production—under capitalism, the relation between the capitalist class and the working class. Therefore the mechanisms for the continuation of sexism and the strategy for eliminating it must be elaborated within the context of the social order in which we live. It is the understanding of the dynamic of our own social reality that will provide the tools for challenging sexism.

Women's oppression is not simply a function of a free-floating set of sexist ideas; rather, it is firmly rooted in the material conditions of women's lives, primarily in the institution of the family. The family is the locus for the continuation of women's oppression not only because of its part in socializing women to their roles in life, nor because of the psychological domination of men within that institution. The primary burden of women within the family is their continued responsibility for extensive household labour, which plays a central role in maintaining the capitalist social order. Domestic labour takes three main forms: the reproduction of the labour force in the form of new workers, (i.e., children); the care of those children and their socialization to the rigours of industrial discipline; the maintenance of the labour force through the day-to-day labour of cooking, cleaning, laundry and shopping; and finally, the provision of emotional services such as tension-managing.

The class nature of women's exploitation in the work place suggests that the women's movement cannot politically separate itself from or ignore the struggle against exploitation of both men and women of the working class. This means allying ourselves with the defensive organization of the working class—the trade unions.

But the subordinate position of women in the work place is not just a function of exploitation. The perpetuation of sexist ideology, which arises in large part from the material conditions of the family, helps to maintain and gives concrete form to this exploitation. For example, the statement that women's place is in the home has been an historical justification for women's low wages and for the pressure on women to vanish into the home during periods of high unemployment. It is only women organizing in trade union caucuses, for example, which can effectively challenge this sexist ideology in the work place and force the trade union movement to take up issues of specific concern to women workers.

Sexist ideology is not confined to the work place; it manifests itself in most spheres of the social order—in the educational system, the media, the legal system. The primary locus for the regeneration of sexist ideology and the perpetuation of women's oppression is not simply the family but the specific form that the family takes within the capitalist mode of production. The fact that women's oppression is rooted in the capitalist family, which exists outside the sphere of commodity production, necessitates the development of an autonomous women's movement to address such issues as child care, domestic labour, violence against women and control of our bodies in order to ultimately challenge the sexual division of labour.

Unlike orthodox Marxists, who argue that the disappearance of exploitation will herald the disappearance of all forms of oppression, socialist feminists understand the dialectical relationship between women's exploitation and women's oppression and thus the necessity for the building of a strong autonomous women's movement. The relative autonomy of women's oppression makes a women's movement essential, but the historical specificity of oppression and its links to the class nature of capitalist society make it insufficient for the achievement of women's liberation. The link between women's oppression and women's exploitation must be concretely expressed in the links between the women's movement and the trade union movement (though not through the submersion of one into the other) and perhaps ultimately in the forging of a strong revolutionary party.

This argument in favour of the autonomous women's movement rests on certain theoretical assumptions, which this paper will investigate in depth: (a) that an historically specific family form exists within capitalism; and (b) that domestic labour is a capitalist form of labour that plays an essential role in reproducing capitalist social relations. A central concern in addressing these points will be the correct application of Marx's theory of capital. In order to apply Marx's theory of capital to the elaboration of the role of domestic labour within the capitalist mode of production, it is essential to distinguish between the inner dynamic of capital and the larger set of capitalist social relations.

The inner dynamic of capital—indeed the moving force of capitalist society—is the reproduction of value, a process predicated on the capital/labour relation. Although this inner dynamic is central to the capitalist mode of production, all of capitalist social relations cannot be reduced to that single relationship; nonetheless, our theory of capitalism as an entire social system must have a relationship to the theory of capital but not be subsumed by it. We must understand the central force that the reproduction of value exerts over all social relations at the same time as we recognize its inability to transform all relations into the wage labour/capital relation. Its inability to effect this transformation, and the continuing existence of social relations outside the labour/capital relation (e.g., the family and the state) do not deny the central strength and integrity of that inner dynamic.

The fact that the inner dynamic has no exact reflection in the real historical world of capitalism (because it is distorted by other capitalist social relations), does not mean the theory of that inner dynamic has no usefulness, or is incorrect. Marx's theory of capital makes no pretensions to include all the variations and historical moments that exist in the "real history of capitalism," nor should its validity as a theory be determined by its ability to reflect, as in a model of the bourgeois social sciences, all historical reality. It is within this framework that the dialectical relationship between wage labour and domestic labour will be examined in this article.

Various forms of labour exist outside of wage labour but are still a part of capitalist social relations. Domestic labour is one of these forms. It is important to specify the nature of domestic labour as a product of capitalist development and a capitalist form of labour without subsuming it under and within the category of wage labour, in the same way as the women's movement cannot be subsumed or contained within the trade union movement or the revolutionary party. Although we cannot use the category of wage labour directly to understand domestic labour, wage labour stands in a dialectical relation to domestic labour. Insofar as the wage labour/capital relation is the *dominant* social relation within capitalist society, there is necessarily a link between the two. The apparent contradiction of this relationship is in fact an expression of the contradictory nature of capitalism as a system of social relations.

In order to understand this contradiction, we must employ the distinction between capital as a process of reproducing value on the one hand, and capitalism as a system of social relations, on the other. The inner dynamic of the reproduction of value has its own logic, which we can specify at a level of abstraction that allows us to understand the central forces at work in capitalist society. It is precisely because this inner dynamic exerts such a force, often hidden, over all arenas of society that we must isolate it. In order to describe the inner dynamic we use certain categories of analysis, particularly those of the commodity and value. These categories have a highly specific application and make sense only at this level of abstraction.

When we turn our attention to capitalism, to the entire system of social relations rather than the abstracted process of the reproduction of value, we must inform our analysis through an understanding of the reproduction of value but we cannot simply appropriate the categories of analysis relevant to that level. So we see that while capital is constantly attempting to transform all relations into market relations, or all forms of labour into wage labour, at the same time capitalism is re-creating the necessity for domestic labour. Although it appears that these two processes cannot exist simultaneously, the fact that they do creates a contradiction for the capitalist social order. Concretely, this takes the form of pressuring women to enter the work force at the same time as trying to maintain the traditional capitalist family form. Indeed it is precisely the contradiction that women's entrance into the labour force poses for capitalism that makes this process potentially so challenging to the social order.

When we consider domestic labour at the level of the reproduction of value, we see that it does not exist as a category of analysis. At this level of abstraction, all labour is commodity-producing labour, value-producing labour, and only commodities can produce other commodities; only two classes exist, capital and labour.

This article will illustrate the role domestic labour plays in the reproduction of capitalist social relations, at the same time showing that domestic labour is not part of the process of reproducing value, and is therefore absent as a category from the theory of capital. The potentially revolutionary nature of women's liberation lies in the understanding of the contradictions between the inner dynamic of capital and capitalism as a system of social relations.

Domestic Labour as a Meaningful Category of Capitalist Social Relations

This section examines the unique nature of the capitalist family form as distinct from other historical forms of the family and concomitantly, domestic labour as a category of labour that emerges with the rise of capitalism. Domestic labour is therefore a capitalist form of labour.

Wage labour is the dominant form of labour within capitalism. The creation of wage labour occurs in the period of primitive accumulation and is the historical presupposition for the capitalist mode of production. Capital as self-expanding value (i.e., the expanded reproduction of value), assumes the existence of a wage labour force and of the capital/labour relation.

Although capital presupposes the existence of wage labour, capitalism is also dependent upon the constant reproduction of a class of free labourers, free

> in the double sense that neither they themselves form part and parcel of the means of production, as in the case of slaves . . . nor do the means of production belong to them, as in the case of peasant proprietors. . . . The so-called primitive accumulation, therefore, is nothing else than the historical process of divorcing the producer from the means of production.[2]

The existence of labour power as a commodity depends upon the separation of the worker from the means of production, which is, in fact, the separation of the family unit from the means of production. "Free" labour is forced to sell its labour power in order for both the labourer and the family to survive.

> Hence the sum of the means of subsistence necessary for the production of labour-power must include the means necessary for the labourer's substitutes, *i.e.*, his children, in order that this race of peculiar commodity-owners may perpetuate its appearance in the market.[3]

The labourer is also free from any direct relations of dependence on the capitalist, unlike the feudal serf, who is tied to the lord. The disappearance of direct relations of dependence is predicated upon the creation of an autonomous economic sphere, which historically takes the form of the split between home and work. Therefore, the creation of a wage labour force in the sphere of commodity production is at one and the same time the creation of a domestic labour force within the capitalist family.

> The owner of labour power is mortal. If then his appearance in the market is to be continuous, and the continuous conversion of money into capital assumes this, the seller of labour-power must

> perpetuate himself, 'in the way that every living individual perpetuates himself, by procreation.'[4]

But although the renewal and procreation of the human species is a universal structural necessity for every mode of production, under the reign of capital, procreation necessarily takes the form of the creation and re-creation of a wage labour force. Thus the capitalist family form—a family which owns no means of production, which is forced to sell a part of its labour power for a wage, and therefore which is dependent on commodities for its survival—is a structural component of capitalism. Domestic labour is that part of the family's labour which helps to maintain and procreate this wage labour force.

It should be stressed that this argument does not deal with the concrete historical reality of women's work, but rather with domestic labour as an economic category, as an abstraction. In fact, this understanding of the category of domestic labour would hold if men did domestic labour. The question of why women traditionally do domestic work requires a separate investigation, predicated on this analysis.

It is only with the creation of wage labour as the dominant form of labour that the possibility of domestic labour as a distinct category exists. This does not mean that one category can be subsumed under or understood solely in connection with the other; rather, it means that the process of primitive accumulation that establishes wage labour as a dominant form of labour also establishes domestic labour as a meaningful category. The existence of wage labour depends upon the existence of domestic labour; thus, domestic labour is one of the presuppositions for the capitalist mode of production and "hence belongs to the history of its formation."[5]

This implies that the capitalist family cannot disappear within the framework of capitalism, and, consequently, that women cannot be liberated within capitalist society. Some people have argued that the separation of women from procreation through the development of socially regulated test tube babies will provide the material basis for women's liberation.[6] Although this is a rather far-fetched argument, exploring its implications helps to illustrate my point. Capitalism depends upon the capitalist family to provide a wage labour force that appears outside of capital's control and that appears to participate in a free and equal exchange on the market-place—an exchange of labour power for wages. If the state were to take over the control of procreation, the wage labourer would no longer be free. His labour power would no longer be a commodity; rather he himself, like a slave, would be a commodity produced, owned and sold by the state.

The test tube baby solution has a second weakness. It implicitly identifies woman's biological capacity to bear children as a source of her oppression. This perspective is a form of biological determinism whose solution is a form of technological determinism—test tube babies. It fails to consider the social historical factors that explain the *form* that childbearing and rearing take in a given society. In the first instance, the liberation of women will not occur through technical invention, nor even technological control, but rather a social reorganization whose priority would be social need rather than profit—a reorganization that would challenge the class structure. As long as capital depends upon the commodity labour power for the reproduction of value, the capitalist family form will be reinforced to provide a wage labour force. As long as the capitalist family form exists, women will be oppressed.

The Reification of the Family

Although the depth of the relationship between the sphere of production and the family is becoming increasingly clear, there is a prevailing myth that the family as a social institution stands apart from the rest of society. It appears that the family has an immutable form which transcends historical forces. It is not enough to ascribe this myth to ignorance; it is important to see how capitalist social relations themselves encourage and create this distortion, this tendency to apprehend only the "natural" fact of the family—its existence—rather than an understanding of the capitalist social relations that give rise to it.

The fundamental difference between the appearance and the essence of capitalism creates such distortions. Marx's concept of the fetishism of commodities is central to understanding the mechanisms of this distortion.

> This I call the Fetishism which attaches itself to the products of labour, so soon as they are produced as commodities, and which is therefore inseparable from the production of commodities.
>
> This fetishism of commodities has its origin . . . in the peculiar social character of the labour that produces them. . . .
>
> In other words, the labour of the individual asserts itself as a part of the labour of society, only by means of the relations which the act of exchange establishes directly between the products, and indirectly, through them, between the producers. To the latter, therefore, the relations connecting the labour of one individual with that of the rest appear, not as direct social relations between individuals at work, but as what they really are, material relations between persons and social relations between things.[7]

Since the social relation between commodity producers expresses itself in the circulation of commodities in the marketplace, it appears that commodities themselves determine the pattern of exchange. "There it is a definite social relation between men, that assumes . . . the fantastic form of a relation between things."[8] Marx was not suggesting that this appearance was simply "false consciousness" for it is generated out of the nature of capitalist social organization itself. Nicolaus suggests, "It [circulation] is only the surface . . . but it is an objective moment of the whole and must be included in its concept."[9]

This fetishism of commodities has a two-told effect. Not only does it make relations that are in reality relations between producers appear as relations between things, but it tends to obfuscate the historical nature of capitalist society. Capitalism appears to be an ahistorical universal rather than an historically determined mode of production over which man has ultimate control.

As I explained in the previous section, commodity production necessitates the development of an autonomous and self-generating economic sphere. This presupposes the existence of a "free" labour force, free from direct relations of dependence, yet forced to sell its labour power in order to survive. The re-creation of the wage labour force is located outside the sphere of commodity production; therefore, the family in which this re-creation occurs appears unrelated to that sphere of production.

Because the family's relation to commodity production is mediated by the exchange between the "free" labour produced in the family and the wage, it appears that the family has merely an external or accidental relation to capitalist social relations, in the same way as it appears that the labourer participates in a free and equal exchange when he sells his labour power for a wage. The family's distinctness from the sphere of production stops at the level of appearance. Although the family has a limited sort of freedom, as does the wage labourer himself, the family is forced to re-create the wage labour force precisely because it is dependent upon commodities for its survival.

When the analysis of the capitalist family stops at the appearance of its separateness, a mystification of the relations in the home occurs. The problems generated within the atomized family are understood as private and individual and the locus of tension becomes the relation between the domestic labourer and the wage labourer. Domestic labour appears only in its "one-sided unity" as a free service to the wage labourer and not in its reality as an integral part of the reproduction of capitalist social relations.

The fetishism of commodities is a function of the relative autonomy of the sphere of circulation from the sphere of production. A similar bifurcation affects our perceptions of the family. Unlike fetishism, which is the personification of things (i.e., commodities), reification is the apparent conversion of social relations into things.[10]

An important manifestation of reification in capitalist society is the seeming disappearance of social relations into commodities, commodities which are then fetishized. In the capital/labour relation, labour power is treated as any other commodity or factor of production. Similarly, reification makes the family appear to be a natural object, a universal disconnected from the capitalist social relations which give rise to it and constantly re-create it. Reification is a function of the relative autonomy of the "free" labourer from the sphere of production, that is, the split between home and work.

The essence of capitalism as an historical form of social relations over which man can exert control is concealed as a function of fetishism and reification. The family suffers from this distortion as it appears to be an ahistorical universal formation which stands apart, not only from production, but from history itself. Like capitalist production, it appears immutable.

Once the historical nature of the family is established, the theory of a continuous system of patriarchy, identified with the family, is called into question. "Patriarchy" is a misleading term because it has no distinct structural reality, and therefore a theory of patriarchy cannot provide us with a satisfactory explanation of women's oppression. Since the family changes with the mode of production, it is more useful to investigate patriarchal *ideas* and to elaborate the way in which their expression and form is mediated by that mode of production. This is the reason that it is correct to speak of patriarchal capitalism (or patriarchal feudalism) but not of capitalist patriarchy.

The Inner Dynamic of Capital: the Reproduction of Value

In *Capital,* Marx elucidates the theory of capital, that is, the ways in which capital, once set in motion, is able to reproduce

itself and expand (thus the inner dynamic of capital is the reproduction of value). Let us briefly examine this theory.

All societies must allocate the total available labour time to meet social needs. But in the capitalistic organization of production, products are not directly produced to meet the needs of the producers or for immediate use. Under capitalism, all products take on the commodity form because they are produced for exchange. A commodity must have some use or no one would want it, but it must also have an exchange value if it is to be equatable with other products and thus exchangeable. In a capitalist society, the division of total social labour to meet social needs takes place indirectly through the exchange process or, what is the same thing, the competitive market.

What makes commodities equatable or exchangeable? It can't be anything natural because their natural properties are unique; so it must be something social. But the only social dimension that all commodities have in common is that they are products of labour. Here again, though, we run up against the obstacle that they are the products of qualitatively distinct types of labour, referred to by Marx as "concrete labour." But under capitalism labour itself becomes a commodity that is bought and sold on the labour market. It is particularly with the development of unskilled labour that the lowest common denominator becomes established and the labour market becomes generalized and standardized. Labour which is indifferent to its mode of application may be considered qualitatively homogeneous and therefore treated purely in quantitative terms, or, to be more specific, treated purely in terms of time, so that two workers working half an hour equals one worker working one hour. Marx calls this homogeneous labour "abstract labour," and it is only in this abstract aspect that labour can form the social substance and social measure of value. As use values, commodities are the products of concrete labour and have particular utilities. As exchange values, commodities are equatable to all other commodities because they express the common measureable social substance, abstract labour.

In order for the equalizing process between commodities to become generalized, a particular commodity must be set aside as an external standard through which the equality of any two commodities can be expressed. This special commodity that makes all other commodities equatable is money. Commodity owners exchange commodities that they do not want through the use of money for commodities they do want, according to the formula C-M-C (commodity-money-commodity).

Capitalists, however, invest money in order to make profits according to the formula M-C-M′. The second M must be bigger than the first or else there is no reason for the exchange. But if we assume all exchanges to be quid-pro-quo, then how can the second M be larger? There must be a commodity that can somehow yield more value than it costs. This commodity can only be living labour power, that is, the worker's ability to work, because once value is embodied in a commodity, it can only be transferred, it cannot expand itself. The industrial capitalist buys labour power and means of production and combines them in a production process that yields a commodity. The profit comes from the difference between the value of the labour power and the new value created by the labourer. This difference is called "surplus value."

The value of labour power is determined by the amount of socially necessary time embodied in those commodities that are necessary to reproduce labour power.

> Therefore the labour-time requisite for the production of labour-power reduces itself to that necessary for the production of those means of subsistence; in other words, the value of labour-power is the value of the means of subsistence necessary for the maintenance of the labourer.[11]

From the point of view of the reproduction of value, we are concerned only with those aspects of the reproduction of labour power that are directly connected with commodity production. In other words, what quantity of commodities (and thus what portion of available socially necessary time) must be allocated to labourers to ensure their continued appearance at work?

Value and surplus value cannot be separated from the process of the production of commodities by means of commodities. The theory of capital specifies the way in which capital expands—its necessary tendency toward accumulation, centralization and concentration through the mechanism of competition; the tendency toward the falling rate of profit and the rising organic composition of capital; the tendency for capital to create and re-create the industrial reserve army; the tendency of capital to revolutionize the means of production and in so doing, to increase the contradiction between the highly regimented organization of the labour process and the private and anarchic ownership of the means of production.

From the standpoint of the reproduction of value, all labour is commodity-producing labour. All areas of production are for exchange and no labour occurs outside of commodity production. When we examine this inner core of capital, the category of domestic labour has no meaning.

Although the inner dynamic of capital is never expressed in a pure form within the capitalist mode of production, Marx's theory of capital is more than an analytical exercise. On the one hand, the laws of motion of capital are not ahistorical abstractions; the wage labour/capital relationship is a concretely historical social relation. Nor are they simply historical generalizations based upon intensive empirical study. Marx makes it clear that he is concerned with tracing the inner dynamic of a fully developed capitalist society and not with the immense diversity of empirical reality. Nor is he addressing primarily questions of historical genesis and evolution. The aim of Marx's theory of capital is to grasp the essential dynamic that governs a whole historical epoch. At the theoretical level the commodity form and the capital/labour relation are treated abstractly, but this is necessary for the sake of theoretical clarity and explanatory power. These concepts are not, however, mere theoretical constructs; for they are based on relationships that exert a dominant determining force in the real world during the entire historical epoch of capitalism.

> It is always the direct relationship of the owners of the conditions of production to the direct producers . . . which reveals the innermost secret, the hidden basis of the entire social structure. . . . This does not prevent the same economic basis—the same from the standpoint of its main conditions—due to innumerable different empirical circumstances, natural environment, racial relations, external historical influences, etc., from showing infinite variations and gradations in appearance, which can be ascertained only by analysis of the empirically given circumstances.[12]

When we are examining the inner dynamic of capital, all labour is transformed into the commodity labour power, and all labour produces a commodity. What is important to the capitalist is that the labourer consumes commodities.

> The labourer consumes in a two-fold way. While producing he consumes by his labour the means of production, and converts them into products with a higher value than that of the capital advanced. This is his productive consumption. It is at the same time consumption of his labour-power by the capitalist who bought it. On the other hand, the labourer turns the money paid to him for his labour-power, into means of subsistence: this is his individual consumption. The labourer's productive consumption, and his individual consumption, are therefore totally distinct. In the former, he acts as the motive power of capital, and belongs to the capitalist. In the latter, he belongs to himself, and performs his necessary vital functions outside the process of production. The result of the one is, that the capitalist lives; of the other, that the labourer lives.[13]

Labour power is an essential factor in the reproduction of capital insofar as it is a necessary condition for that reproduction. The working class' "individual consumption" of commodities from the sphere of production results in the reproduction of labour power and the necessity for labour power to sell itself in exchange for continued means of subsistence.

> By converting part of his capital into labour-power, the capitalist augments the value of his entire capital. He kills two birds with one stone. He profits, not only by what he receives from, but by what he gives to, the labourer. The capital given in exchange for labour-power is converted into necessaries, by the consumption of which the muscles, nerves, bones, and brains of existing labourers are reproduced, and new labourers are begotten. Within the

> limits of what is strictly necessary, the individual consumption of the working class is, therefore, the reconversion of the means of subsistence given by capital in exchange for labour power, into fresh labour-power at the disposal of capital for exploitation. It is the production and reproduction of that means of production so indispensable to the capitalist: the labourer himself. The individual consumption of the labourer . . . forms therefore a factor of the production and reproduction of capital.[14]

In analyzing the reproduction of value, Marx deliberately and consistently refers to the reproduction of labour power as the "individual consumption" of the working class. This is not simply a sexist oversight concerning domestic labour within the family. Rather, from the point of view of capital, only labour that participates in the reproduction and expansion of capital, that is, which produces value, is of any concern.

Any labour involved in consumption of these commodities allocated to the reproduction of labour power, whether it be eating them (is this not expending labour?), cooking them, shopping for them or whatever, is irrelevant. Similarly, the "form" of the "individual consumption" of the working class is also irrelevant. The way in which the worker consumes those commodities, either by eating bread and cheese directly purchased or by sitting down to a meal prepared by a domestic labourer is of no concern. "The fact that the labourer consumes his means of subsistence for his own purposes [and by extension, in his chosen way], and not to please the capitalist, has no bearing on the matter."[15]

The only concern of capital is that the process of individual consumption occur. And in fact, capital has no worries on this score, precisely because of the hidden coercion that is exercised on the wage labourer to sell his labour power to survive. The individual consumption of the working class "provides, on the one hand, the means for their maintenance and reproduction: on the other hand, it secures by the annihilation of the necessaries of life, the continued re-appearance of the workman in the labour-market."[16] Marx reminds us that production and consumption are not identical, but that production and consumption are moments of one process, in which production is "the point of departure for realization and hence also its predominant moment."[17]

Capitalism as a System of Social Relations: the Role of Domestic Labour

Although it is important to specify the inner dynamic of capital in order to isolate its essential working capitalism as an historic mode of production is unable to transform all relations into market relations. It is therefore important not to equate capitalism with the narrower concept of the reproduction of value, thereby emptying it of any specifically historical content and reducing it to a limited set of categories.[18] Paradoxically, it appears that capitalism requires a certain amount of non-commoditized relationships, such as motherhood, for example. Domestic labour exists outside the marketplace, and as we have already shown, participates in the reproduction of the labour force. Capital is unable to make the direct transformation of domestic labour into wage labour, which implies a level of secondary contradiction beyond that of the wage labour/capital relation between other capitalist social relations and the laws of motion of capital.

As we have shown, domestic labour is not part of the inner dynamic of capital and as such, the amount and kind of domestic labour is not regulated by the process of reproducing value. Yet, domestic labour as an economic category is generated out of the rise of capitalism and is a capitalist form of labour informed by the laws of motion of capital.

Domestic labour is essentially a two-fold labour. First, it mediates the production of commodities and the provision of services by the state with the "individual consumption" of the working class.[19] Domestic labour transforms commodities to make them usable without transferring value or adding new value, and, as such, is the form of the individual consumption of the working class. Second, it "produces" both the replacements for the wage labour force and the domestic labourers.[20]

The following section will examine the current debates on domestic labour in the light of the above perspective. Much of the debate centres around four questions: Does domestic labour produce the commodity labour power? Does domestic labour affect the value of labour power? Does domestic labour produce value?[21] Does domestic labour produce use value?[22]

The posing of these questions is not simply a theoretical game. Methodological clarity can allow us to deepen our understanding of the nature of capitalist reality and provide tools for investigation of social relations, such as the state, that stand apart from the capital/labour relation. Similarly, understanding the precise nature of the relationship between domestic labour and capitalism will facilitate the emergence of a potent political strategy for the women's movement.

However, in view of our earlier discussion, the asking of these particular questions seems incorrect. Domestic labour is not a category in the theory of capital. Further, it is impossible to separate these questions (as they are really all the same question) because of the inextricable link between commodity production and value production. Nonetheless, these questions must be addressed as such in order to refute the misunderstandings that abound in the literature. It is hoped that a direct rebuttal of these points will expose the fallacies of the questions.

DOES DOMESTIC LABOUR PRODUCE THE COMMODITY LABOUR POWER?

The ability of the labourer to work is called "labour power," and must be clearly distinguished from his labour, which is the actual work that he does. The worker sells his labour power for a wage. Through this exchange process labour power is transformed into a commodity, one which has a very special nature.

Like any other commodity, labour power has both a use value and an exchange value. The use value of labour power is its labour or the specific qualitative work of the labourer. The exchange value of labour power "is determined, as in the case of every other commodity, by the labour-time necessary for the production, and consequently also the reproduction, of this special article."[23]

The first special aspect of labour power is that it is the only commodity that produces value. Further, its use value, labour, produces more value than the labour power is worth, or conversely, the exchange value of labour power is less than the value it produces. In a ten-hour day, perhaps only five of the hours are necessary for the labourer's subsistence; the other five hours constitute the basis for the exploitation of the labourer by the purchaser of that labour power. As Marx explains, "the daily cost of maintaining it, and its daily expenditure in work, are two totally different things. The former determines the exchange-value of the labour-power, the latter is its use value."[24]

Labour power is reproduced in the sphere of production, insofar as the value of labour power is a portion of the commodities produced in the sphere of production. In the aggregate, the reproduction of labour power is the reproduction of the dominant class relations of capitalist society.[25]

But the labourer, as wage labour, the potential embodiment of labour power, is reproduced outside of the sphere of production, in the family. And the labour which goes into producing (bearing and raising children) and reproducing (daily maintenance) the labourer is to a large extent performed by the domestic labourer, not the labourer himself. (Of course, the domestic labourer and the wage labourer can be one and the same, as in the case of a mother who works outside the home or a man who does his own housework. This underlines the fact that this analysis is concerned with economic categories, not physical persons.) Domestic labour does not produce or even reproduce labour power; rather it participates in the process of reproducing the labourer himself, as wage labour.

The "product" of domestic labour, the wage labourer, is not the means of realizing value and is therefore not intended for exchange. For it is not the labourer who is sold as a commodity (as would be true of a slave), but rather the capacity of the labourer to work, his labour power, which is sold. Insofar as domestic labour does not produce a commodity, it cannot participate in the production of value, because only commodities embody value.

DOES DOMESTIC LABOUR AFFECT THE VALUE OF LABOUR?

We have shown that domestic labour does not produce the commodity labour power, but can it affect the value of labour power? The value of labour power is relevant to the capitalist in that it determines the proportion of socially necessary time that must be allocated to the working class. It is the aggregate of commodities necessary to reproduce the entire working class, not a single individual. The value of labour power is an abstract conceptualization and will always include whatever magnitude of commodities is necessary.

There are two ways in which it has been suggested that domestic labour might affect the value of labour power. First, it might increase the value appropriated by the capitalist. In order to do this it would have to affect the amount of socially necessary labour time needed to produce the workers' means of subsistence. Second, domestic labour might lower the value of labour power by decreasing the actual amount of commodities allocated to the working class.

Let us take up the first issue. No amount of domestic labour can alter the time it takes to produce those commodities. This would imply that domestic labour increases relative surplus value. (Relative surplus value depends upon a decrease in the value of labour power, that is, a decrease in the portion of the working day necessary to produce the commodities essential to the production of labour power.)

A reduction of necessary labour time is most easily effected by producing commodities more efficiently (or increasing the productivity of labour). Subsequently, they will embody less value and less value will be allocated to workers. This can be accomplished through a reorganization of work, a more efficient division of labour or through improved technological methods. These developments in the mode of production will increase the productivity of labour, and thus decrease the value of labour power.

> Such a fall in the value of labour-power implies, however, that the same necessaries of life which were formerly produced in ten hours, can now be produced in nine hours. But this is impossible without an increase in the productiveness of labour. . . . Hence, the conditions of production, *i.e.*, his mode of production, and the labour-process itself, must be revolutionised. By increase in the productiveness of labour, we mean, generally, an alteration in the labour-process, of such a kind as to shorten the labour-time socially necessary for the production of a commodity.[26]

Marx continues, "Hence there is immanent in capital an inclination and constant tendency, to heighten the productiveness of labour, in order to cheapen commodities, and by such cheapening to cheapen the labourer himself."[27]

Domestic labour cannot affect the amount of relative surplus value the capitalist appropriates. To argue this is to incorrectly imply that the "form" of the individual consumption of the working class, that is, the specific way in which the domestic labourer transforms commodities, affects the value of labour power.[28] For example, if the domestic labourer is more efficient in her use of food, this in turn would affect the relative surplus value of the capitalist.

This argument illustrated again the problem of attempting to appropriate the categories of value analysis relevant to the reproduction of value to those spheres outside of the commodity sphere. The domestic labourer in the family does not produce a commodity nor does domestic labour affect the value of labour power. Domestic labour can neither increase the value appropriated by the capitalist (by increasing relative surplus value) nor lower the value of labour power (which is whatever sum of commodities).

But can domestic labour affect the actual amount of commodities (the magnitude of the value of labour power) allocated to the working class? The magnitude of the value of labour power is the range and extent of the needs of the working class. Marx specifies that "the number and extent of his so-called necessary wants, as also the modes of satisfying them, are themselves the product of *historical development*" (my emphasis).[29] Therefore the *actual* amount of commodities is not relevant to the process of producing value. The answer to the question, "How many commodities will be allocated?" must be found in an investigation of particular stages in the development of capitalism (such as monopoly capitalism), and an examination of specific historical ingredients. This is not to imply that the study of a particular stage in capitalism will ignore the theory of capital; in fact, it will be predicated upon it. Such an investigation will be concerned with the systematic distortions that affect that inner dynamic to produce a complex historical reality.

If we pose the question, "Can domestic labour in a particular stage of capitalism decrease the amount of commodities allocated to the working class?", the answer is still no. The amount of commodities available to the domestic labourer is in no way determined by her actual domestic labour, but rather by the stage of development of capitalism and the level of class struggle. The capitalist clearly has an interest in limiting the amount of the so-called needs of the workers because the magnitude of the value of labour power directly influences the actual amount of surplus value that the capitalist will appropriate. Thus the capitalist will attempt to allocate only the minimum necessary to reproduce the working class. This minimum will take into account the kind of working class that the stage of capitalist development demands, especially as capitalist development is increasingly predicated upon the availability of skilled and educated workers.

The actual allocation of time between necessary and surplus labour is a reflection of the central contradiction of capitalism—the wage labour/capital relation—whose historical reality is the class struggle. The domestic labourer may be involved in this class struggle, for example, in food riots, which may in turn affect the amount of commodities at her disposal, but her actual domestic labour (e.g., her personal decision to have a garden or to make her own clothes) will not affect the amount of commodities.

It is also true that domestic labour can, in specific *historical* instances, provide substitutes for commodities. For example, in a cycle of high unemployment, when the trade union movement is weak and wages are pushed down, the intensification of domestic labour may occur (e.g., "stretching the dollar"). However, this intensification must be explained at a conjunctural/historical level, not as a general effect of the laws of motion.[30]

CAN DOMESTIC LABOUR PRODUCE VALUE?

Domestic labour does not produce the commodity labour power nor does it affect the value of labour power. Nor can it produce value. Domestic labour is unlike wage labour in precisely those ways which stamp wage labour as value-producing.

Unlike wage labour, domestic labour is not a commodity. The ability to labour, labour power, becomes a commodity when it is exchanged for a wage. Precisely because it is unwaged, domestic labour cannot find its quantitative understanding in abstract labour and socially necessary time. And because only abstract labour can produce value, domestic labour cannot produce value. It has no relation to the social relations in which value is produced, that is, a situation in which labour can be abstracted.

Domestic labour does not directly receive a wage. But although it is unwaged, it is a form of labour essential to capitalist social relations. The fetishism of the wage form makes all labour done in the productive sphere appear to be paid and only labour that is paid relevant. Yet all wage labourers do unpaid labour, which is the source of surplus value for the capitalist. However, the unpaid labour of the domestic labourer is qualitatively different from the surplus labour performed by the working class in the sphere of commodity production. Domestic labour is neither necessary labour nor surplus labour from the point of view of capital.

Similarly there is no distinction between necessary and surplus domestic labour time. The time involved in executing domestic labour[31] is a matter of importance only to the domestic labourer herself. No increase in the amount of domestic labour can affect the amount of value (the quantification of abstract labour) produced in the sphere of production.

We can conclude that the value of labour power and the time embodied in those commodities is not equal to the time necessary to actually reproduce the labourer. It must be underscored that this does not imply the equation of domestic labour time with socially necessary labour time, nor does it suggest that domestic labour contributes to the production of value or affects specifically the value of labour power.[32] Domestic labour neither produces value, nor by extension surplus value, nor does it have an exchange value. The integration of commodity-producing labour, value production and the process of exchange finds no mirror image in the execution of domestic labour or the "production" of the wage labourer.

DOES DOMESTIC LABOUR PRODUCE USE VALUES?

Some of the people engaged in the debate on domestic labour have argued that domestic labour does not produce value, but rather that it produces use values. This argument makes no attempt, and rightly so, to insert domestic labour into the inner dynamic of capital, but nonetheless it is still incorrect. Implicit in the argument that domestic labour produces use values is the comparison between domestic labour and that labour which produces directly for consumption. Domestic labour, which is dependent upon commodities, is not the direct satisfaction of needs with the produce of labour, for clearly, neither prepared foods, vacuum cleaners nor disposable diapers are the products of domestic labour. Domestic labour *actualizes* or *transforms* use values, but it does not create them.

To argue that domestic labour produces use values is to further imply that it is a form of labour untouched by capitalism, and that the family in which domestic labour occurs is a pre-capitalist holdout. A brief examination of the dominant characteristics of the pre-capitalist economy, an economy whose motive force was consumption rather than the expansion of capital, directly challenges these assumptions. (It should be pointed out that the following does not correspond to a specific historical moment, but is an historically informed abstraction.)

Production in the pre-capitalist economy was centred in the family, rather than in an autonomous economic sphere. The family form was independent and self-sufficient. Its ability to reproduce itself without substantial exchange was predicated on the availability (although not the ownership) of the means of production, primarily the land. It produced for immediate consumption, thus the process of production and of consumption were under the direct control of the family. It was a small-scale, labour-intensive organization that was duplicated in each family unit.

Marx explains that "it is the tendency of the capitalist mode of production to transform all production *as much as possible* into commodity production" (my emphasis).[33] This process is experienced historically as the increasing separation of the means of production from the worker and concomitantly from the family, and of the separation of production from consumption. This process of primitive accumulation does not leave the family untouched (a pre-capitalist holdout) nor does it transform it into a mirror of commodity production (a factory to reproduce labour power). Once commodity production is established as the dominant mode, it affects all arenas of society, even those outside of commodity production itself.

With the transformation of production for direct consumption into commodity production for exchange domestic labour emerges as a unique form of labour that is increasingly dependent on commodities. So too are the survival and the reproduction of the family unit. Household production is now mediated by the marketplace, by the whole sphere of commodity production; that is, production and consumption are indirectly rather than directly related. The production of the traditional family is now transformed into two processes—on the one hand, commodity production, and on the other hand, labour of transformation or domestic labour.

But the internal reorganization of the family takes a qualitatively different form from the organization of work in the sphere of commodity production, which is premised on the extraction of surplus value and designed for efficiency. Although domestic labour is increasingly dependent on commodities, the intervention of commodities does not affect the organization of work itself, which remains isolated in individual units without much increase in the division of labour or in productivity. And because surplus value is not extracted from the family, efficiency is irrelevant.

The capitalist family form is not a pre-capitalist holdout but in fact a presupposition of the capitalist mode of production, insofar as it supplies a class of wage labourers who are forced to sell their labour power for a wage. The capitalist family appears similar to its pre-capitalist form in that it is highly atomized, but in fact, in the context of highly developed commodity production, it is inefficient and reduplicative. It is a unit in which the tasks and the meaning of these tasks have altered.

With the development of capitalism, the concept of use value becomes meaningful only as one aspect of a commodity, which cannot exist apart from exchange value. Use value is not a free-floating concept that can be appropriated to describe any form of useful labour; it is an historically specific concept related to the commodity. Because domestic labour does not participate in commodity production, it is incorrect to argue that it produces use values.

In this section, I have tried to demonstrate that domestic labour is not a relevant category to the reproduction of value. I have also tried to show that domestic labour and the capitalist family are presuppositions for the existence of the capitalist mode of production. Finally, I have specified the role of domestic labour within capitalist social relations.

A major methodological critique of a number of the contributions to the domestic labour debate emerges from these formulations. Too often, the inner workings of capital have been confused with the real and explicit history of the stages of development of the capitalist mode of production. This has taken the form of trying to understand domestic labour's role as part of the reproduction of value, and of misunderstanding the dialectical relation between domestic labour and wage labour.

Such an analysis applies the categories such as commodity and value, which are relevant to wage labour, to domestic labour. *This distorts the nature of the categories, which are not abstract formulations that can be applied to any form of labour, but historically specific categories, which apply to the wage labour/capital relation.* The categories do not exist abstractly on their own, nor do they exist independently–they are part of an integral whole dependent upon the social relation of wage labour to capital in the sphere of commodity production. Domestic labour is part of capitalism, but predicated upon a particular set of social relations, molded by the dominant relation, but relatively autonomous. It is not possible to simply extrapolate the categories of one social relation of capital, although it be the dominant one, to another social relation within the same dominant mode.

Certain important political implications emerge from this understanding of domestic labour's relation to capitalism. If we were to argue that domestic labour produced value, it would be logical to assume that capital would eventually invade the household and attempt to more efficiently organize the appropriation of surplus value. This in turn implies that the specific form of the family under capitalism is not necessary to its reproduction, and that it can and probably will disappear.

The Industrial Reserve Army

The inner dynamic of capital does not include domestic labour; furthermore domestic labour has no effect on the reproduction of value. At the same time, we have asserted that the laws of motion exert a level of control over all aspects of capitalist society. In what ways do these laws of motion affect domestic labour? To answer this question, we have to consider, not domestic labour, but the wage labour that the domestic labourer is increasingly forced to perform in the sphere of production.

We have consciously avoided equating domestic labour with women's labour. An adequate understanding of women's labour depends upon an examination of the interaction between women's domestic labour and women's wage labour. It is women's labour in the aggregate that is affected by the laws of motion of capital; and particularly the allocation of women's time between domestic labour and wage labour. The specificity of the division of labour time can only be considered at the historical level, but we can examine the process of the accumulation of capital as it creates and re-creates the industrial reserve army and affects the participation of women in the wage labour force.

The process of accumulation takes different forms depending on the particular stage of development of capitalism. We will not address the conjunctural dynamics of the process of capitalist accumulation—for example, the historical transformation of use value production into commodity production—but rather consider the general mechanism for the realization of labour power within the established capitalist mode of production. In so doing, we will elaborate the relation between women's wage work and women's domestic work in the context of the laws of capitalist accumulation.

With the advance of accumulation, the proportion of constant to variable capital changes as a function of increased productivity, that is, an increase in the percentage of capital allocated to raw materials and machinery in relation to that used to purchase labour power. Concurrently, the demand for labour power falls; however, as the total magnitude of capital increases, the demand for labour power also increases, but it continues to represent a smaller proportion of the expenditure of capital.

Thus capitalism produces concomitantly with its rate of growth, a relatively redundant population of labourers, what Marx calls a "surplus population." This reserve does not depend on an absolute increase in population, but on a reorganization of production.

Surplus population is both a result of accumulation and also the motive force for it. For it provides a "disposable industrial reserve army" available for exploitation whenever the expansion of capital requires a new group of workers. The availability of the industrial reserve army puts pressure on the wages of the working class through competition for jobs.

The particularity of women's wage work informs women's relation to the industrial reserve army. Women's work, in all stages of capitalism, is segregated in sectors that generally demand lower skill, pay lower wages and often depend on transient labour, home work or part-time work.

Unemployed women form an industrial reserve army for women's sectors. When production expands and creates new areas in the economy, women will compete with men for access to that sector. Gradually the sector becomes identified as either male or female. Since women's labour power is traditionally undervalued, capital would prefer to hire women. This exacerbates the pressure on the industrial reserve army of men. However, once a sector is defined, women no longer compete with men for the same jobs, and when women are unemployed they do not force the wages of men down. Frequently when women are unemployed, they fall back into the family.[34]

When women are pulled into the wage labour force, the amount of time available for domestic labour decreases. It is clear that the simultaneous performance of both domestic labour and wage labour leaves less time for domestic labour. Since the amount of domestic labour has no effect on value reproduction, we cannot discover laws to explain the allocation of labour time between domestic labour and wage labour.

Any radical increase in women's participation in the labour force must be understood in the context of the stages of development of capitalism. An adequate exploration demands an historical study of the particular stage—monopoly capitalism or early capitalism—informed both by the theory of capital and an understanding of the nature of domestic labour.

Women working for wages has an effect on the amount of time allocated to domestic labour. Does it also affect the amount of commodities available to the domestic labourer and the family? In trying to address this question, it is crucial to establish the unit of analysis as the family. The reason that the value of labour power is calculated as the sum of commodities necessary to reproduce the wage labourer and his replacements is precisely because of the key role that the capitalist family plays in producing the labour force. When we consider the relationship between the value of labour power and women working for wages, it must be done in this context. The extension of the number of workers does not alter the value of labour power, the aggregate proportion of socially necessary time allocated to reproduce the working class. Marx says on this point:

> Machinery, by throwing every member of that family on to the labour-market, spreads the value of the man's labour-power over his whole family. It thus depreciates his labour-power. To purchase the labour-power of a family of four workers may, perhaps, cost more than it formerly did to purchase the labour-power of the head of the family, but, in return, four days' labour takes the place of one, and their price falls in proportion to the excess of the surplus-labour of four over the surplus-labour of one. In order that the family may live, four people must now, not only labour, but expend surplus-labour for the capitalist.[35]

The value of labour power does not change with the entrance of women into the work force. Whether or not the actual amount of commodities (or the magnitude of the value of labour power available to the household) increases is a conjunctural question related to the stage of development of capitalism—for example, the level of productivity of the working class, the location in the business cycle and the level of class struggle (as manifested in the development of trade unions and the political stability of the state).

Certain contradictions arise for capital out of the necessity for women to fulfill domestic responsibilities in addition to performing wage labour. Part of the contradiction relates to the bearing and raising of children, the labour force of the future. No law of population emerges, but there is a contradiction between the immediate extraction of surplus value from women as wage workers and the long-run production of the conditions of that extraction in the form of children.[36]

These contradictions do not necessarily posit the disappearance of the family. The resolution of the contradiction in the short term may take many forms: new forms of work organization and the division of labour, provision of state services, etc. If we step back and consider the long-term possibility of the disappearance of the capitalist mode of production itself, we see a different picture. Marx points out that "the historical development of the antagonisms, immanent in a given form of production, is the only way in which that form of production can be dissolved and a new form established."[37] However, "no social order ever disappears before all the productive forces, for which there is room in it, have developed; and new higher relations of production never appear before the material conditions of their existence have matured in the womb of the old society."[38]

The capitalist family form, although wrought by contradictions, will not disappear until a new mode of production is established, but these very contradictions posit both the basis on which the struggle for socialism occurs and the necessity for an autonomous women's movement.

> But in eroding (not removing) the material basis for the family as an institution and drawing women into wage work, capital has been eroding the material basis for that form of oppression, and it now finds itself faced with demands for setting up the preconditions for equality, such as nurseries, to which it cannot hope to accede, and with demands, which if seriously pursued, could threaten women's role as a cheap labour force. Thus again, the labour process of capital is producing its own opponents.[39]

Conclusion

The distinction between the theory of capital and the historical reality of capitalism as a system of social relations (in which the reproduction of value is one part), establishes the basis for an understanding of domestic labour. Such an approach avoids both a distorted abstraction of the categories of value and an historical understanding that is only a compilation of empirical data. It begins with the fact that domestic labour is a capitalist form of labour located in a capitalist family.

The development of the capitalist mode of production illustrates that the laws of motion of capital are systematically distorted by historical events. Capitalism develops through a series of stages that are generated from the contradictions of the process of accumulation, which is evidenced in what is referred to as the "business cycle of capital." The contradictions of this process lead to the increasing importance of a state structure that will operate in the interests of capital as a whole. Part of the function of the state is to ensure that the reproduction of labour power occurs. This can take many historically specific forms: the establishment of minimum wages, the specification and control of working conditions, the appropriation of a part of the surplus value and the redistribution in the form of services. The state's relation to the family has no general laws of motion, but can be understood in conjunctural terms.

It is within the context of the stages of capitalist development that we pose a variety of questions. What is the effect of the socialization of domestic labour and the increased participation of women in the labour force? Under what conditions is domestic labour intensified? What is the actual content of domestic labour? How much time does it take? What is the effect of domestic technology and the expansion of consumer goods production on the household? When do women move into the labour force, remain at home or combine both jobs? What happens with large families, single workers? What influences the level of wages? What is the developmental dynamic of the "family wage"? When and why does child care change in form? Under what impetus does the state socialize services or remove them? How do women participate in the class struggle? What is the role of the family in the class struggle?

To answer these questions is beyond the scope of this paper. But there exists a rich social history which is approaching such problems. For a correct analysis to emerge, these questions must be posited within a many-layered framework that takes into account the laws of motion of capital, the nature of domestic labour as a capitalist form of labour and a stage theory of capitalist development.

NOTES

1. I wish to thank Mariana Valverde and Jane Springer for support and criticism, and Robert Albritton for his invaluable aid, and for doing my share of the domestic labour while I was writing this article.
2. Karl Marx, *Capital,* Vol. I (Moscow: Progress Publishers, 1954), p. 668.
3. Ibid., p. 168.
4. Ibid.
5. Karl Marx, *Grundrisse* (Harmondsworth: Penguin, 1973), pp. 459-60. This section is helpful in understanding the distinction between the presuppositions of the capitalist mode of production and the laws of motion of capital.
6. See, for example, Shulamith Firestone, *The Dialectic of Sex* (New York: Bantam, 1970).
7. Marx, *Capital,* Vol. I, pp. 77-78.
8. Ibid., p. 77.
9. Martin Nicolaus, Foreword to the *Grundrisse,* p. 30.
10. See John Holloway and Sol Picciotto, "Capital, Crisis and the State," *Capital and Class,* 2 (Summer 1977), p. 79, where they consider the relation between commodity fetishism and the state:

"This abstraction of the relations of force from the immediate process of production and their necessary location (since class domination must ultimately rest on force) in an instance separated from individual capitals constitutes (historically and logically) the economic and the political as distinct, particularised forms of capitalist domination. . . . [T]his real, historically determined separation of the economic and the political as two forms of class domination gives rise to illusions about the autonomy of the 'state' from the 'economy.' . . . The so-called autonomy of the state is but one aspect of commodity fetishism."

11. Marx, *Capital,* Vol. I, p. 167.
12. Karl Marx, *Capital,* Vol. III (Moscow: Progress Publishers, 1959), pp. 791-92.
13. Marx, *Capital,* Vol. I., p. 536.
14. Ibid., pp. 536-37.
15. Ibid., p. 537.
16. Ibid., p. 538.
17. Marx, *Grundrisse,* p. 94.
18. Jairus Banajii, "Modes of Production in a Materialist Conception of History," *Capital and Class,* 3 (Autumn 1977), pp. 1-45, where the author draws out the implications of this approach to the concept of the mode of production.
19. Furthermore, we could say that the value of labour power is increasingly made up of commodities purchased with the wage as well as services provided by the state. The latter is not a free gift but in fact a part of the wage of the working class that is directly appropriated by the state.
20. Mary Carter, "Review–Housework under capitalism," *Revolutionary Communist,* 2 (May 1975), pp. 45-50. This review highlights the distinction between reproducing labour power and reproducing the labourer.
21. On the issue of domestic labour creating value, see especially Wally Seccombe, "The Housewife and Her Labour Under Capitalism." *New Left Review,* 83 (Jan.-Feb. 1974); Mariarosa Dalla Costa, *Women and the Subversion of the Community* (Bristol: Falling Wall Press, 1972). Those who argue that domestic labour produces value tend by implication to see domestic labour as producing or reproducing the commodity labour power. See Marlene Dixon, "On the Super-exploitation of Women," *Synthesis,* 1 (Spring 1977),

pp. 1-12; Hodee Edwards, "Housework and Exploitation: A Marxist Analysis," *No More Fun and Games*, 5 (July 1971), pp. 92-100; Peggy Morton, "A Woman's Work is Never Done," in *Women Unite* (Toronto: The Women's Press, 1972), pp. 45-69.

22. Those who do not argue that domestic labour produces value tend to take the position that domestic labour produces use values. See Margaret Benston, "The Political Economy of Women's Liberation," *Monthly Review*, 21 (Sept. 1969), pp. 13-27; Ira Gerstein, "Domestic Work and Capitalism," *Radical America*, 7 (Fall 1973), pp. 101-130; Lisa Vogel, "The Earthly Family," *Radical America*, 7 (Fall 1973), pp. 9-50; Margaret Coulson, Branka Magas and Hilary Wainwright, "The Housewife and Her Labour Under Capitalism—A Critique," *New Left Review*, 89 (Jan.-Feb. 1975), pp. 59-71; Jean Gardiner, Susan Himmelweit and Maureen Mackintosh, "Women's Domestic Labour," *Bulletin of the Conference of Socialist Economists*, 4 (June 1975), pp. 1-11; Terry Fee, "Domestic Labour: An Analysis of Housework and its Relation to the Productive Forces," *Review of Radical Political Ecnomics*, 8 (Spring 1976), pp. 1-9.

23. Marx, *Capital*, Vol. I, p. 167.

24. Ibid., p. 188.

25. An extreme case of confusion on this point can be found in Joan Smith, "Women and the Family," *International Socialism*, Nos. 100 and 104. She argues that the development of labour and the development of the family can be seen as two forms of production, that is, a mode of production and a mode of reproduction.

26. Marx, *Capital*, Vol. I, p. 298.

27. Ibid., p. 303.

28. See Fee, "Domestic Labour."

29. Marx, *Capital*, Vol. I, p. 168.

30. This intensification may affect the actual "modes of satisfying needs," which can be separated into three categories: first, needs that are satisfied through commodities; second, those satisfied through services paid for either by taxes (i.e., state-provided) or directly; and finally, those needs that are satisfied through domestic labour by the transformation of commodities or the provision of unpaid services. Different stages in the development of capitalism will exhibit a varying balance of these modes, although certain historical trends may emerge. Another important historical question will concern the manipulation of these needs by the capitalist class.

31. See Ben Fine and Laurence Harris, "Controversial Issues in Marxist Economic Theory," in *Socialist Register,* Ralph Miliband and John Saville, eds. (London: Merlin Press, 1976), pp. 141-79. Fine and Harris suggest that assigning significance to the quantification of domestic labour time is a neo-Ricardian approach. See also John Harrison, "The Political Economy of Housework," *Bulletin of the Conference of Socialist Economists* (Winter 1973), pp. 35-52; Seccombe. "The Housewife and Her Labour."

32. See "Women's Domestic Labour" in *On the Political Economy of Women* (London: Stage One, n.d.), p. 10.

33. Karl Marx, quoted in Meredith Tax, *The Wageless Slave and the Proletarian* (Mimeo, n.d.).

34. Veronica Beechey, "Some Notes on Female Wage Labour in Capitalist Production," *Capital and Class,* 3 (Autumn 1977), pp. 45-67.

35. Marx, *Capital,* Vol. I, p. 373.

36. Paddy Quick, "The Class Nature of Women's Oppression," *Review of Radical Political Ecnomics,* 9 (Fall 1977), p. 45.

37. Marx, *Capital,* Vol. I, p. 458.

38. Karl Marx, *A Contribution to the Critique of Political Economy* (Montreal: Progressive Books, n.d.), p. 12.

39. "Women's Domestic Labour," p. 15.

WOMEN'S DOUBLE WORK DAY: TWENTIETH-CENTURY CHANGES IN THE REPRODUCTION OF DAILY LIFE

Bonnie Fox

Linda Briskin makes an important point: there is a contradiction between capital's drive to turn all labour into wage labour and its perpetual need for privatized domestic labour, a contradiction most poignant for women. This article is an attempt to show how married women's growing involvement in the wage work force is a logical product of their key responsibility to balance household wage income against the family's daily needs.

The notion that women's domestic labour represents a balancing act of continual adjustment of wage income and personal work inputs to ensure the reproduction of family life is seen here to arise out of the analysis that domestic production results in use value and not value. In arguing that domestic work is use value production, the article takes up many of the questions BRISKIN *raises. Specifically, it disagrees with her conclusion that domestic labour cannot affect surplus value. More generally, it attempts to show the way in which the household labour process is influenced by changes originating in the sphere of capitalist production—because the means of domestic production are commodities and the expected product is subject to marketplace definition. Finally, the article describes how the increased activation of the domestic labour reserve is understandable in light of changes in the extent to which men in working-class households have been able to support a household of dependents, changes in the organization of household production and changes in what is assumed to be necessary for existence.*

Introduction

The assumption that women's entry into wage work or the sphere of socialized (i.e., cooperatively organized) production is the route to their development of class consciousness has been a common one among Marxists. Many Marxists have taken for granted that when women become wage workers the material conditions and social relations of this role become the primary influences that shape their work lives and their consciousness. Consequently, it is believed that it should be possible to organize women workers in the same way (many) men have been organized. However, married women in the work force remain primarily responsible for the privatized household work that provides for family reproduction. This fact is probably the key reason why many women have been resistant to unionizing attempts in the work place. It is also the reason why I think we should begin our attempts to understand both the causes and the consequences of women's growing assumption of a double work load by focussing on the work women do in the home.

The strategies we develop for organizing women in the labour force will certainly depend on the causes of this trend. Clearly, unless the reasons for increasingly seeking wage work are the same for all or most women, a number of organizing strategies must be developed. And these strategies will vary depending on whether economic compulsion pushed women or perceived opportunities pulled them into the work force.

It is commonly agreed that married women represent a "reserve army of labour," that the growing entry of married women into the labour force represents the activation of a labour reserve latent in the household production sphere.[1] As developed by Marx in the culminating chapter of Volume I of *Capital,* the concept of a reserve army refers to the tendency of capitalist production to generate a surplus population of labourers that provides the competitive pressure regulating wages.[2] In using the concept to describe women, theorists like Harry Braverman have supplied a partial explanation of the growing involvement of married women in wage work. Specifically, Braverman and others have enumerated the functions of this female labour pool. Because their main work is in the home, married women represent a population that can be mobilized for large-scale production during periods of labour shortage, one that is likely to retreat when no longer needed and one that provides cheap and thus potentially competitive labour. However, a functional explanation such as this leaves unanswered the question of how the changing labour needs of capital are felt as pressures or incentives by women in the home. It leaves unspecified the *mechanism* by which changes in the economy are translated into changes in the household.

The way in which this reserve labour pool of female household workers has been progressively activated in recent decades is my key concern here. If the cause is structural, and due to long-term changes, then capital may have problems cyclically turning its changing labour needs into pressures moving women in and out of the home. If the causes are less deep-seated, if, for example, changing wages spurred the movement of women into the labour force, then we can expect capital to more easily move the female labour force in and out of the home.

Examining the trend of the growing involvement of married women in wage work also means probing the possibility of a changing material foundation of the household. For the reasons behind the trend may imply a closer tie between the household and capitalist production than was the case earlier in the twentieth century. The proletarian condition may now entail the necessity for both adults to sell their labour power to support a family. And the domestic labour process may have changed in such a way that it is now directly attuned to the process of commodity production. Surely the nature of the link between the private household and capitalist production must be understood by those involved in the struggle to liberate women.

In this article, I shall critically review other explanations of the increase in married women's involvement in wage work,

Because these explanations derive from specific theories of household production and its relationship to capitalistically organized commodity production, I shall then briefly criticize some of these key theories. I shall outline an alternative theory of household production, addressing the issue of how domestic labourers not producing commodities are nevertheless affected by capitalist production. Next, I shall speculate—with the aid of census data from both Canada and the United States—on causes of the influx of married women into wage work. Finally, I shall briefly explore the political implications of my argument.

Explanations of the Influx of Married Women into Wage Work

Since 1940, in both Canada and the United States, there has been a substantial increase in the involvement of married women in wage work. While the percentage of single, divorced and widowed women who are in the labour force changed insignificantly between the turn of the century and 1970, labour force participation rates for married women rose substantially, especially in recent decades. In the United States, slightly more than 5 percent of married women were counted as "gainfully occupied" at the turn of the century. In 1940, 15.6 percent were in the labour force and by 1970, after a steady rise in their rates of involvement, 40.2 percent were in the labour force.[3] This rising incidence of married women's employment outside the home was not due to a heightened incidence of marriage among younger women. In fact, the increases were greater over time for older women, 35 to 64 years of age, than they were for younger women. In Canada, as well, the trend of women's growing involvement in wage work was generally due to older, married women. The participation rate of married Canadian women rose from less than 4 percent ("gainfully occupied") in 1941 and 9.5 percent ("wage earners") in 1951 to 22 percent and 37 percent (in the labour force) in 1961 and 1971, respectively.[4]

Unfortunately, the theories of household production offered so far have been unable to explain the trend of married women's increased involvement in wage work. None of the theories elucidates the way structural changes in the economy were translated into pressures women experienced (or opportunities they perceived) that made them seek wage work. In other words, the explanations deriving from analyses of the relation between household production and capitalist production have not specified the *causal mechanism* through which system-level changes work themselves out at the level of the individual household. To the extent that theorists writing on women's domestic labour have developed explanations of the trend of married women's growing assumption of a double work load, these explanations typically have not followed from their analysis of the link between the household and capitalist production. Consequently, though the elements of a thorough explanation of the post-World War II trend have been offered, they have not been fit together in a way that provides general laws about how capital mobilizes its domestic female labour reserve.

Margaret Benston's theory of the household as a sphere of use value production—an historic holdover from pre-capitalist societies, outside market relations and governed by personal relationships—emphasizes the basic distinctiveness and even separateness of domestic production and capitalist production.[5] In Benston's analysis, only the functional requirements of capital that are met by the private household tie the two production spheres together. In fact, for Benston, these household functions seem to explain the existence of the family and even the allocation of women's time between domestic work and wage work. Probably because her argument begins with functions or results instead of causes and does not attempt to explain organic connections between the household and the economy, it generates a weak explanation of the trend of married women's increased involvement in wage work.

Benston merely invokes Marx's notion of a reserve army of labour to explain the trend. Unfortunately, she offers no explanation of why women who are doing what is (according to her analysis) unalienated work in the home have come increasingly to seek alienated work for wages. And the fact that real income rose during the 1950s and 1960s, when the major increases in married women's participation in the labour force occurred, begs such an explanation. Yet the household is simply assumed to release its primary worker in response to the periodic demands of capital for additional labour.

Clearly, some change must occur in the cycle of women's production of family subsistence, or in the relation between that production and capitalist production, before domestic labourers will move into wage work. Benston mentions the growing "underemployment" of women in the household, due to the transfer of productive activities and services from the home to capitalist industry and the state. She apparently then *assumes* a compulsion sufficient to prompt women to seek work additional to their household responsibilities. Her only explanation of a force motivating women's behaviour focusses on the mechanism urging them back into the home, and not on one compelling them out of it. (She argues that ideology, the "cult of the home," is the device capital periodically invokes.) In short, Benston's use of Marx's reserve army of labour concept, without modification or amplification to fit the current situation of women, demonstrates no structural connection between household production and commodity production that would result in a response by household members to capital's changing needs.

Unlike Benston, Wally Seccombe attempts to specify what moved married women into wage work.[6] The explanation appears to follow from his argument that because domestic labour is a form of independent commodity production (of the commodity labour power), it is at least indirectly subject to laws of motion that govern all forms of commodity production. In other words, Seccombe argues that the law of value extends into the household ("indirectly impinges upon it") and allocates women's time between household work and wage work.

His specific argument rests on the fact that productivity rose faster in the sector of the economy producing wage goods than it did in the household in the post-World War II period. Women could thus acquire more use values working in the sphere of capitalist production for wages than they could working the same amount of time producing similar subsistence goods in the household. It therefore increasingly made "economic sense" to enter the work force.[7]

This part of Seccombe's argument bears a striking similarity to one made by bourgeois economist Jacob Mincer, whose modification of the consumer choice model to explain women's work behaviour remains most popular with neo-Keynesian economists.[8] According to that model, women choose among wage work, housework and leisure in allocating their time. The resulting combination of the three activities represents a maximization of personal utility or taste. One factor determining the relative proportions of each use of time is what is known as the "substitution effect." It is, in fact, the key element in Mincer's explanation of women's growing involvement in wage work during a period of rising real income. Specifically, when real wages rise, the "opportunity cost" of refraining from wage work also rises. So leisure and, for women, domestic labour, become relatively more "expensive" uses of time. Since women's wages rose from the late 1940s on, the fact that it became increasingly costly for women to stay out of wage work provides, for Mincer, sufficient explanation of their increased labour force participation.

In this argument, women's *choices* about how to allocate their time are central. Moreover, it is assumed that in making these choices female household workers are rational (in the economic sense), that is, calculating time-maximizers. For neo-Keynesian economists, this maximalist model of human behaviour apparently rests on the notion that human beings have an innate desire to maximize "utility." In fact, women working in the home no doubt often attempt to rationally organize their schedules, and their behaviour may even at times fit a maximalist model. But the structural mechanism by which such a result occurs is not elaborated in the consumer choice model.

An argument that domestic labour involves commodity production would entail the notion that the law of value, which is expressed through marketplace competition, provides the mechanism that imposes a rational ordering of time on the household worker. However, such an analysis would have to demonstrate how the market mechanism extends into the household, quantifies the work performed by the household worker and compares it with other labours.

Wally Seccombe does not attempt to argue that market pressures governing all commodity production are at work in the household—although the logic of his discussion indicates such a position. His argument ultimately departs from Mincer's because Seccombe assumes that economic compulsion was the key component in the changing pattern of work for married women. He argues that productivity increases in the wage goods sector of the economy occurred in the context of an inflating social (i.e., market) definition of the number and quality of commodity goods necessary for family subsistence. This raised the value of labour power in spite of the potential that productivity increases provided for its lowering. Thus, Seccombe argues, domestic labourers experienced pressures to produce more (than was possible) in the household, which was falling further and further behind the wage goods sector of capitalist production with respect to productivity.

Unfortunately brief, but ultimately quite provocative, Seccombe's explanation of the trend is only a partial one. For example, although Seccombe mentions changes over time in men's wages as the other factor (besides changes in productivity) that is potentially disruptive to the household cycle that reproduces labour power, he never considers actual trends in men's wages. This omission is perhaps the result of his focus on *women's* work instead of *family* reproduction. Yet because domestic labour essentially involves the responsibility for the reproduction of labour power on a daily and a generational basis, through the provision of family subsistence, the household (and not the individual) is the unit of analysis most suitable for analyzing changes in women's productive role.

Seccombe also neglects to explore the composition of the items increasingly assumed necessary for subsistence and the changing material conditions (e.g., the means of production) of household work. In assuming perfect substitutability between the products of labour at home and labour in the wage goods sector of the economy, Seccombe fails to ask whether women are still able to produce, at home, the means of family subsistence. In contrast, Patricia Connelly makes a strong case that a form of economic compulsion progressively encouraged married women to seek work for wages, pointing out that the commodity content of what is necessary for family living has grown over the years.[9]

This insight and others already suggested can be used to formulate a more systematic explanation than has so far been offered of the trend towards married women's growing involvement in wage work. In attempting to provide this explanation, I shall concentrate on the mechanism by which workers not producing for the market are made to feel market pressures. I think that specification of the mechanism calls for an analysis of the changing material conditions of women's household work, examining, for example, the means of domestic production and the product of domestic labour. Unlike other attempts to explain married women's growing involvement in wage work, this approach reveals differences among women. And perhaps the greatest weakness with past explanations of the trend is the assumption that one explanation is sufficient for all women.

Obviously, an analysis of changes in the household labour of family reproduction must flow from a theory of domestic labour and its relation to capitalist production. Let me, then, elaborate such a theory before proposing an explanation of the growing importance of wage work in the lives of married women.

Marxist Analyses of Household Production

I have already indicated what I see as the key shortcoming in Benston's analysis: it seems to accurately describe the character of the domestic work process but reveals no organic connection between that process and capitalist production. The household is conceptually left hanging in space, a holdover from pre-capitalist times—despite its clear shaping by capitalist development. Yet the attempt to correct for this apparent absence of any connection between the household and the capitalist work process (namely the argument that domestic labour is simple commodity production, governed by the law of value) seems to me to ignore real differences between domestic work and work that produces material products or services for the market.

A great deal of household labour is socially necessary for the production and reproduction of labour power, which under capitalism assumes the form of a commodity. Nevertheless, it seems clear that Marx's abstract model of capitalist production, developed in Volume I of *Capital,* locates that labour outside the sphere of the production and reproduction of self-expanding value (i.e., capital) and even outside any process that produces the value embodied in labour power. This is only implied in the body of *Capital*; it is implicit in the logic of Marx's value analysis. However, he stated it directly in material that has only recently been published in English:

> In fact, of course, the worker must sustain his capacity for work with the aid of means of subsistence, but this, his private consumption, which is at the same time the reproduction of his labour power, *falls outside the process of producing commodities* [emphasis added].[10]

In Marx's economic theory, the working day is divided into two parts: necessary labour time, during which the worker reproduces the value of his subsistence, incorporated in money form in his wage and in real form in the commodities exchanged for the wage; and surplus labour time, during which the worker creates surplus value for the capitalist. The value of the worker's labour power is determined by the value of the means of subsistence the worker must acquire as commodities on the market. Thus, the worker's labour power is exchanged for the wage which, in turn, is exchanged for subsistence commodities. The worker's labour power, the money wage, and the package of subsistence commodities that the wage purchases are, therefore, value equivalents.[11] Their equivalence is one instance of the general assumption, in *Capital,* that exchange involves things of equal value. The assumption is necessary to the labour theory of value, which rests on the fact that value does not arise in the exchange process, but rather is created in the process of production.

Because of the equivalence of the time socially necessary (i.e., given the average level of skills and the highest level of technology) for the reproduction of labour power and that for which the wage is payment, it seems to me that only labour that produces the *commodities* the worker consumes adds to the value of his or her labour power. The most obvious reason for this is that if the socially necessary time spent in the household labour that ensured the maintenance of the male wage earner contributed to the value of his labour power, it is unlikely that he could produce for the capitalist an equivalent amount of value (plus surplus value).[12] For, even today, despite the aid of "fast foods" and permanent press clothing, about 26 hours of household work per week on average seem to be necessary.[13] In determining the value of labour power, these hours would be additional to the hours of labour embodied in the commodities and services domestic labourers purchase and use in carrying out their weekly household work. Of course, there are significant differences between the productivity of labour in the household and that in the capitalist work sector, so the hours spent in the household are not strictly comparable with those spent working for wages (unless the latter involve service jobs). Nevertheless, given the large time requirements for necessary household work and recognizing that in the decades prior to the development of easy-care fabrics and "fast foods" domestic labour took even more time than it does today, we must at least question the quantitative possibility of including time spent in domestic tasks in the calculation of the value of labour power.[14]

There is a more compelling reason why only labour that

produces the commodities and commercial services required by the wage labourer can contribute to the value of his labour power. It is simply that not only must the labour time socially necessary to produce labour power be equal to the "necessary labour time" spent in the sphere of capitalist production, but also that there must be a mechanism that quantifies and compares these two labour times. Of course, the market is the point at which this quantification and eventual equalization usually occurs. Through market mechanisms, when commodities are exchanged, the labours that contributed to their production are abstracted from their particular concrete qualities and quantified–and thus compared. Then, because of competition, different producers are continually subject to the law of value, which works to reduce the labour time socially necessary for all production.

Household work differs from other work processes chiefly because exchange (i.e., the market) does not mediate between the labour performed by the woman and the commodities the family must buy, or that performed by the wage worker under the aegis of capital and partly embodied in the wage. Domestic labour is never abstracted, never quantified, because it is never subject to market forces such as competition. In other words, there is no (market) mechanism which would force a woman's labour time downward to equal the social average of necessary domestic labour (i.e., no competition) or which could receive the use values she creates and return their value in the shape of the universal equivalent, money.

Unlike family farmers, for example, the results of domestic labourers intensifying (or diminishing) their efforts towards the reproduction of labour power–which is a commodity–will not be more (or fewer) products that will earn them more (or less) cash on the market. When times are hard, family farmers can intensify their work efforts, produce more and earn more cash in market sales (assuming each family farm is so small that its products have no effect on prices). Household workers in the same situation cannot double their efforts, produce a higher quality labour power and thus earn more in (husband's) wages. (They would probably intensify their domestic efforts during hard times, but with an entirely different effect—one that I shall discuss below.)

In short, household production is not aimed at the market. Consequently, there is no competition among domestic labourers to produce a cheaper commodity, husband's labour power, for they have invested nothing in its production that must be recovered. "Time is money" in the capitalist work place, not in the household. In sum, then, the value relations in Marx's theory require that the value of labour power be determined by labour time socially necessary for the production of basic subsistence commodities.

For the same reasons that it is problematic, given the logic of Marx's theory, to argue that domestic labour creates value, it is problematic to argue that the surplus labour performed by the female domestic labourer (working longer than is necessary to produce the equivalent of her means of subsistence) is simply appropriated by capital. John Harrison makes such an argument (although he maintains at the same time that domestic labour is solely use value production).[15] Basically, Harrison seems to ignore the process through which surplus value is appropriated by capital. He apparently assumes that the exchange process can generate surplus value, that in buying something that embodies more value than the wage represents, the capitalist can appropriate a surplus. Of course, surplus value can arise only in the process of production. Profit can, however, be made in exchange. But even profit cannot result from the exchange between labour and capital, because the capitalist does not buy the commodity labour power and then sell it. Instead, the capitalist uses labour power; he productively consumes it. And it is only at the point of use—when work is being done for capital—that surplus value is created and appropriated (because the wage represents less value than the worker creates).

Wally Seccombe's early argument that domestic labour produces value withstands some of the specific criticisms raised so far, yet in avoiding these problems it yields to others.[16] An example is the proposition that the law of value allocates women's time between wage work and household work. In avoiding the problem of dangling value (i.e., that the domestic labourer adds to the value of labour power more than the equivalent the wage worker can produce in the paid part of his work day), Seccombe arbitrarily sets the value created by domestic labour equal to the value of the part of the wage earner's wage that goes towards the housewife's necessary means of subsistence. This formulation is a radical departure from the labour theory of value (whereby value is created according to the labour time socially necessary for production), because it holds time to be irrelevant in the determination of the value created.

The way in which market mechanisms usually impose the law of value on individual producers is precluded for domestic labourers in Seccombe's argument. In Marx's model, producers who take more time in the production of a commodity than is socially necessary are forced by prices, which because of competition follow the social value of products, to reduce their labour time to that socially necessary. According to Seccombe's argument, however, if the time socially necessary to domestic labour were to decrease, there would be no consequent decrease in the worker's wage. The market mechanism relating the household to the exchange of commodities (and to other households) is absent. Thus, there is no pressure on the domestic labourer to reduce her labour time in the event of a change in socially necessary labour time. In Seccombe's argument, one wonders how the law of value could operate, because for him, time is irrelevant in determining the value that domestic labourers produce.

An Alternative Analysis of Domestic Production

I have argued that the domestic labourer is not producing for market exchange. As a producer, she does not have the relationship to the market that characterizes the work of commodity producers. Consequently, she does not aim her work at producing more, more efficiently, because such an effort cannot result in a higher value of the product labour power and a higher wage.

If, as I argued above, the value of the worker's labour power depends solely on the value of the necessary commodities that compose his means of subsistence, domestic labour creates no new value, but simply transfers the value of the commodities consumed to the worker's labour power. As well, however, the work a woman does in the home can *substitute for* commercial goods and services. So, to the extent that domestic labour *generally* substitutes for purchases of goods and services, it effects a reduction in the value of wage workers' labour power.

In other words, the work done by married women in the household determines the mixture of homemade goods (and services) and commercial goods (and services) that compose the worker's and his family's subsistence. To the extent that domestic labour *generally* performs certain essential services, it reduces the *socially necessary* labour time embodied in commodities and services necessary for subsistence and thus reduces the (social) value of labour power. This social value of labour power is the equilibrium point around which wages move.

In terms of the determination of the value of the *individual* worker's labour power, to the extent that his wife can substitute products of her labour for commercial products (which are defined by a certain amount of value and must be purchased), she can reduce the value of the individual wage worker's labour power and thus "stretch" his wage. In short, household production can improve the level of living a wage will purchase. Consequently, in times when the working-class family is financially squeezed, the domestic labourer can either intensify her work at home or try to find wage work. The former course of action involves a substitution of the use values she produces and the services she provides for commodities which, when purchased, raise the cost of daily living and (in value terms) add to the individual value of her husband's labour power. In effect, she is attempting to reduce the individual value of the wage earner's labour power below, or keep it even with, its social value, which partly (and with a time lag) determines the wage he will attract. This would be the logical course of action when real wages fall or the prices of commodities deemed necessary to subsistence rise.

Jean Gardiner, in her first article, seems to be making the same argument:

> The contribution which domestic labour makes to surplus value is one of keeping down necessary labour to a level that is lower than the actual subsistence level of the working class. For example, it could be argued that it is cheaper for capital to pay a male worker a wage sufficient to maintain, at least partially, a wife who prepares meals for him, than to pay him a wage on which he could afford to eat regularly at restaurants.[17]

The argument, in short, is that domestic labour has an effect on the value of labour power to the extent that its universal performance of necessary tasks reduces, at the level of society, the commercial goods and services necessary for labour power's reproduction. That is, domestic labour may reduce the labour time socially necessary for the reproduction of labour power that determines its value. In the individual family, domestic labour can, if it is more intense or productive than average, reduce the value of the man's labour power; that is, a woman's efforts in the home can reduce the cost of daily rejuvenation of the capacity for work. In part, the durable means of production a "housewife" has will affect her ability to decrease these costs of reproduction; as well, the product expected of her, the socially defined standard of living, will have a major effect on this ability.[18]

While domestic labourers direct their efforts to the satisfaction of human needs, these needs are, of course, objects of social construction. So, unlike in the use value production characteristic of pre-capitalist social formations, the fact that personal needs govern the household work process does not mean that there is a clear point at which the job is done. Rather, because needs are socially defined, and because capital requires consumption boosted by need creation (through advertising, for example), domestic labour does not have a built-in, well-defined termination point. The domestic labourer, the mother, the wife is ultimately responsible for meeting her family's needs, for ensuring its material welfare and its satisfactory "personal life."

Those things expected of the home environment, those considered necessary for relaxation and recreation, those deemed essential for rearing children, the quality and variety demanded with respect to food and clothing, etc., are all defined by a capitalist marketplace. It is partly because these standards of family life and personal needs are continually inflating that "a woman's work is never done." Moreover, through this continually changing (and inflating) product of household work capitalist production influences domestic work. Therefore, to the extent that "housewives" experience an absolute scarcity of time each day, it is partly because the task they have come to expect of themselves is virtually unbounded.

As well, in some households there exists an absolute scarcity of the means of household production because the incoming wage is simply too low for purchase of the commodities essential for family subsistence. Certainly, many primary wage earners do not earn a "family wage." In the event of this scarcity of means of production, the domestic labourer is forced to attempt to allocate her time rationally. The extent to which she can do so does, of course, depend on the facilities available to her (e.g., household appliances) and the extent to which children's needs interfere. For children's needs are probably the biggest obstacle to achievement of an economically rational allocation of the household worker's time, if this compulsion towards its achievement does exist.

In short, what is production for the domestic labourer is, at the same time, family consumption. This is perhaps the crux of the difference between domestic labour and commodity production. Because use value, and not value, is salient, any compulsion to reduce the domestic labourer's production time must be balanced against pressures to increase her work in the household and thus enhance family consumption (or family welfare). Because household work is, simultaneously, family consumption, there are two opposing forces perpetually at work in the household: one to decrease work time and the other to increase it. Depending on the nature of an inflation in the product expected of the domestic labourer–namely, family subsistence–it may or may not make sense for the domestic labourer to intensify her efforts in the home.

Besides the influence of the marketplace on the product of domestic labour, there is another difference between household work and the use value production characterizing precapitalist social formations. Although the domestic labourer owns her means of production, they are acquired only through the continual sale of labour power. From one day to the next, the domestic labourer can continue to reproduce the means of family subsistence only if wages continue to flow into the household. In other words, even focussing exclusively on the domestic labour process, it is clear that proletarianization is the basic condition of most housewives. Their class position is the same as that of their husbands.

Nevertheless, within the working class, women have special interests. They occupy a unique position because of their sex. Domestic labourers are dependent on a *man's* wage (or on state subsidies). This is so even if female household workers are themselves wage earners, because men's wages are the only ones typically high enough to cover the costs of family subsistence. Proletarian women are, in a sense, doubly dependent.

Because the means of household production are commodities, at the point of their acquisition, capital's needs and those of the family confront each other squarely. The prices by which the capitalist covers his costs and realizes surplus value are the cost of life itself for the working-class family. During some periods, like in the 1950s and 1960s in North America, when productivity increases are substantial and real wages are increasing, the contradictory nature of the interests of the working-class family and capital are not evident. Indeed, the working class benefits during such times from the heightened consumption resulting not only from increased industrial productivity, but also from the wage increases won through class struggle. However, during periods of inflation, when wage gains are reversed, price increases stand in clear opposition to the interests of working-class reproduction.

That the means of household production are commodities has another, less apparent implication. It means they are not necessarily as efficient or useful as they might be. It means, more generally, that capital shapes the materials of domestic labour and thus shapes the labour process itself. Domestic labour is affected not only by the choice of items manufactured for the household, or their construction (e.g., "labour saving" appliances that scarcely save any effort) but also by the way in which domestic means of production are sold, that is, the expectations created in the campaign to sell them. Thus, for example, standards with respect to cleanliness of clothing and variety of meals have no doubt risen over time and consequently affected women's domestic work.[19]

Focussing on the means of household production highlights a distinction which, at least until very recently, has existed between working-class and middle-class households. Until recently, working-class women have had to continually purchase not only their nondurable means of production (e.g., food) but also the use of those durable goods necessary for housework (e.g., laundry facilities). Middle-class domestic labourers came to own virtually all of their durable means of production (i.e., household appliances) in the decades before and after World War II. This difference has consequences for women's participation in wage work, as I will attempt to show below.

Basically, I think that because household means of production are commodities, and because the product of a woman's efforts—namely, the family's continued existence, its standard of living—is socially defined and variable, the household work process and its worker are continually influenced by forces emanating from the sphere of capitalist production. Let us examine the way in which this framework allows an explanation of the trend of increasing involvement of married women in wage work.

The Increased Involvement of Married Women in Wage Work

The changes underlying the substantial rise in the work force involvement of married women after 1940 in both the United States and Canada were quite compelling: the labour force participation rate of American women with children under six years of age increased fully 181 percent between 1948 and 1970, despite a continued and glaring dearth of day care facilities.[20] Thirty percent of American women with young children were in the work force in 1970 and they represented 21.3 percent of the female work force.[21]

While it would seem that only economic compulsion could cause the growing assumption of an extra workload by women least free to handle it, real incomes rose steadily in both Canada and the United States from the late 1940s to the early 1970s.[22] For example, in Canada, median real incomes of male family heads increased about 142 percent between 1951 and 1971. Even the real incomes of the lowest 25 percent of male Canadian family heads rose about 59 percent between 1951 and 1971.[23]

More to the point, in Canada the increases over this period in the money earning activities of married women do not appear to have been greater for women from lower income households than for those from higher income households. As Table 1 shows, when the 1931 and 1971 populations of Canadian families are divided into fifths according to husbands' incomes, and women's "gainful occupation" in 1931 is compared with their involvement in paid jobs in 1971, we find that percentage increases over this period were greater for higher husbands' incomes. The very high percentage increases for women from high income families were due to their very low involvement in wage work in 1940. Nevertheless, by 1970, the extent to which these women worked for money was high enough that the negative relationship between

Table 1: Wives' labour force participation by husbands' relative income, for Canada, 1931 and 1971

Population Fifths (by husbands' income)	1931 Gain-full Occupation Rates	1971 Rates of Involvement in Paid Civilian Work	Percentage Point Increase	Percentage Increase
low 1	5%	24%	19	380
2	4%	34%	30	750
3	3%	33%	30	1000
4	2%	32%	30	1500
high 5	1%	26%	25	2500

Sources: Dominion Bureau of Statistics, *1931 Census of Population*, Vol. V, p. 686; Statistics Canada, data from Public Use Sample Tape, 1971. Percentages are approximate.

Table 2: Wives' labour force participation by husbands' relative income, for the United States, 1940 and 1970

Population Fifths (by husbands' income)	1940 Labour Force Participation Rates	1970 Labour Force Participation Rates	Percentage Point Increase	Percentage Increase	Approximate Increase in Numbers
low 1	22%	67%	45	205	5,066,000
2	18%	61%	43	239	4,920,000
3	17%	58%	41	241	4,187,000
4	13%	53%	40	308	4,239,000
high 5	7%	47%	40	571	4,146,000

Sources: U.S. Bureau of the Census, *1940 Census of Population.* Additional Reports, p. 151; *1970 Census of Population.* Subject Reports, PC (2)-8A, p. 377.

husbands' incomes and wives' involvement in wage work of 1931 seems to have disappeared. (However, if the poorest 20 percent of families is ignored the negative relationship remains.) Women from the middle 60 percent of families, according to husbands' incomes, had the highest involvement in wage work in 1971. Moreover, it was these families that experienced the highest percentage point increase in women's wage earning activities between 1931 and 1971.

In the United States as in Canada, between 1940 and 1970 the percentage increase in the labour force participation rates of married women was greater the higher the husbands' incomes. Again, as shown in Table 2, it is because the involvement in wage work was relatively so low for married women from higher income families in 1940 that the percentage increases over the 30-year period were so high for these women. Moreover, unlike the situation apparent in the Canadian data, in 1970 in the United States there was still an inverse relationship between husbands' incomes and wives' labour force participation rates. That is, while the differences in work force involvement among women with husbands of different incomes decreased over time, in 1970, women whose husbands made lower incomes were still more likely than those whose husbands' incomes were higher to be employed outside the home.

Furthermore, between 1940 and 1970 in the United States the increases in the numbers of women in the labour force were higher for both of the lower two-fifths of families than for those from each of the higher three-fifths of families. The percentage point increase in the labour force participation of married women, between 1940 and 1970, decreases as husbands' incomes rise. In other words, in the United States there were slightly higher absolute increases in women's labour force involvement over time for women from lower income households than for those from higher income households.

The most compelling conclusion that emerges from this brief examination of the empirical evidence is that dramatic increases occurred for married women from all income groups.

There was, in both countries, a tremendous rise both in terms of percentage gain and absolutely, in the labour force participation of women whose husbands' incomes place them in the higher income segments of the population. The common situation towards which married women from all income groups are moving is involvement in a double work day, involving domestic labour and wage labour.

I have criticized bourgeois economists for explaining the trend by arguing that after World War II women *chose* to move into a work sector where they could maximize their output. Wally Seccombe refers to the compulsion to which all married women were increasingly subject. I concluded that efforts to explain women's behaviour, specifically efforts to look for the source of this compulsion, must begin with close examination of changes in household production.

Focussing on changes in domestic production, particularly in the control over means of production and the relationship between these household means of production and the socially defined standard of living, it is first of all clear that there are differences among women. The pressures married women have experienced vary and the manner of coping with them has no doubt varied because of differences ultimately attributable to income and resource differences. Perhaps these differences can be reduced to variations in control over means of household production. Whatever the crucial source of the differences, the trend of rising involvement of married women in wage work, which was due to an increased entry into the work force of women from all income groups, calls for explanations specific to the material circumstances of the different classes of women involved. I shall refer, in this paper, to differences between working-class and middle-class women. However, since the distinction between these two groups is, for my purposes here, one of income (and resources) only, it can be seen as a distinction between upper income and lower income working-class women.

Before examining the question of the increased "supply" of married women for wage work, however, there are several points to note about changes in the "demand" for labour. First, the numbers of unemployed men, released from jobs by a dizzying procession of technological improvements in productivity, would not have been sufficient to meet the inflating demand for labour, especially for clerical workers and service workers, that occurred after World War II. So, women workers were needed and, at least in the United States, the population of unmarried women was too small to fill the rising demand.[24]

Second, the expansion of the economy in the twentieth century and the growing number of jobs for women cannot be separated from the substantial transfer, over the course of the century, of many production and service tasks formerly carried out in the home to the sectors of capitalist production and the state. With the shift of the population from rural to increasingly dense urban areas, the production of foodstuffs left the household; especially since the 1920s, food processing has been progressively taken over by the large food conglomerates; and in the last decade, the restaurant industry has made considerable progress towards assuming responsibility for the preparation of meals. The fabrication of women's and children's clothing has also been transferred from the home to the factory since the turn of the century, although the work involved in the cleaning and maintenance of clothes has moved back into the home (despite a trend apparent, especially in the 1920s, towards commercial assumption of the task). Education, health care and other social services have also grown substantially, not so much assuming tasks formerly carried out in the home as extending the amount of state (or private professional) involvement in people's personal lives.

These changes in the distribution of labour processes that sustain life and produce and reproduce labour power, essentially a shift from privatized household production to socialized production, underly the shift in women's work from domestic labour to wage labour. They are crucial not only because they indicate the basis for the rising needs of capital and the state for wage labourers, but also because they represent changes in the conditions of women's production in the household, in the conditions of the reproduction of labour power on a daily and on a generational basis.[25]

When working-class households are examined from the perspective of the production and reproduction of subsistence, it appears that they have consistently, over the course of the twentieth century, required wages additional to those contributed by the chief male earner. In other words, lower income, working-class families have persistently needed a second wage. So, changes in capital's need for labour are sufficient to explain the increased involvement of these women in the labour force.

In the United States, from the first decade of the twentieth century (excepting depression years and war years), estimates were made of the minimum budget necessary for a family of four to live in "health and decency," estimates based both on decisions by panels of experts about essential subsistence goods and the actual choices of goods made by working-class women.[26] A comparison of these estimated minimum incomes with the mean incomes of all males working for wages or salaries reveals the startling fact that as many as 50 percent of such men, before and after World War I, through the 1920s and probably since the late 1940s, have not earned incomes sufficient for the subsistence of a family of four. Moreover, virtually all of the means of subsistence for working-class families were in the form of commodities. That is, working-class families have bought virtually all of their means of subsistence since at least the beginning of the twentieth century.

From studies of American working-class households in the early decades of the twentieth century, it is clear that families living in cities rarely had land sufficient to grow vegetables or fruit.[27] In fact, household facilities were often insufficient to allow the domestic labourer to contribute much in the way of homemade goods. The sheer drudgery of doing the necessary cooking and cleaning without running water or central heating, coupled with significant overcrowding both inside and out, must have inhibited activities like sewing, canning and even baking bread.

In the United States, as late as 1940, only 58 percent of urban dwelling units had central heating, only 78 percent had gas or electric cooking stoves, and only 56 percent had mechanical refrigeration.[28] In 1940 in Canada, only about 56 percent of urban dwelling units had a furnace for heating, only about 61 percent had gas or electric cooking stoves and only 31 percent were equipped with mechanical refrigeration.[29] When women have to distribute water manually, when they must continually tend the fire for cooking and heating, when they are forced to shop daily because of lack of refrigeration, their working time for necessary chores is severely lengthened and the possibility of homemade goods substantially restricted.

By 1950 in the United States, fewer than 15 percent of urban households were without gas or electric cooking stoves and mechanical refrigeration,[30] so middle-class and a substantial proportion of working-class households had these facilities. A similar statement might be made about Canadian households, by the early 1960s.

So, partly because working-class women lacked the means of household production necessary to produce many use values for their families, they were unable to substantially contribute to the daily reproduction of labour power.

In fact, the standard of living for working-class households was very low. Diets typically consisted of bread, tea, butter and jam, some milk and meat and no vegetables or fruit (unless in season). Within such a diet, only bread could be homemade—and it was apparently cheaper to buy than to make. However, many working-class households had sewing machines, even in the absence of much furniture; and housewives often made and remade their own and their children's clothing. Nevertheless, in low income households the housewife was unable to make up for the man's low income.

We should recognize, however, that women's domestic work was nevertheless essential, and their skills at shopping had a substantial effect on the family budget. Several early American studies of working-class households concluded that differences in the standard of living occurred among families with the same income because of differences in the skills of the housewives.[31] Their skills at shopping and managing money—activities bourgeois sociology has relegated to the trivial category of "consumption"—were especially crucial, and no doubt meant the difference between healthy survival and perpetual sickness or discomfort for many families.

If women have been unable to substantially reduce the costs of family subsistence by replacing homemade goods for things that must be purchased, and if men's wages have typically been insufficient to meet the subsistence needs of the working-class family, where did additional cash come from in the early part of the twentieth century? It appears that children were the most significant secondary contributors to family coffers. In the United States, in 1910, 18.4 percent of children 10 to 15 years of age and 59.4 percent of children 16 to 20 years of age worked for wages; in 1920, 8.5 percent of children 10 to 15 years of age and 52.3 percent of children 16 to 19 years of age did wage work. While 89 percent of children 10 to 15 years old attended school, only 30.5 percent of people 16 to 20 years old went to school in 1920.[32] In Canada, in 1931, while only about 3 percent of married women worked, over 54 percent of children 15 years and older, in families with both husband and wife present, earned money during the year.[33] The mandatory age for school attendance was lower and more often ignored early in the century, and the school year was shorter than it is now.

The situation had, of course, changed dramatically for children and young adults by the 1970s in North America. In the United States in 1970 only 35 percent of people 16 to 19 years of age did work for wages (and then usually only after school), while 96 percent of 15-year-olds and 74 percent of 16 to 19-year-olds were enrolled in school.[34] Underlying the extension of formal education requirements are changes in the economy, such as the shift towards service occupations, which meant changing labour needs. Consequently, the mandatory attendance of children and young adults at school for longer and longer periods of time was both an indirect and a direct cause of women's increased entry into the work force. Capital's labour requirements have changed and families have increasingly lost their likely second wage earner to educational training.

The story is more complex, however. It would be historically inaccurate to assume that very few married working-class women contributed financially to the running of the household. There was, in fact, considerable underestimation in the censuses of the numbers of married women who earned wages. Census figures were highly sensitive to the predelictions and biases of the enumerators, and it was typically assumed by census enumerators that wives and mothers did not work (for money). Besides assumptions on the part of enumerators, married women were not likely to consider themselves to be "working," even if they were.[35]

Because many of the ways in which married women earned cash involved extensions of their normal domestic services and chores, such activities were easily overlooked. Moreover, many of these jobs were deliberately defined as unworthy of the label "gainful occupation." Taking in boarders or lodgers was officially ignored unless the numbers involved were large. Domestic chores like washing and ironing, carried out for cash, were likely to be overlooked by both census enumerators and the women involved. Accordingly, the 1920 American census reported only 9 percent of married women to be "gainfully occupied." Yet a private study carried out the same year in Rochester, New York, found that although only about 9 percent of married women worked outside the home, about 25 percent of them earned money.[36] More importantly, home economist Hazel Kyrk concluded, after examining many private studies done in the 1920s, that about 20 percent of married women in American cities contributed financially to the running of the household at that time.[37]

In conclusion, there is strong evidence that through the twentieth century a sizeable and constant proportion of families has experienced the need for income additional to that earned by the male family "head." That is, competition among workers and other material factors have worked to drive the wages of many male workers down below the value of their labour power. Consequently, the wages of an additional family member were a necessary condition for the daily reproduction of many working-class families, especially since limited means of household production precluded much production of homemade substitutes for commercial goods. At the same time, the supply of potential additional workers eroded over time, especially because of educational requirements imposed on children and young adults. The pressure to earn wages was then transferred to housewives, whose domestic labour had meanwhile lost much of its drudgery, and who had traditionally contributed whatever cash they could anyway.

In the United States, there is evidence, even in the censuses, that the fairly recent increases in married women's labour force participation do not represent drastic increases in the occurrence of wage earners additional to the adult male. According to the censuses, in the United States the percentage of households with three or more wage earners did not increase between 1930 and 1970. The percentage of households with two or more wage workers even stayed about the same between 1930 and 1950.[38] After 1950, however, the percentage of households with two or more wage earners increased considerably. In other words, the increase in the participation of married women in wage work occurred for a larger proportion of households than is accounted for by the trend of replacement of the wages of married women for those earned by other family members. Perhaps this increase in the number of households with two wage earners represents the beginning of the need for a second worker on the part of middle-class or higher income working-class families.

More puzzling than the growing involvement of working-class women in wage work is the increased involvement of middle-class women. However, an examination of their changing means of production and consequent changes in the organization of their household production, as well as changes in the socially defined product of domestic work, sheds some light on this trend. A sizeable proportion of married middle-class women has owned the durable means of their household production throughout the twentieth century. As these aids to household work improved, middle-class women benefited in terms of decreased drudgery but also in their ability to contribute materially to family living.

Through the twentieth century, middle-class women were better able to earn money than their working-class sisters. For example, larger houses were better equipped to admit boarders or lodgers. Home ownership, in fact, made it more likely that a married woman or a widow would take in boarders or lodgers.[39]

Early in the century, many of these families lived on enough land, whether in the country, on the edges of the city or even in the city, to grow vegetables and fruit. Women in these households could produce significant amounts of food for their families. Since they also sewed many of their own and their children's clothing, these women contributed substantially, materially, to family subsistence. Moreover, homemade food and clothing were seen as superior to commercial products.[40]

Nevertheless, as the century unfolded, the things comprising the North American standard of living, the necessary means of family reproduction, were increasingly attainable only through cash. A larger and larger proportion of family necessities were things the domestic labourer could not provide through her own efforts at home (e.g., a car, a college education for the children). In short, cash became more and more the medium of access to items making up a larger and larger bulk of the middle-class budget.

Orthodox economists usually refer to "rising expectations" as a catch-all explanation for that proportion of the influx of married women into wage work that they cannot otherwise explain. The notion, as these economists use it, is deceptive rather than wrong. For, while it is probably true that the standard of living has risen over the past few decades, in that the average person expects to own and does own more things now than before, one would be hard pressed to distinguish necessities from luxuries. The orthodox economists imply that new entries to the list of things people expect to have are mostly the latter. That, I think, is incorrect. A family car, for example, is a necessity of North American living; post-secondary schooling is necessary for the reproduction of many types of labouring capacities. The means of family subsistence or (in value terms) the items determining the value of labour power, are historically defined. Because of the changing requirements of capital, both for different types of labour power and for continually increasing sales, these means of subsistence have been substantially redefined and expanded in North America since World War II.

The household efforts of middle-class women have, consequently, become increasingly less efficacious for reducing the costs of family reproduction. Homemade substitutes for a family car or a college education, for example, are nonexistent. Consequently, much of the influx of married women into the work force (especially the entry of women whose husbands' incomes are not low) was probably due to a kind of economic compulsion—namely, an effort to provide for their families things they increasingly felt were necessary.

In value terms, the value of labour power has risen, perhaps most because of rising educational requirements facing the next generation of workers. The household has experienced a rising cost of living. (From the perspective of capital, if surplus value was not to be reduced according to the rise in the value of labour power, more value had to be created. That is, the economy had to absorb more workers.)

Finally, in the case of middle-class women especially, the changing organization of domestic labour must not be overlooked as a factor promoting the influx to wage work. Because the household means of production owned by women in the early decades of the twentieth century were crude, domestic labour must not only have been long and arduous, but also the tasks very labour intensive and not easily integrated with each other. For example, the week's clothes washing or baking was likely to be carried out all at once and not spread over the course of a week. The week was the unit of time during which the full round of household chores was carried out.[41] Given these conditions of domestic labour, it would have been difficult for the primary worker in the home to work additionally outside the home. Moreover, extending the time spent on regular household tasks—all of them, in order to accommodate a boarder, or one of them, like washing or ironing for people in other households—would have fit in more with the organization of the work than would the absence of the woman from the house for long periods.

When the household means of production changed, and when, after the 1940s, middle-class families began to be able to afford the new household appliances, the time necessary for household chores was reduced, the gap between labour time and production time widened for many tasks, and the day became increasingly the unit of time over which the full round of housework was spread.[42] Specifically, modern household appliances reduced labour time considerably by freeing the household worker from the obligation to be present throughout the performance of a task like the washing of clothes. Consequently, a number of household chores could be performed simultaneously and the full round of housework chores performed (in smaller amounts) each day. This more integrated organization of household work gives the domestic labourer some time to work outside the home. As well, of course, the simple reduction of labour time involved in housework means full-time work outside the home is now possible for the domestic labourer.[43]

Conclusion

This article is an attempt to outline the way in which household production, the sphere of privatized labour by which daily subsistence is provided, is tied into capitalist commodity production. I specifically addressed the question of how capital's changing needs for female labour have been translated into pressures experienced by female household workers, who represent the major labour reserve today. I assumed that provision of the family's means of subsistence, in consumable form, is the chief outcome of domestic labour. Then, I focussed on differences among women with respect to the ownership of and access to the domestic means of production and changes over time in the relationship between these means of production and the socially defined product of household work. These changes, in addition to related changes that occurred in the organization of the domestic work process, contributed to the fairly recent movement of married women into wage work outside the home.

I should point out here that before a complete explanation of the growing involvement of married women in wage work can be formulated, however, a more thorough understanding of the changing labour needs of both capital and the state is necessary. The nature of the jobs women hold (e.g., how many are ones formerly undertaken in the home and what proportion of them are productive of surplus value) and the extent to which women are segregated from men in waged jobs are some of the questions that must be addressed before we will understand the long-run significance of the trend. As well, a full explanation of the trend must include the role of the state, through its "welfare" programs, in ensuring that working-class families always find wage work more attractive than "the dole."[44]

One implication of the explanation of the trend that I have offered is that working-class or lower income households harbour a female labour reserve perpetually in need of wage work. Domestic labourers from working-class households have been increasingly activated for wage work over the course of the twentieth century, and changes in demand for labour alone probably explain their growing involvement in work outside the home. They have been a labour pool that capital can mobilize as it needs, then, and they will probably continue to hold this role since many working-class women still remain outside the work force. Middle-class women, on the other hand, are increasingly involved in the work force as a result of long-term structural changes in the mode of the production and reproduction of family subsistence and of labour power. Their involvement, in the short run, is probably a function more of changes in their own life cycle than of capital's needs for labour and offers of jobs. In short, aside from the question of the types of jobs women normally hold, only part of the female reserve can be expected to be responsive to capital's cyclical labour needs.

Another implication of the trend is fairly clear. The household is increasingly in a structurally vulnerable position.[45] Because of changes over the past century, household means of production are increasingly commodities. With respect to the durable means of production or household appliances, this has meant an easing of the burden of housework but also an increased fragmentation of the work process and probably a rising feeling that household work is not really work. The commoditization of household means of production has tied women more closely to capitalist production by organizing their domestic labour so that it is easier for them to be periodically absent from the home, by socializing them to work with machines and by adding to the family expenses that put pressure on women to take up work for wages. Moreover, because the nondurable means of production have become almost exclusively commodities, women are less and less able to reduce the costs of family reproduction—in part because they have lost the skills involved in making homemade products.

The fact that more and more households depend on the wages of two workers leaves them fragile. That is, while the value of labour power has risen, men's wages have perhaps not risen so fast—certainly not in the 1970s—and so the wage work of women has become necessary for family maintenance. Moreover, the influx of married women into the labour force means capital does not have to grant such high wage increases to workers, for these workers know that their families are not solely dependent on their wages.

While it is true that having two members in the work force protects households from financial disaster, in practice it does not bring much security. Rather, the feeling of well-being which, in many cases, accompanies the inflow of cash from two sources probably causes families to take greater financial risks, to acquire more debts than they would if the man were the sole support. In short, a basic structural fragility may be reinforced by the consumer decisions taken by many families.

Clearly, the pressures that are driving married women into the work force are not uniform. They are different for different women, and consequently the double work day affects women in different ways. For lower income, working-class women, the assumption of a double work load arises out of a clear and absolute need. It is these women for whom work in the sphere of socialized production can lead to increased class consciousness; and these women are now in a work situation in which it is possible to organize collective action against capital. As the economy becomes less and less stable, these women are likely candidates for growing working-class militancy.

Women whose husbands' incomes are near the higher end of the income scale, however, cannot be expected to identify themselves with the working class as a whole. Since their participation in wage work resulted from an inflation in the level of living and, since their earnings contribute to the purchase of things that only a few decades earlier were luxuries, middle-class women working a "double day" will probably not be responsive to efforts at unionization. Moreover, these women cannot be appealed to as women working out of absolute necessity—they do not think they are working out of necessity and, indeed, many are not.

Because consumer issues represent the "heart of the matter" with respect to domestic labour—because the means of domestic production are in the form of commodities—the political struggle most likely to engage these women will be one over prices. The growing commoditization of domestic means of production ties the household ever more closely to capitalist production, thus placing it increasingly at the mercy of larger economic forces. As monopoly prices forge a tighter stranglehold over the household, women should increasingly come to realize the family's weak position. Organizing housewives remains very difficult, however, because of the privatized nature of their work. Shopping occurs in a social sphere, but one in which the people who rub elbows are, in most cases, strangers. Perhaps the most effective long-run strategy for organizing housewives to overthrow a system oppressive especially to women is the organization of consumer cooperatives. Such activity will not only begin the construction of alternative distribution forms, but it will also forge relationships among housewives based on the activity in which the contradictory interests of capital and the working-class household are most obvious.

NOTES

I wish to thank John Fox, who patiently and lovingly contributed both directly and indirectly to this paper. I am grateful as well to Wendy Donner, Bill Johnston, Susan Mann, Thelma McCormack and Wally Seccombe for helpful criticisms of earlier versions of the paper. Finally, comments and support offered by the late Richard Frucht were of inestimable value to me.

1. Many writers, and increasingly non-Marxists, use the term. But there are two sources that especially develop the argument as it applies to women. Harry Braverman's important work, *Labour and Monopoly Capital* (New York: Monthly Review Press, 1974), argues that married women constitute a latent form of reserve army. Patricia Connelly, in *Last Hired, First Fired* (Toronto: The Women's Press, 1978) borrows substantially from Braverman but extends the argument theoretically and details it with Canadian data.

2. Karl Marx, *Capital,* Vol. I (Moscow: Progress Publishers, 1954), pp. 589-607.

3. U.S. Bureau of the Census, *Historical Statistics of the United States: Colonial Times to 1970* (Washington, D.C.: U.S. Government Printing Office, 1975), p. 133.

4. Dominion Bureau of Statistics (hereinafter, DBS), *1941 Census of Canada* (Ottawa: Queen's Printer, 1946), Vol. I, p. 140 and Vol. VII, p. 165; DBS, *1951 Census of Canada* (Ottawa: Queen's Printer, 1953), Vol. I, p. 26-1 and Vol. IV, p. 11-11; DBS, *1961 Census of Canada* (Ottawa: Queen's Printer, 1963), Vol. I, Part 2, p. 28-1 and Vol. III, Part I, pp. 17-18; Statistics Canada, *1976 Census of Canada* (Ottawa: Queen's Printer, 1978), Vol. V, Part 5, p. 10-2.

5. Margaret Benston, "The Political Economy of Women's Liberation," *Monthly Review,* 21 (Sept. 1969), pp. 13-27.

6. Wally Seccombe, "Domestic Labour—Reply to Critics," *New Left Review,* 94 (Nov.-Dec. 1975), pp. 85-96.

7. How the operation of the law of value fits into this argument is not clear in the article. The point seems to be that labour is moving from a sector of low productivity to one of higher productivity. In other words, the *effect* of the move is similar to that resulting from the operation of the law of value. That, of course, does not necessarily mean the law of value was responsible for the outcome.

8. Jacob Mincer, "Labor Force Participation of Married Women: A Study of Labor Supply," in National Bureau of Economic Research, *Aspects of Labor Economics* (Princeton: University of Princeton Press, 1962).

9. Connelly, *Last Hired.*

10. Karl Marx, *Capital,* Vol. I, trans. Ben Fowkes (New York: Vintage Books, 1976), p. 1004.

11. Marx, *Capital,* Vol. I, pp. 164-93.

12. I shall refer to the wage earner as "he," and assume the simplest case—the household in which a man is the chief wage earner.

13. Joann Vanek, "Time Spent in Housework," *Scientific American,* 231 (Nov. 1974), pp. 116-20. The article summarizes time budget studies of housework, studies that have accumulated over the past 50 years in the United States. Recent data show that housewives who are also involved in wage work spend, on average, about 26 hours per week on domestic chores. So, we assume that this is the minimum time required for such work.

14. Of course, there is no simple, exact equation between the value of a particular labour power and the value produced by that labourer working for capital during the part of the day the wage covers. Only at the level of the whole working class is the value of labour power equal to value produced during "necessary labour time." And this equalization is in a constant process of disruption; it is an historical tendency, pure only in the abstract. Moreover, when one moves from a high level of abstraction to the level of concrete situations, the assumption that wages equal the value of labour power and the value produced during "necessary labour time" gives way to the question of how the levels of particular wages are determined. Historical and market forces enter the discussion when one moves to the empirical level of *prices.*

    Even in discussing the value of labour power, that is, the quantity of commodities (of a certain quality) assumed necessary for subsistence, historical forces are clearly at work. Marx specified an "historical and moral" element in the determination of the value of labour power. In other words, he pointed out that the standard of living is clearly socially and culturally defined: the quantity of means of subsistence, or commodities assumed necessary for living, is subject to social—and marketplace—definition.

15. John Harrison, "The Political Economy of Housework," *Bulletin of the Conference of Socialist Economists* (Winter 1973), pp. 35-52.

16. Wally Seccombe, "The Housewife and Her Labour Under Capitalism," *New Left Review*, 83 (Jan.-Feb. 1974), pp. 3-24.

17. Jean Gardiner, "Women's Domestic Labour," *New Left Review*, 89 (Jan.-Feb. 1975), pp. 47-58. I should point out that this argument is not the same as the one Harrison seems to be making, though its conclusion is the same. I agree with both Harrison and Gardiner, however, that domestic labour *can* indirectly lead to higher surplus value appropriation by capital. (The way in which Harrison sees this occurring is different from this first argument by Gardiner.)

    In attempting to refute this notion, Maxine Molyneux, in "Beyond the Domestic Labour Debate," *New Left Review*, 116 (July-Aug. 1979), pp. 2-38, makes the serious mistake of confusing the price and the value of labour power (i.e., the empirical realization and the abstract property). She refers, in one place to the value of labour power being determined by the "wage bargain" (p. 11), and, in another, to an influence on it by inflation (p. 12). At one point, she agrees that domestic labour may be important "in cases where the *value* of male labour power has fallen below the family wage and the dependent housewife . . . redoubles her effort to stretch the family wage" (p. 12), when she means the situation where the *price* of male labour power—or the wage—falls below the *value* of labour power (which covers the whole family's reproduction). Yet clearly, the value of labour power is determined by the labour time socially necessary for its production, and not supply and demand, inflation, or the outcome of the bargaining between capital and labour—all of which influence labour power's price.

    It is on empirical grounds (and thus at the level of *price*) that Molyneux attempts to argue against the theory of domestic labour as use value production which *can* substitute for commodities and thus *can* generally reduce labour power's value. Molyneux says that it is in cases where workers' labour power has a low value (she means low wages) that the domestic labour input is often lowest—not highest. She seems to expect that if the argument were correct, high inputs of domestic labour would lead to lower *wages*. This is a misunderstanding of the argument. Only because she confuses price and value can she assume the argument to imply that domestic labour affects the wage.

18. The other labour process, besides the wage goods sector of the economy, in which labour power is produced and its value determined is in the service occupations, especially in education. The part of the wage that goes for taxes (and is paid out of the pockets

of labour and capital) pays for social service inputs to the production of labour power, and an approximate value equivalence is maintained between the value of labour power and that produced during necessary labour time. It would be misleading, however, to think that the laws of motion governing most forms of commodity production operate in the service sector. For services, like education, cannot really be thought of as commodity production. The product of education belongs not to educational workers or to the owner of their means of production but to the individual who walks away at the end of the process. He or she is the one who sells the product, labour power. Consequently, partly because no commodity is produced directly for the market, productivity increases in education (and other social services) are neither crucial nor frequent. To the extent that there are pressures to increase efficiency, or productivity, or simply to cut costs, they arise because education and other social services are costs to capital and to labour.

19. A content analysis of *Ladies Home Journal,* from 1890 to 1970, indicated an inflation in expectations about the variety of meals, which was partly a result of an advertising campaign to convince housewives to use canned food. See Bonnie Fox, *Women's Productive Role in the Household and the Wage Work Force in the Twentieth Century* (Doctoral dissertation, University of Alberta, 1980).

20. This dramatically high percentage increase, higher than that experienced by American women with older children, was actually largely due to the fact that the percentage of women with very young children who were in the labour force in the late 1940s was so low. The increase over this period in numbers of women in the work force was, in fact, higher for women with children over five. Nevertheless, by 1970 in the United States a high proportion of women with very young children was involved in wage work.

21. U.S. Bureau of the Census, *Historical Statistics,* p. 134.

22. Gabriel Kolko, in "Working Wives: Their Effects on the Structure of the Working Class," *Science and Society,* XLII (Fall 1978), pp. 257-77, states that the decade between 1930 and 1940 witnessed the largest increase in the labour force participation of American women in order to support his argument that economic necessity caused the influx of women into wage work. Unfortunately, such a conclusion is risky at best, largely because the changes in measurement between the 1930 and 1940 censuses were major. In 1930, the census attempted to measure people's customary or *habitual activity,* employing the "gainfully occupied" concept; in 1940, the census switched to measuring *current activity* in the

week preceding the enumeration. Revised figures are so sensitive to different assumptions and arguments that conclusions based upon them are extremely hazardous.

23. Median incomes of heads of Canadian husband-wife families:

	Current dollars	Constant dollars
1951	$1,795	$1,795
1961	$4,116	$3,254
1971	$7,039	$4,337
First quartile incomes:		
1951	$1,688	$1,688
1961	$2,726	$2,155
1971	$4,349	$2,680

Sources: DBS, *1951 Census of Canada,* Vol. III, p. 128-2; Statistics Canada, *1961 Census of Canada,* Vol. II, Part 2, p. 104-1.

24. See Valerie Oppenheimer, *The Female Labour Force in the United States* (Berkeley: Institute of International Studies, 1970) for empirical evidence of the disjuncture between estimates of the pools of married women, or those without husbands, and the demand for female workers.

25. The cause-effect relationship is not one-directional, however. For the availability of women no doubt encouraged the transfer of jobs from privatized to socialized production. Eli Ginsberg, in "The Job Problem," *Scientific American,* 237 (Nov. 1977) pp. 43-52, reported that about three out of five jobs created in the United States between 1950 and 1976 were "undesirable" with respect to wages, fringe benefits, regularity of work, working conditions and job security. That is, a majority of the jobs created in this period were tailor-made for women.

26. The Bureau of Applied Economics, Inc., *Standards of Living: A Compilation of Budgetary Studies.* Vols. I and II (Washington, D.C.: Bureau of Applied Economics, 1920, 1932); National Industrial Conference Board, *Family Budgets of American Wage Earners: A Critical Analysis,* Research Report No. 41 (New York: The Century Co., 1921); Eunice Knapp, "Family Budget of City Worker," *Monthly Labour Review,* 72 (Jan. 1951), pp. 152-55; Helen Lamale and Margaret Stotz, "The Interim City Worker's Family Budget," *MLR,* 83 (Aug. 1960), pp. 785-808; Jean Brackett, "New BLS Budgets provide yardsticks for measuring Family Living Costs," *MLR,* 92 (Apr. 1969), pp. 3-16.

27. Louise B. More, *Wage-Earners' Budgets: A Study of Standards* (New York: Henry Holt and Co., 1907); Robert C. Chapin, *The Standard of Living Among Workingmen's Families in New York City* (New York: The Russell Sage Foundation, 1909); Margaret Byington, *Homestead: The Households of a Mill Town* (New York: Charities Publication, 1910); Esther Little and William Cotton, *Budgets of Families and Individuals of Kensington, Philadelphia* (Lancaster, Pennsylvania: New Era Printing Co., 1920); Leila Houghteling, *The Income and Standard of Living of Unskilled Laborers in Chicago* (Chicago: University of Chicago Press, 1927).

28. U.S. Bureau of the Census, *Census of Housing* (Washington, D.C.: Government Printing Office, 1943), Vol. II, Part 1, pp. 20, 23, 36, 40.

29. DBS, *1941 Census of Canada,* Vol. I, p. 400 and Vol. IX, pp. 59, 247.

30. U.S. Bureau of the Census, *Census of Housing* (Washington, D.C.: U.S. Government Printing Office, 1953), Vol. I, Part 1, pp. 1-6, 1-9.

31. More, *Budgets,* p. 210; Chapin, *Standard of Living,* p. 322; Byington, *Homestead,* p. 75.

32. U.S. Bureau of the Census, *1920 Census,* Vol. IV, p. 474, 376; *1950 Census,* Vol. II, Part 1, p. 1-206.

33. DBS, *1931 Census,* Vol. V, pp. 686-87.

34. U.S. Bureau of the Census, *1970 Census. Subject Reports.* Final Report PC(2)-5A (Washington, D.C.: Government Printing Office, 1973), pp. 1-25. The statistics actually conceal the differences between children's involvement in wage work in the early part of the century and now. For to be counted as gainfully occupied, wage work had to be one's major activity, while to be listed in the labour force one had only to work for as little as an hour the week of the enumeration.

35. This tendency would be especially consequential when what was being measured was not current behaviour, as is involved in the "labour force" concept, but usual status, which is what the earlier notion of "gainfully occupied" aims to capture.

36. Reported in Hazel Kyrk, *Economic Problems of the Family* (New York: Harper and Brothers, 1933).

37. Kyrk, *Economic Problems,* p. 132.

38.

Year	Percentage of Households with Two or More Members in the Labour Force	Percentage of Households with Three or More Members in the Labour Force
1930	32%	11%
1940	31%	10%
1950	30%	7%
1960	44%	8%
1970	51%	11%

Sources: U.S. Bureau of the Census, *1950 Census, Special Reports* P-E No. 2A; *1960 Census.* Subjects Reports PC(2)-4C; *1970 Census. Subject Reports* PC(2)-8A.

39. Gwendolyn Hughes, *Mothers in Industry: Wage-Earning by Mothers in Philadelphia* (New York: New Republic, 1925).

40. The Fall 1886 issue of *Ladies Home Journal* deplored the adulteration and general inferiority of canned foods. In the 1920s, Robert and Helen Lynd, in *Middletown* (New York: Harcourt, Brace & World, 1929), reported a clear preference for homemade food of all kinds over commercial substitutes. They also noted that before the 1920s, bakery bread was seen as a working-class food.

41. See Meg Luxton's *More Than A Labour of Love* (Toronto: The Women's Press, 1980) for excellent descriptions of changes over time in household technology and the material conditions of domestic labour.

42. Labour time is simply the amount of time spent in active labour; production time is the amount of time it takes for the task, or for the production to be complete. It is Marx's distinction; see *Capital,* Vol. II (Moscow: Progress Publishers, 1956), pp. 245-47.

43. As a factor which facilitated women's entry into wage work, we must not forget their increased isolation in domestic labour. Over the course of the century, and largely because of education, those household members available during the day for help with household chores have been removed from the home. Moreover, there is decreasing contact with neighbours as daily shopping at neighbourhood groceries has given way to weekly shopping at large supermarkets. And if the need for companionship has been a prod urging women to seek wage work, their involvement in socialized production is probably a welcome end to the isolation of domestic work.

44. See Frances Fox Piven and Richard Cloward, *Regulating the Poor: The Functions of Public Welfare* (New York: Vintage Books, 1971).

45. Kolko, "Working Wives."

THE EXPANDED REPRODUCTION CYCLE OF LABOUR POWER IN TWENTIETH-CENTURY CAPITALISM

Wally Seccombe

In his second article, Wally Seccombe takes a more dynamic and speculative look at the way labour power is reproduced. Specifically, he asks how privatized domestic labour is combined with labour performed in the state sector (in the area of education, for example), to produce labour power. Although his chief concern is the domestic labour process and the way that process is shaped by the law of value, by examining the state sector he is breaking through the old boundaries of the "domestic labour debate."

A critical question is whether labour power is able to realize its full value in regular sale. FOX, *in her article, argues that the labour power of a constant proportion of households failed to realize its value through the twentieth century, at least until 1970; Seccombe argues here that the labour power of the whole working class is less and less able (especially in the 1970s) to realize its value. Because of the contradiction between the form and the function of the wage, the take-home pay of the proletariat fails to cover the full costs of labour power's expanded reproduction. Consequently, according to Seccombe, the state must step in to subsidize and regulate this non-capitalist production in the interests of capital in general.*

Part of the reason labour power decreasingly realizes its value is because labour inputs to its production have so increased, especially in the educational sector. Seccombe solves the puzzle of how capital attempts to cover the consequent rise in the cost of labour power and, in the process, complements the previous article's explanation of the changing "supply" of female labour with an explanation of capital's changing "demand" for it. Having discussed how the working class experiences increasing difficulty in maintaining and realizing the full value of its labour power during the current period of capitalist stagnation and cuts in state social expenditure, he concludes by suggesting appropriate political responses to the capitalist austerity drive in the 1980s.

Domestic labour is one of several labours integral to the reproduction of labour power in capitalist societies. All of the labour that goes into the production of commodity goods and services purchased with the wage—labour expended in education, health care and in the building and maintaining of the infrastructure of the urban residence (electricity, water, sewage, etc.)—combine with domestic labour to reproduce labour power on a continuous and expanding basis. But how is domestic labour, which is conducted in the interior of the private working-class household, shaped in relation to these other labours, which, taken together, reproduce labour power on an expanding scale? Or, to pose this question in the form in which I will endeavour to answer it here: how does the law of value shape the reproduction cycle of labour power?

I want to address this question at two levels: (a) at the (constituent) level of individual household units, whose members are employed by individual capitals; (b) at the (aggregate) level of the whole working class, living apart from capital and reproducing itself, but engaged by total social capital in the production of the social product.

In the first part of this article, proceeding at the level of individual households, I will extend the analysis of the simple reproduction cycle of labour power (which is developed in my first article in this book), to consider the ways in which the working-class household is forced to adjust its own subsistence strategy to make ends meet. The management of the household's resources "on a sound economic basis" involves the allocation of labour time, in a way that obeys and expresses the action of the law of value as it presses on the individual household from two directions: first, from the labour market, reflecting the exchange value that the labour power offered by a household for sale is able (or unable) to realize; and second, from the retail market of consumer goods and services, reflecting the exchange value required to purchase a given set of commodities comprising the household's means of subsistence.

In the second part of this article, I will proceed at the aggregate level of the working class. After a ground-clearing discussion of the peculiar nature of the commodity labour power and the processes of its valorization, I will offer a provisional analysis of the long-term tendencies of private capital and the state in the aggregate production of labour power in the developed capitalist countries in the twentieth century. This involves (a) the capital-deepening development of Department II, under the impetus of relative surplus value extraction; and (b) the growth of the state sector provision of standardized inputs to labour power's production (residential infrastructure, education, minimal health care) under the impetus of shifting these costs from the wage fund of private capital onto the general tax fund of the state.

I will argue that these two contradictory tendencies have run up against their own limits and have now generated a virulent crisis in the valorization of labour power, manifest in mass unemployment, falling working-class living standards and rising per capita costs of producing labour power. This is part of the global crisis of capital accumulation that afflicts the world economy as we enter the 1980s.

Capitalist states have now plunged into reverse gear, attempting to reprivatize the costs of labour power's production and force working-class households to shoulder the additional burden. Finally, I want to consider, very briefly, effective ways of combatting this austerity drive.

Domestic Labour and the Law of Value

From the standpoint of wage workers as sellers of labour power, their households are atomized units competing against one another, usually in a buyer's market. They are forced to sell in order to survive, and to compete with other sellers in order to realize the value of their only commodity. In this they have no choice. Individual households must accept the verdict of the labour market against their labour power and adjust their resources and labour time accordingly, in order to defend and enhance its exchange value.

Through this proletarian compulsion, the law of value shapes domestic labour in individual working-class households, influencing, in a sluggish fashion, its intensity, its duration and its composite tasks. What do I mean by this?

The essence of Marx's claim for the law of value is that in all forms of commodity production, a certain characteristic form of regulative interaction occurs between the spheres of exchange and production, more or less strongly as the case may be.[1] The circulation of commodities in exchange acts to enforce a dynamic adjustment on labour expenditure (kind, intensity, duration) in separate disassociated production units. The producers are compelled to respond in an economically rational and characteristic way, employing quantitative calculations against a uniform monetary standard. They are compelled to organize the productive forces at their command and to spend their labour time so as to optimize the anticipated exchange value of their product on the market. And, by the same token, (selling in order to buy), they endeavour to minimize their costs for means of production in the market. They therefore adopt, in one form or another (and their consciousness of what they are doing may vary), a market criteria of cost/price accounting. This includes, implicitly, even *before* it is widely sold on the market, an e(valu)ation of the worth of their own labour power and the exchange value efficacy of exerting it in various ways. Thus, labour power has already been evaluated and allocated in exchange value terms (however weakly this may be occurring) prior to its mass appearance in proletarian commodity form. The empirical verification of this distinct exchange value form of economic calculation among private commodity producers is evidence for the operation of the law of value among them.[2]

The law of value is unleashed when independent units of commodity production have *no choice* but to exchange their products on the market and when they have some discretionary leeway in the arrangement of their productive forces in order to do so. Two preconditions apply here:

1. These units are unable to withdraw from the market by reverting to production for use without suffering a sharp drop in their standard of living. They are, therefore, forced to pay heed to the rewards and the punishments of changing exchange values for the commodities they buy and sell.
2. These units have the capacity to adjust their labour power and other productive forces at hand according to the verdict (actual or anticipated) that the market renders directly against their commodities and indirectly against their labour expenditure. This leeway involves:

(a) the exchangeability of one labour process for another;
(b) some capacity to obtain, through purchase and manufacture, new (superior) productive forces to replace outmoded ones;
(c) flexibility in the exercise of labour vis-à-vis duration, intensity and task-mix;
(d) some mobility of the producers from one location and economic unit to another.

I will argue that these conditions pertain, in a partial and awkward sense, in the sphere of proletarian subsistence. Here we have individual household units which are unable to withdraw from the market, which must, therefore, shape their labour in conformity with the principle of optimizing their only commodity's exchange value in a competitive market. These units have a limited capacity to adjust their labour accordingly. They can intensify domestic labour, shift its focus or seek a second wage. They can also change location, in order to be able to sell their only commodity in a new market. In all these ways, they are in a position to obey the law of value in the constant struggle to "make ends meet" by operating the household in "a businesslike fashion." Within the framework elaborated above, I therefore want to pose the value question for domestic labour in the proletarian household in the following way: Does the domestic labourer calculate and allocate her labour time according to implicit standards which reflect the dominance of exchange value over use value criteria? How does the law of value *tend* to equilibrate domestic labour and bring it into relation with surrounding labours via the consumer and the labour markets?

A central argument of my initial *New Left Review* article on domestic labour was that domestic labour, while unproductive of surplus value, did indeed create value; it was an integral and necessary labour input to the production of the commodity labour power, which realized its full value upon sale.[3] Although I do not find that argument wrong, *per se*, it tended to pose, implicitly, a sterile either-or question–does, or does not, domestic labour create value? I had answered that it did. My critics replied that it did not–being a labour of direct use–and in this way we dug conceptual antimony, in which the domestic labour debate became stuck. To have a "position" in this debate was often merely to line up on one or another side of this well-chewed bone of contention.

The problem with this framework was that the law of value is a dynamic set of tendencies and a regulative/disruptive force that operates more or less strongly, encountering various degrees of resistance in different social formations where commodity production is prevalent. And it does so with different strengths in various regions of these social formations.

The question of the law of value's presence or absence is,

therefore, always a relative and an historical one. It cannot be answered by recourse to ahistorical criteria and essentialist definition.[4]

Is, then, domestic labour in the modern working-class household a labour of direct use or a labour of exchange? It is both—in awkward combination. It is a labour for the direct use of household members. It is also a labour that is compelled to defend the exchange value of their labour power on the market. The way in which the housewife balances these conflicted imperatives will be taken up in the next section.

Does the law of value have an impact upon domestic labour? In my first article, I answered no to this question.[5] I made the mistake of equating the law of value with the direct organization of the labour process by capital and equating abstract labour with proletarian labour. Coulson, Magas and Wainwright, in their critique, pointed out that this position was in direct contradiction to my assertion that domestic labour created value.[6] They were perfectly correct in this. In my response, I shifted my terrain: "I am here much more interested in how the law of value impinges indirectly upon housework, where I formerly emphasized that it did not do so directly."[7]

The problem with this response, while it was moving in the right direction, was that it revealed the dubious character of my prior formulation without tackling it head on. For the fact is that the law of value *never* operates directly in organizing a labour process. Its characteristic action is "behind the backs" of the producers, as Marx so graphically put it. It only operates through competition in the market. It is expressed, in essence, as an interior compulsion of the producer to obey the anonymous dictates of the market under the pain of losing out competitively against other producers and suffering a loss of monetary income. For capitalists this is a loss of profit, while for petty proprietors and wage labourers, it is a loss of necessary subsistence income. In either case there is a compulsion to compete on the market and to organize the labour and the material inputs to one's commodity production accordingly.

Household Strategies for Securing Subsistence

Within the limits of the proletarian condition, working-class households constantly strategize their optimal course for securing the means for their own subsistence. They confront two great imperatives here which they strive, in a trade-off, to reconcile:

1. They strive, through their own labour, to maintain and, wherever possible, to improve their living standards.
2. They seek to limit the labour effort required to do so (both its intensity and duration) in order to avoid the exhaustion and degradation of their labour power and to enjoy their leisure time.

The trade-off between these two imperatives is by no means unique to the proletariat. It has preoccupied every labouring class in world history. What is unique to the modern working class is the specific way in which these imperatives confront its household units and the way in which they strive to manage it.

The proletariat is freely compelled to take an active interest in safeguarding and enhancing both the use value of its labour power for itself and the exchange value of its labour power for regular sale to capital. These two life necessities are by no means congruent with one another. They engender a conflicted set of trade-offs with which the working-class household is constantly forced to grapple. One of the primary facets of "sound household management" is to juggle these imperatives and to secure their prioritization within the household. But before examining this process, I will briefly outline each of them in turn.

1. The labour power of the working-class household is not merely a commodity to be sold and consumed by capital elsewhere. It is also the capacity to live, to enjoy oneself, to seek the satisfaction of one's own physiological and social needs. Domestic labour is unmistakably shaped, quite directly in the household, by the needs and demands of family

members. In this sense, housework is a labour for consumption, for direct use. While the household struggles to obtain a larger money income, it does so to meet its own needs, to incorporate new needs into its daily lifestyle and, secondarily, to relax the pressures on domestic labour to meet these new needs. The struggle of the working-class household to maximize its living autonomy from capital is a struggle to assert its own human needs against the anonymous pressures of the law of value.

2. The size and regularity of the household's income, and the external labour it must expend to obtain it, will determine the leeway within which the needs of the household's members are expressed. Therefore the exchange value of its only commodity must always be safeguarded. This is the constant external compulsion (internalized in the proletarian as a free labourer) through which the law of value rules over the allocation of the household's resources and the management of its labour power. The assertion of personal needs must be reconciled with this imperative.

Furthermore, workers take an active interest in how their labour power is consumed by capital. This is unusual for commodity sellers. Most are indifferent to the nature of the consumption of their commodity as long as it is being consumed, the market demand for it remains strong and its exchange value can be realized.

But since the seller of labour power does not part with it in the market, but in capitalist production, she/he is forced to take an active interest in how capital elects to consume it. This is the context for struggle over working conditions, health and safety on the job, etc.

The working class may labour in two separate locations but it cannot possibly make an absolute separation between them. For what happens to it in one sphere crucially affects its capacities to live and labour in the other. This cuts both ways, on a day-to-day basis. The imperatives of these two spheres are in constant tension.

The way her/his labour power is (ab)used in capitalist production will critically affect the proletarian's capacity to live–to stay healthy, to live a long life, to enjoy her/his leisure time. And, obversely, the worker on her/his own time must safeguard the utility of her/his labour power for capital to meet the employer's standards on the job. Domestic labour must ensure that the labour power employed by capital is in a usable form, according to the latter's standards and modes of consuming it.

These two imperatives, the use value of the household and of the labour exercised therein, and the exchange value of labour power sold to capital for use elsewhere, implicitly form two "standards" that shape domestic labour. In their equilibration with one another, they determine the duration, intensity and task composition of the labour of the working-class household.[8] The management of tension between family members, which is so characteristic of women's domestic roles, is in essence an attempt to reconcile these imperatives. Thus, when her husband, the primary wage earner, is sleeping prior to his next shift, the noisy play of the children must be stifled by a stern intervention in defence of the exchange value of his labour power. On the weekend, however, that criteria can be relaxed. She may organize a family outing in which her children are treated to their favourite entertainment as a compensation for the previous day's suppression of their play. To be able to manage both of these standards "each in their proper time and place" is the mark of a competent housewife and mother.

In family household planning and decision-making, these imperatives are also traded off against one another. The contentious issue of overtime provides a simple example of how this works. Working overtime brings in an additional income, raising the exchange value realized by the household's labour power. But, on the other hand, it disrupts the household's social life. The further exhaustion of the worker makes it harder for her/him to hold up her/his end at home. Thus, it is often undertaken as a sacrifice of today's needs–an investment in the household's future use value—"for retirement" or "for the children's education" or "for next Christmas."

Consider the familiar working-class investment in the future—eduction, or the acquisition of a skilled trade. A household may elect to forego a part of its income and/or leisure time today in order for one of its members to enroll in a night course or an apprenticeship program, thereby enhancing the potential use value of its labour power for capital and, hopefully, the future exchange value of its labour power.

The second wage option is another familiar proletarian trade-off. The additional income of the wife, nowhere near her husband's, will nevertheless secure in commodity form, goods and services that will enable her to reduce her domestic labour time. The household's living standards will thus be raised while her total labour time is increased but not doubled.[9]

All the major decisions of household budgeting and management can be analyzed in light of the trade-off between these imperatives. On the one hand, decisions are made with rational economic calculation to allocate the household's resources in begrudging conformity to the law of value. On the other hand, the household strives for independence and autonomy in its private life, holding at bay tomorrow's dull compulsion to enhance the exchange value of one's labour power in order to enjoy one's leisure time today. The proletarian household remains caught in the tension between the pursuit of its own needs and the external compulsion to which it must submit in order to survive. It is the housewife/mother who manages this tension through her labour.

If we now combine elements of the examples given above, we can approximate the decision-making process whereby a household adjusts various elements in the reproduction cycle of its labour power to meet a new economic conjuncture. For example, say a wife returns to wage work part-time as soon as her youngest child is in school, so that her husband can cut out overtime and enroll in night school. He is hoping to pick up a skill (and certificate) which will enhance his use value attraction to prospective employers, raise his potential earning power and act as an insurance against lay-off. They are counting on him being able to gain a raise after completing the course, so that she can leave the labour market to bear and raise another child. In the meantime, she is using some form of contraception. They are pinching pennies, cutting back on meat in the family diet and cooking less with expensive, prepared foods. Domestic labour is therefore being intensified; and she is pressuring him to assume responsibility for getting the dinner started, since she too is out working all day, and his shift ends an hour earlier than hers. The trip they took last summer on his vacation time is out this year, because she cannot afford to quit work and has no holiday time coming to her. As a consolation, they have decided to fix up the back porch and yard, so they can have their friends over and sit out back on hot summer evenings.

This is the familiar stuff and substance of decision-making in working-class households: strategizing to arrange their labour time in such a way as to keep it within limits, while at the same time striving to enhance their living standards. The compulsion of the law of value is in evidence in forcing a market "rationality" upon their decisions.

The household budget is the unit of proletarian account. In the confines of its rationality, women's needs and interests are normally subordinated. This is an important and subtle aspect of women's subordination in the family which occurs through an apparent symmetry of sacrifice. Both the primary breadwinner husband and the housewife/mother toil "for the sake of the family" and both share the fruits of their labour with other family members. The unequal value of their respective labour powers on the market, however, impresses an unequal division of labour upon them.

Her wage work, in the above example, is consciously conceived as being supplementary and temporary, while he enhances the future exchange value of his labour power. This will widen the wage gap between them, because she will quit her job to raise another child as soon as he can secure his sought-after pay raise. The most pernicious thing about this is that it all makes a certain perverse economic sense from the standpoint of the household unit. Whose labour power is more valuable to the family unit on the labour market? His, of course. Would it make "economic sense" for him to disrupt his employment and weaken his future earning power to stay at home with their pre-school-age child while she works for a smaller wage? Of course not. But it "makes sense" for her to do this. These "economic facts of life" are so banal that the collective choices households make on the basis of them seem natural and are taken for granted. They are, in fact, a complex reflection of the law of value which enforces its socially irrational rationality on household units freely compelled to play by its rules.[10]

In discussing the way in which working-class households strategize their subsistence arrangements to defend the exchange value of their labour power, while meeting their members' personal needs, I have assumed a static real wage rate and a stable value for labour power. In fact, of course, such homeostasis is rare. I want now to consider two types of variation in the value of labour power to see how they affect domestic labour: (a) a real wage difference between two households; (b) a net drop in real wages taken across the entire body of the working class over a given time period.

For the first case, compare two single wage families with the same number and aged children, one with an income of $18,000 and another with an income of $12,000. For both, the productivity of their domestic labour is much lower than the average productivity of labour embodied in the bundle of commodities they purchase with their wages. But the $18,000 household has more leeway than the $12,000 unit to reduce domestic labour time through the purchase of superior household appliances, prepared foods, etc. In further commoditizing its means of subsistence, it tends to shift labour time out of the household into consumer goods industries where labour productivity is much higher. The productivity of its remaining domestic labour is subsequently raised, because the houseworker is now outfitted with superior means of producing subsistence.

The $12,000 family is not so fortunate. A new dishwasher may be on the market, but the family budget cannot afford it, and the housewife must continue to wash every dish by hand. The productivity of her labour falls further behind her counterpart in the $18,000 household, with the result that her domestic labour time is increased while "the product" she produces is inferior. This family's labour power is being devalued relative to the other and the housewife can do little to compensate. The fact that she creates value (at an abysmally low productivity) does not mean she has an instrumental role in the overall valorization of labour power. Her labour does make a difference (which is why the family has an incentive to intensify it) but it is a minor difference compared to the changes in the labour time socially necessary for the production of other aspects of the commodity labour power occurring in the consumer goods and state sector.

Secondly, in the past few years there has been a fall in real wages across the entire working class in the developed capitalist countries. This has provoked a compensating intensification of domestic labour. Housewives try to stretch the family budget by shopping more carefully, cooking more from basic staples and mending old clothes instead of buying new ones, etc.

How do we explain this shift? We know that capital is experiencing increasing difficulty achieving its own valorization. For its part, the working class has an increasingly difficult time maintaining the full value of its commodity; labour power begins to lose value. The proletariat contests this loss but it suffers a number of setbacks and partial defeats. Real wages fall and labour power is devalued. These real wage decreases force the working class to decrease the productivity of the labour it brings to bear upon the production of its labour power.

When housewives prepare more meals from basic staples, purchase fewer new clothes and mend the old ones more often, they are replacing the labour embodied in the commodity goods they no longer buy with their own labour. But their own labour is of much lower productivity than the labour it replaces. In prosperous times, with real wages rising, it would be completely irrational for housewives to shift their labour back into the household in this manner. It would be contrary to their own interest in enhancing the use value of their households and reducing their own labour time and intensity. But capitalist stagnation and falling real wages reverse the developmental logic of the law of value. Now housewives are forced to lower the average productivity of the labour producing labour power in order to preserve, as best they can, the use values of the household.

It is well understood by Marxists in other areas of the capitalist economy that a generalized capitalist crisis produces an active antagonism between the use value and exchange value of commodities, conflicting with the logic of their simultaneous production. This conflict is also engendered in the production of the commodity labour power. The intensification of domestic labour, as real wages fall, is made in defence of the use value of the household and everything consumed therein. What had previously vanished as domestically necessary labour time (what had become unnecessary, on the average) now creeps back into the household, marking a regression in the development of the working class' mode of subsistence.[11] This is a regression that visits its greatest burdens upon women.

The Peculiar Nature of the Commodity Labour Power

Marx termed labour power a "peculiar" commodity. He considered it to be unlike other commodities in four basic ways:

1. As the only living commodity, the use value of labour power has the capacity to generate more value in its consumption than is necessary to replace it.

2. Embodied, as it is, in a person, labour power is not alienable in the market upon sale. Its seller is compelled to accompany its buyer (the capitalist) directly into the latter's sphere of consumption.

3. The value of labour power reflects a cultural element above and beyond the physical requisites of its reproduction, this element varying with the normal living conditions of the working class in a given country in a given period.

4. The capacity of living labour power to acquire and consolidate new needs through the struggle of its owners against capital represents a unique feature of the realization, in the market, of its value.

In this section I would like to discuss two additional peculiarities, with which Marx did not grapple, and which have not been seriously addressed by subsequent generations of Marxists.

The fifth peculiarity of labour power is that there is a permanent disjunction between the function of the wage and its form under capitalism. The wage functions, as Marx correctly insists, to reproduce labour power from one day to the next and from one generation to the next. It does so by covering the costs of its private production in proletarian households. But there is no direct relation to this function in the way wage rates are adjusted and established. Worker A and Worker B, who do the same job, are paid the same rate, in spite of the fact that A has a pregnant wife at home with three pre-school-age children, and B is single and lives on his own. A capitalist may pay them at different rates but not because of differences in their subsistence costs; rather he adjusts their pay according to his own competitive principles of attracting labour and differentiating and dividing his labour force. The fact that the wage he pays A is spent in part reproducing a new generation of proletarians, while B's is not, is of no immediate concern to the capitalist. He seeks only to reduce their pay as far as he practically can and still get a full day's labour out of them. The private wage system is thus a very rough and imprecise mechanism in funding the reproduction of labour power.

It is the working class that adapts to capital's fluctuating wage rates and employment fortunes, and not vice versa. If households were not able to exercise a genuine flexibility, the capitalist wage system would break down, unable to reproduce a new generation of proletarian labour power. Since I have already discussed many aspects of this flexibility, I will review them briefly here.

1. Most couples consciously control family size, space births and create saving funds when they first get married, in order to get over the "hump" in the domestic life cycle when women are pinned down at home with the care of infants and the growing household must rely solely on the husband's income for subsistence.

2. The working class historically has displayed a remarkable flexibility in fitting its domestic groups to the available housing stock–doubling up, if necessary, renting out rooms to borders, building additional rooms on houses wherever possible, etc.

3. The working-class household is able to adjust its labour in several different directions to secure additional income: moonlighting, overtime, women's external wage work, piecework in the household, selling petty commodities locally (bread, garden vegetables, etc.).

4. As well as managing to save modest funds, households go into debt to cover major purchases and get over the phases of the life cycle when there is a peak drain on resources.

5. A large part of the household's flexibility is an adjustment of its needs to its purchasing power. The "historical and moral element" which Marx included in the value of labour power refers precisely to the creation of new needs (above and beyond the physiological floor of bare subsistence) which can only be consolidated through a rising living standard.

Since wages are not adjusted to differential needs, there can never be, under capitalism, a uniform consolidation of new needs in the proletariat. The cultural variable that Marx included in the value of labour power is, therefore, always differentiated within a national working class, as well as between national sections of the proletariat. There is never a time when one particular subsistence pattern (e.g., the single male wage/female housewife model) becomes uniform across the entire breadth of the working class of a given country; differentiated wage rates and stratified needs make this impossible.[12]

In addition to the working class' own flexibility in adapting its subsistence means to the capitalist wage system, the state has historically been compelled to step in to supplement and rationalize.[13] This has been accomplished through a whole range of transfer payments based upon legally specified criteria of entitlement: old age pensions, baby bonuses, unemployment and health insurance, injured workman's compensation, welfare, etc.

These payments have been called "the social wage," which is, perhaps, a useful term in highlighting the inadequacy of the private wage. They do not take the form of a wage, however, nor are they part of a market contract. These funds are allocated by means of legislated eligibility criteria and dispensed through an arbitrary bureaucratic monopoly. There is nothing comparable here to the proletarian prerogative of employer choice.

Social security provisions have generally been advocated and fought for by the labour movement, social democratic parties and organizations of the oppressed. This support is certainly justified by the considerable material assistance which these programs provide the working and unemployed poor. (Their reduction today must be fought as well.) However, there has been far less awareness of the insidious way these programs are implemented; their eligibility criteria are often used by state functionaries to police the living arrangements and private lives of their recipients. Illegitimacy and cohabitation out of wedlock, for example, are often supressed through the threat of a withdrawal of funds and other supports. Male breadwinners/female dependency relations are reinforced in marriage by the eligibility criteria of income maintenance programs.[14] In all of these ways the state indirectly cultivates the "legitimate" family norm in the heart of the working class and punishes diversity in living arrangements.

The sixth peculiarity of labour power as a commodity under capitalism is that it is not produced by capital. Neither the household's nor the state sector's inputs to labour power's production are capitalist. This raises a real problem for a value analysis of this commodity. For, if we confine "the value of labour power" strictly to the labour time necessary for the production of wage goods in Department II, as Marx appears to do in most of Volume I, then there is no correspondence at all between "the value of labor power" and its real production (or replacement) costs. In Marx's day, when the state sector inputs to labour power were relatively minor, this omission was not so problematic as it is now when there is a massive and costly state contribution to this commodity's production. So, how should we proceed?

Marx argued that the basic value determination of labour power was not one of its peculiarities: "The value of labour power is determined, as in the case of every other commodity, by the labour time necessary for the production and consequently also the reproduction of this special article. . . . Its value, like that of every other commodity, is already fixed before it goes into circulation since a definite quantity of social labour has been spent upon it.[15]

What is this "definite quantity of social labour" that has been spent upon labour power before it enters into circulation? There is no compelling reason to exclude from this quantity all the non-capitalist labours of labour power's production. To the contrary, the very conception of labour power's valorization becomes incoherent and practically irrelevant without their inclusion.

One might argue (some have) that Marx did not have these labours "in mind" when he equated the value of labour power with the real costs of its replacement. That is debatable. In places he mentions education and medical care as necessary costs which boost the value of labour power. However, he considered them to be entirely secondary, and the capitalist or non-capitalist organization of these inputs is not clearly specified in *Capital.*

But this is an essentially theological debate over the "real meaning" of sacred texts. The relevant question is how to treat the valorization of labour power today, within a coherent Marxist framework, soundly based on the labour theory of value. In a few places in *Capital,* Marx goes beyond his normally restricted treatment of labour power's valorization and furnishes some highly suggestive clues which have been neglected by subsequent generations of Marxists. I would like to examine the contemporary implications of two such passages in some detail here.

> The value of labour power is determined by the value of the necessaries of life habitually required by the average labourer. The quantity of these necessaries is known at any given epoch of a given society, and can therefore be treated as a constant magnitude. What changes, is the value of this quantity. There are, besides, two other factors that enter into the determination of the value of labour-power. One, the expenses of developing that power, which expenses vary with the mode of production; the other, its natural diversity, the difference between the labour-power of men and women, of children and adults. The employment of these different sorts of labour-power, an employment which is, in its turn, made necessary by the mode of production, makes a great difference in the cost of maintaining the family of the labourer, and in the value of the labour-power of the adult male. Both these factors, however, are excluded in the following investigation.[16]

In the first three sentences of this passage, Marx formulates the determination of labour power's value in an entirely standard manner, reminiscent of a dozen or more similar passages in Volume I of *Capital.* But then he adds "two other factors that enter the determination of the value of labour power," and proceeds, after two tantalizing sentences, to bracket them for consideration at a later point. Marx saw this exclusion as being entirely consistent with the simplified value assumptions upon which Volume I of *Capital* was based. "I assume," he writes, following directly from the passage cited above, "(1) that commodities are sold at their value; (2) that the price of labour power rises occasionally above its value but never sinks below it." These were not assumptions about capitalist reality; they were the restricted, simplifying assumptions of Volume I. Elsewhere in Volume I, Marx writes:

> Despite the important part which this method [driving the price of labour power beneath its value] plays in actual practice, we are excluded from considering it in this place, by our assumption, that all commodities, including labour-power, are bought and sold at their full value.[17]

Capital, it bears repeating, is an unfinished work. Marx never returned to these "two other factors" in any sustained passage of the four existing volumes. It should not be inferred from this omission that Marx considered these factors unimportant. He comments that the employment of women and children "make a great difference" in the value of male labour power; and he considered the driving down of the price of labour power beneath its value to be one of the major counter-tendencies to the tendency of the falling rate of profit.[18]

The first extra factor Marx terms the "expenses of developing that power." He is, as I understand it, considering a specific development cost above and beyond the costs of household subsistence ("the quantity of necessaries" mentioned in the preceding sentence). This category includes all forms of training, education and specialized non-domestic health care supplied in the state sector–precisely those inputs to labour power which have been exponentially expanded since Marx's day. Marx comments that these costs "vary with the mode of production."

The permanent revolutionization of the productive forces that characterizes the capitalist mode of production necessitates the continuous revolutionization of its living productive force, labour power, above and beyond its household maintenance. Therefore, this specific expense tends to rise with the development of capitalism, despite real deskilling tendencies operating in the opposite direction. I do not want to claim that this is what Marx "really meant" by the sentence I have cited. I would insist, however, that he *is* clearly setting out an additional component of labour power's replacement cost, above and beyond household subsistence, and that the massive rise of state education and health care expenses in the twentieth century can be assessed within this framework. Marx sets the wage up as a straightforward equivalent of household subsistence (the necessaries of the wage goods package purchased as commodities entirely from Department II), suggesting that these extra development costs would not necessarily be covered and paid for via the take-home pay of the private wage, as indeed they have not been in the twentieth century. In this respect, Marx's treatment of labour power's valorization in *Capital,* while skeletal, is sound and quite amenable to development once we move beyond the simplifying assumptions of Volume I.

The second extra "factor entering the determination of the value of labour power" is the employment of "different sorts of labour power"—men and women, adults and children. This "makes a great difference in the costs of maintaining the family of the labourer and in the value of the labour power of the adult male." In another passage Marx expands upon this idea:

> The value of labour-power was determined, not only by the labour-time necessary to maintain the individual adult labourer, but also by that necessary to maintain his family. Machinery, by throwing every member of that family on to the labour-market, spreads the value of the man's labour power over his whole family. It thus depreciates his labour power. To purchase the labour-power of a family of four workers may, perhaps, cost more than it formerly did to purchase the labour-power of the head of the family, but, in return, four days' labour takes the place of one, and their price falls in proportion to the excess of the surplus-labour of four over the surplus-labour of one. In order

> that the family may live, four people must now, not only labour, but expend surplus-labour for the capitalist. Thus we see, that machinery, while augmenting the human material that forms the principal object of capital's exploiting power, at the same time raises the degree of exploitation.[19]

Note in this passage that Marx takes the family unit, not the individual wage labourer, as his starting point. He begins by discussing the value of labour power in family unit terms and ends by treating the rate of exploitation in the same fashion. This is an exemplary methodological premise for contemporary study, not only of women's labour but of the whole question of the allocation of the working class' total labour time between the sexes and between the two production sites.

We begin by calculating the number of hours the average proletarian household spends in wage labour; the proportion of that time its members work to create the equivalent value (v) of their total wage income; and the remaining portion, which is surplus (s) unpaid labour time. Capital's problem is to raise the proportion of s to v or the rate of surplus value. If we now calculate this proportion at the level of *household units,* we obtain a new perspective on absolute and relative surplus value.

In the developed capitalist countries it has generally been assumed that raising the rate of surplus value by absolute means—by prolonging the working day—ended in the mid-nineteenth century with the advent of the twelve and later the ten and finally the eight-hour day. From that point on, Marxists have tended to assume that capital's sole means of raising the rate of surplus value was by relative means—or by reducing the labour time necessary to generate the wage fund and the average bundle of wage goods, thus shifting the proportions of s to v without prolonging the working day. This was, in fact, the dominant trend in the latter half of the nineteenth and the early part of the twentieth centuries, when the working-class household's average number of hours in wage work diminished. But, particularly since the Second

World War, the number of hours an average household spends in wage work has been steadily increasing by means of the mass re-entry of married women into the paid work force. From the standpoint of proletarian households, this is a tremendous extension of the working day, reflecting capital accumulation by absolute means.

For Marx, as soon as the stage of primitive capital accumulation was surpassed, the relative means of raising the rate of surplus value was central. There is nothing wrong or outmoded about this basic insight. Indeed, I would argue that the shortening of the time in which wage workers of both sexes toil to recuperate their private means of household subsistence was a vital element in the long boom after the Second World War. The problem arises not *within* the phenomenon covered by the ratio of s to v, but by the fact that v, as Marx defined it, does not cover the *public* costs of producing labour power and it is these costs (and labour time inputs) which have been rising exponentially since the Second World War. Thus, in concentrating solely on the private sphere of capitalist production (and even if we include the sphere of private households) we cannot reflect the real costs of labour power, nor the total labour time necessary for its contemporary production, until we include the state sector inputs in our calculations.

Thus, I will argue, the relative means of surplus value extraction have been choked off by the swelling public or socialized fraction of v, which has more than offset reductions in the private component of v. In the face of this stagnation, capital has reverted to the old absolute means by "wage-spreading"—involving a greater and greater proportion of married women as second wage earners. It is the mass contribution of female surplus labour time to capital, via their entry into wage work, which has indirectly funded the replacement of domestic labour with intensified state sector inputs (education and health care being the major ones) in the contemporary reproduction cycle of labour power.

I should not leave the impression here that capital accumulation proceeds through the simple alternation of the absolute and relative modes of surplus value production—first absolute, then relative, and then back to absolute. In reality, they are often combined, in a highly contradictory way, because these two modes involve opposite tendencies in the consumption of labour power by capital. Under the impetus of absolute surplus value production, capital moves to extend the working day beyond established limits. Under the impetus of relative surplus value production (and a rising organic composition of capital) capital drives to expel living labour from production.

The combination of these opposites leads to a socially irrational situation, which Marx noted in his day and which is very much in evidence today. Mass unemployment arises in combination with the widespread practice of compulsory overtime, through which employers circumvent the limits of the normal eight-hour shift. Thus, capital exhibits a tendency towards increasing *unevenness* in the distribution of labour time (and wages) among the mass of the population available for wage labour. And capital accumulation militates against the redistribution of available work among willing (and needy) hands. The social consequences of this perversity are profound and manifold.

In the first place, workers are pitted against technological changes which promise to *reduce* necessary labour time, because such changes threaten to throw some of them out of work. But secondly, unemployment/overtime throws ever larger numbers of people onto the welfare roles or some form of state subsidy. Thus, private wages cover a decreasing proportion of the total subsistence costs of the masses, as the regularly employed proletariat, with its shrinking nuclear and sub-nuclear units, sheds layer upon layer of sporadically employed, dependent populations. With no chance to secure regular employment, these strata fall into a semi-proletarian condition and, lest they starve or riot, are caught in the miserable safety net of the welfare state. Here they are barely sustained, shuffling back and forth between low-wage, high-turnover jobs and the welfare rolls. In this way, the welfare state reinforces the secondary labour market and indirectly props up a sordid array of sweat shops and marginal operations, many of which would go out of business were they forced to pay living wages for steady work.[20]

As Marx pointed out over a century ago, private capital functions with a practical indifference to the stable reproduction of the working class' labour power over time. Both the (absolute) drive to extend the working day and the (relative) drive to expel living labour from production exhibit this indifference, in different ways. The state is ultimately the only agency which can compensate (however miserably) for this divergence between the imperatives of competing capitals and the long-run interests of stable capitalist reproduction. The seeds of the welfare state, administering subsistence for a mass of sub- and semi-proletarian strata, are thus to be found buried in the socioeconomic structure of the capitalist mode of production.

The Development of the Consumer Goods Sector

Before moving on to investigate the state sector inputs to labour power's production, it will be useful to review the development of Department II production in twentieth-century capitalism and its effect on the working-class household's labour and the value of its labour power.[21] Constant revolutionization of the productive forces is a hallmark of capitalism. The progress of technological revolutions can be seen to proceed from the centre to the periphery, as it were. A scientific breakthrough occurs in a basic mode of machine power; it is then harnessed and rendered industrially applicable. Once a new technology can be effectively harnessed to the mass production of machine components, which themselves embody that technology, then the take-off point for a wave of capital accumulation based on relative surplus value production has been reached.[22] These industrial applications soon find their way into Department II and, before long, they are being conceived and tested for the household as well. Initially, new technologically sophisticated consumer durables are within the grasp only of wealthy households. But as their value is cheapened, the markets for these goods broaden and soon they cease to be luxury goods and become mass consumer necessities, within the reach of normal wage incomes.

Consider the vast improvements in the last century which have taken place in various standard working-class household commodities, for example:

(a) consumer durables–washing machines, vacuum cleaners, refrigerators, stoves, sinks, bathroom fixtures, etc.
(b) foodstuffs–frozen foods, canned goods, semi-prepared and precooked packaged foods, fast foods, take-out foods etc.
(c) housing–building materials, synthetic fibres, furnaces, hot water tanks, etc.
(d) private transportation–the automobile.

These developments have been accompanied by massive improvements in the infrastructure of urban residences–electricity, running water, sewage systems, garbage disposal, sidewalks, roads, streetcars and buses–most of which have been supplied in the state sector as public goods built mainly by private firms on contract. Improvements in all of these areas represent a considerable shift of necessary labour time from the household into the consumer goods industries and the state sector. This shift is accompanied by a marked rise in the productivity of domestic labour time which, in these specific task areas (meal preparation, house cleaning, clothes washing, etc.) has sharply reduced the labour time domestically necessary. These shifts fulfil the logic of the law of value.[23] Labour is tending to flow from sectors of low productivity (the household) to sectors of higher productivity (Department II), which then induces a secondary reciprocal improvement in the productivity of the more backward sector.

All of these developments cheapened the value of labour power while enhancing the use value of households. But they also reduced the flexibility of the proletarian family. Married women could no longer reconcile homemaking with income producing activities. It was not wage labour per se, but regular factory and office work in uninterrupted shifts, far away from home, which became practically impossible for women with pre-school-age children. The reduction of married women in industry was thus closely associated with the capital deepening of Department II, the thoroughgoing commoditization of the means of subsistence and the separation of residential and industrial areas in urban development.

As wage labour intensified in the (by now predominantly male) core industries, greater attention to the restoration of the primary breadwinner became necessary on the home front. This was facilitated in turn by real improvements in household appliances and basic amenities so that housewives were able to reduce the long hours they formerly spent in washing, cooking and housecleaning to turn their attention increasingly to the personal care of children and husbands. This shift was the domestic correlate of the expansion of capital on the basis of relative surplus value production.

The mass influx of married women into wage labour in the past forty years has furthered the commoditization of the means of proletarian subsistence. The second wage has been instrumental in purchasing additional consumer goods which have, to a certain extent, reduced domestic labour time and raised its productivity. Marx refers to a similar shift in the reproduction cycle of labour power, occurring in a very different period of employment for married women over a century ago.

> Since certain family functions, such as nursing and suckling children, cannot be entirely suppressed, the mothers confiscated by capital, must try substitutes of some sort. Domestic work, such as sewing and mending, must be replaced by the purchase of ready-made articles. Hence, the diminished expenditure of labour in the house is accompanied by an increased expenditure of

> money. The cost of keeping the family increases, and balances the greater income.[24]

The Expansion of the State's Role in Reproducing Labour Power

Alongside and ultimately in contradiction with the deepening commoditization of the private household's means of subsistence in the twentieth century is the tremendous increase in socialized investment in labour power through the expanding state sector. In all developed capitalist countries, without exception, the state has deepened its involvement in the production of labour power. Both transfer payments to private households and the direct provision of socialized services in the state sector have been increased exponentially.[25]

It is the state sector's inputs which have raised the real cost of labour power relative to other commodities in the twentieth century. Since the productivity of state sector labour in the social services lags far behind the average productivity of labour in the capitalist sector (and Department II in particular), the contribution of this input looms larger and larger in the overall cost structure of labour power. And because these costs have not been covered by real wage increases of a comparable size, they must increasingly be subsidized out of the general tax fund which, in turn, consumes a larger and larger portion of the total social product (or GNP), subtracting value, via taxation, from the spheres of households and businesses.[26]

Thus, we are face to face with a central contradiction of contemporary capitalism: the long-term tendency towards the socialization of labour power's production has collided with the (value) limits of labour power as a private commodity.[27] The result is an overall crisis in the valorization of labour power, which has made its own important contribution to the global crisis of capital accumulation in the Seventies. Capitalist states now want to reverse the trend of the past forty years towards an increasing socialization of labour power's production. They are attempting to reprivatize the costs of labour power and reduce the state sector contribution to this commodity's production. Whether they can succeed in inflicting this reversal on the working class remains to be seen.

How did this situation arise? Here it is necessary to briefly comment on the role of the state in the development of the capitalist mode of production. I will limit myself to a number of basic points.

The capitalist mode of production is distinguished from all previous class modes known in history by the absence of direct extra-economic coercion in the daily harnessing of labour and the extraction of the surplus product by the ruling class. The working class, under capitalism, owns its own labour power and surrenders it to capital through a free exchange of commodity values in the labour market. This unique condition engenders a phenomenal separation of the socioeconomic and the political-state regions of capitalist social formations.

The resulting *autonomy* of the socioeconomic region should not be misunderstood, as if often is. It does *not* reflect a self-sufficiency of private capital within the sphere of its own reproduction. For, far from engendering conditions of a minimal state (as free market ideologues would imagine), the structured separation of spheres gives rise to an immense counterpressure, expressed through the growth and intervention of the state, to furnish and to regulate those general preconditions of the capitalist mode of production which are *not* generated and reproduced, on a stable basis, within the sphere of capital accumulation.

Private capitals, under the compulsion of competition, are in no position to furnish a whole series of "public goods and services" which the state, in the (class) interest of capital-in-general, must itself provide and/or supervise. The two critical commodities, money and labour power, for example, are not, and cannot be, privately produced by capitalist firms. Their general provision and regulation therefore falls under the purview of the state, capital's only agency that is external to the spheres of capitalist production and commodity circulation and is unitary in form.

We have seen that the private household is the primary site for the reproduction of labour power. In the first article, I discussed how private capital is structurally indifferent to labour power's production; and tends, without external regulation, to jeopardize and destabilize its long-term reproduction. The state is thus compelled to play a major role in supervising, at arm's length, the private household's production of labour power, and progressively, in taking over more and more aspects of this process as capitalism industrializes. This compulsion to expand the state's role in the production and regulation of labour power does not operate automatically, as a byproduct of capital accumulation and reproduction. It operates through the mobilization and direction of the state's resources under the impact of class struggle. Nor is this long-term trend irreversible under capitalism. The reorganization of the state and the rearrangement of its priorities are ultimately a matter of protracted political struggle, both between and within the major classes.

If the enlargement of the state's role in the production of labour power is not "given" automatically in the logic of capital accumulation, there are nevertheless strong pressures originating within the accumulation process which have, until recently, persuaded most sectors of the bourgeoisie in the developed capitalist countries to go along with, if not to support enthusiastically, this expansion.[28]

Private firms seek to minimize their costs in order to maximize their profits. Whenever they can cut their labour bill they will do so. But they are also interested in enhancing the use value of the labour power they employ in order to raise its productivity, and they would prefer not to pay for this improvement. The logic of these two imperatives—to enhance the use value of labour power, while cutting (or keeping down) its private purchasing price—creates a tremendous force driving towards the socialization of labour power's production through increasing wage supplementation and direct provision of social services such as education and health care. Thus, the private wage's coverage of the means of proletarian subsistence is breached and the state steps in to pick up the difference.

But here private capital is faced with a paradox. It has succeeded in driving the price of labour power far beneath its real value. This shores up the rate of profit in the short term. However, the long-term effect of this breach is to shunt an increasing proportion of labour power's production into the state sector. This eventually constricts the expansion of Department II. In other words, the consumption of commodities by private households, spending wage income, is fenced in by the increasing provision of alternative public goods, collectively consumed, and funded by draining private (tax) revenue from households and businesses. This is the situation which has gradually developed in the Seventies and which bourgeois governments throughout the West have pledged themselves to reverse.

Let us look more carefully at the state social services that have become increasingly involved in the training and repair of the proletariat's labour power in the twentieth century. I want to consider them first from the standpoint of their relative productivity and second from the vantage point of their funding via taxation. Both affect the value of labour power in critical ways.

Productivity. Within a capitalist economy where labour's alienation is generalized, the most efficient mechanism for enforcing labour discipline, raising labour productivity and allocating labour rationally within an organization is the market mechanism of private profit. Departments of the state lack any such mechanism.

State services such as education and health care lack a clear bottom line (comparable to profit) from which to gauge their efficiency and make a cost-benefit analysis of their labour process. Their activities are labour intensive and they do not obey the capitalist impetus towards a rising organic composition of capital. They also lack a direct feedback from the market in terms of their "product," which is an individual worker.

For all of these reasons, the productivity of state sector labour falls far behind the productivity of labour in capitalist firms. The real costs of these inputs rise correspondingly. They force the real value of labour power upward (relative to other commodities produced with a superior average productivity), and, in the process, breach the private wage, so that the difference must eventually be picked up through increased taxation.

Taxation. Who pays for these costly services and who benefits from them? The short answer to this is that it depends on the overall balance of class forces. We are reminded of Marx's comment on the overhead costs, accruing in the first place to the state, of the upkeep of paupers in various sectors of the unemployed: "Capital knows how to throw these [costs] for the most part, from its own shoulders on to those of the working-class and the lower middle class."[29] Such a class struggle perspective on taxation is not generally reflected in *Capital,* where Marx tends to treat all taxes, regardless of their immediate source, as a subtraction from the pool of surplus value available to the total social capital.

As taxation (as a proportion of GNP) has grown, both the burdens of its extraction and the modes of its expenditure have become major bones of contention in the class struggle. To leave this question of taxation where Marx did in *Capital* disarms us in the face of these developments. First, let me briefly modify Marx's treatment to include the sphere of private households. We then arrive at the following: taxation diverts value from the private economy of businesses and households; as such it constitutes a drain on private revenues. Those tax revenues (i.e., taxes on profit) which would otherwise be directly available to capitalists for investment, constitute a drain on surplus value because they withdraw from circulation money capital which would have been capable of generating additional surplus value. Those tax revenues coming from non-capitalist households, on the other hand, divert funds from the private purchase of consumer goods. They detract from the capacity of capital to realize surplus value by selling commodities at value to the households of the final consumers.

By distinguishing between the effects of taxation on the *generation* of surplus value in capitalist production and its *realization* in exchange, we can augment Marx's treatment. We uphold his basic point—that all taxation constitutes a drain on private capital accumulation—but we retain a substantial (class) distinction concerning the source of tax revenue.

If all taxes depress capital accumulation initially by their withdrawal of revenues from the private economy of households and businesses, this does not determine what the ultimate impact of socializing these funds will be. Here, everything depends on the *use* to which the state puts these funds. Will the state's provisions enhance the general conditions for private capital accumulation, and, in this way, successfully offset the initial drain; or, will it fail and act as an eventual drag on the pace of capital accumulation?

This is an extremely complex discussion which would take us far away from the subject of this article. I will therefore be brief and schematic. The state's expenditure will tend to boost capital accumulation in the long run if it: (a) opens up new fields for capitalist expansion and/or facilitates the acceleration of the turnover time of capital investment; (b) raises the productivity of labour power that capital is able to exploit by harnessing productive enterprise.

We are concerned here with the second type—that is, state sector provisions that attempt to raise the productivity of labour. Under what circumstances will investments in education and public health care succeed in boosting the rate of capital accumulation in the long run, and when will they fail and drag down this rate?

Take an example of an expenditure on public education. The Ontario government has recently recognized a shortage of indigenous, skilled manual labour in the province. As a result, the Tories are moving to upgrade secondary and post-secondary polytechnical institutes in this area. This expenditure may eventually result in a cohort of graduates who have greater skills in various trades and are more precisely matched to the skill requirements of private employers. If these graduates are then hired by employers in sufficient numbers and their additional training is turned to productive advantage (creating a higher rate of surplus value), private capital will be able to recuperate this social investment, to reprivatize and recapitalize it. The original expenditure in public education will, in the long run, give a lift to the pace of private accumulation, despite its short-term drain.[30]

If, on the other hand, this educational expenditure (a) does not raise the use value of a given cohort of labour power appreciably, or (b) the cohort is not then employed by productive capital in such a way that its special training actually raises its productivity; then the original expenditure will act as a long-term drag on capital accumulation and will never be fully recapitalized.

We are now in a position to venture some very provisional arguments about how the growth of state social expenditure on labour power's preparation and repair is affecting the overall pace of capital accumulation today. Let us continue to use the example of the educational system.

The training and motivation of skilled and willing workers to labour under conditions of general alienation, is, by its very nature, a complicated and costly business. The lack of a real stake in the product of one's own labour is an immense deterrent to motivation; and motivation is the key to genuine learning. Schools are presented with the job of educating a class of free labourers, who must be able to think for themselves in order to survive as beings responsible for securing their own livelihood in complex, urban societies. At the same time, the schools have to prepare a work force that will tolerate its own alienation in labour, that will learn to consider it natural and inevitable and not to reflect critically upon it; and yet that will be motivated to work hard to get ahead. No wonder schools fail by the standards of professional educators, for this is a highly contradictory and volatile package. Generally, as a labour process becomes more highly socialized, it becomes more difficult to inculcate skills and attitudes that require considerable mental work and social cooperation. Schools must motivate people to perform such tasks to a high standard, simultaneously stifling their desire for control over their working conditions and a stake in the product of their labour. There is, in sum, an irrationality buried at the core of the educational process under capitalism that undermines the principles of scientific rationality upon which it is ostensibly based.

Taylor, with his principles of scientific management, provided an answer to this dilemma through the fragmentation of tasks and the complete appropriation by management of all leeway and decision-making in the socialized labour process. Harry Braverman, in *Labor and Monopoly Capital,* brilliantly exposes the specifically capitalist (as opposed to industrial) logic of scientific management.[31] He nevertheless accepts Taylor's thesis, as if, from capital's standpoint, the principles of scientific management had solved all the essential problems of harnessing alienated labour to the pump of surplus value. But this is far from true.

Braverman's emphasis on deskilling and the degradation of labour in twentieth-century capitalism is entirely one-sided.[32] He misses the counter-tendency, equally critical to capitalist accumulation, of skill upgrading and technical sophistication in many sectors of the modern labour force. This is part and parcel of the revolutionization of the productive forces that is a hallmark of capitalist development.

The tendency of labour under capitalism to ever greater abstraction is not adequately captured in the unilateral deskilling perspective. The other side of labour's abstraction is its ever-growing versatility, a tendency that Marx describes eloquently:

> Modern Industry . . . through its catastrophes imposes the necessity of recognising, as a fundamental law of production, variation of work, consequently fitness of the labourer for varied work, consequently the greatest possible development of his varied aptitudes.[33]

Here was the essential rationale for the development of compulsory universal education in capitalist states—precisely to ensure this versatility, to "educate" this freedom and to wean it from subversive and intoxicating ideas.

Given labour's widespread and ever-increasing mobility, there is little incentive for firms to intensively train their employees; and the practices of apprenticeship are undermined by labour's general interchangeability. Schools, for their part, cannot efficiently undertake the training of specialized industrial skills because the economy is unplanned; the matching of skills to jobs takes place through an open market, where conditions of supply and demand for particular kinds of labour are in constant flux and almost impossible to anticipate ten to fifteen years in advance. To "aim" students towards particular occupations, which they will freely enter several years hence, is a permanently problematic enterprise under capitalist conditions. The only recourse is to offer a class-streamed, regionally standardized educational program with an extremely diffuse skill repertoire and to cultivate a completely uncritical, numbed response to future conditions of alienated labour. This is a very costly program.

But the current crisis of education in the West is not due primarily to changes internal to the school system. None of the irrationalities I have addressed are particularly new for capitalism; nor are they suddenly more severe than they were ten years ago. Rising per capita costs were tolerable in the long post-World War II boom, when economic expansion enabled private firms to harness the system's graduates effectively and put them to productive use. The critical current problem of the school system is *external.* Private capital is stagnating; its productive forces are not advancing rapidly; it is therefore unable to fully engage the labour force that is flowing out of the school system. As a result, this huge socialized investment in labour power is being squandered.

Two types of waste occur here: "overeducation" and unemployment. "Overeducation" is now a generally recognized phenomenon in all the developed capitalist states. This, of course, does not involve absolute overeducation (whatever that would mean), but overqualification *relative* to the job market and skill requirements of employers. On the one hand, the school graduate cannot realize the value of her/his education in higher wages; on the other hand, employers cannot use the training their employees have received and turn it to profitable advantage. They thus resist paying at a rate formerly consummate with the employees' qualifications. "Overqualification" is one symptom of a general devaluation of labour power.

Another aspect of the crisis of labour power's valorization is mass unemployment, which is now exceeding 17 million workers in the developed capitalist world. By deepening the per capita investment in public education, health care and social security for the proletarian masses in the twentieth century, capitalist states eventually altered the effect of unemployment on capital accumulation, to the detriment of capital. The reserve army of labour is, of course, a chronic and recurring feature of capitalism, as Marx correctly pointed out. By being available to compete for scarce jobs, the unemployed help keep wages down and employed labour in line, under the threat of being replaced by those who would work harder and/or for less. The unemployed today still serve these functions for capital. What then has changed?

The key change is the overhead cost of carrying the unemployed on some form of social security, with the rudiments of health and a minimal education, so that they can remain in a fully competitive position in all job categories across the span of the entire economy. These overhead costs were practically negligible in Marx's day; but today the mass squandering of idle labour power, educated and socially secured from starvation at considerable cost, increasingly offsets the traditional benefits, from capital's standpoint, of the effects of the unemployed upon the employed. The failure to secure a solid day's productive labour from this mass is indeed becoming a burden, not only on the working-class taxpayer, but on private capital accumulation. The reserve army of labour, a fundamental lever of capital accumulation in the nineteenth century, has thus become less and less effective in this role in the latter part of the twentieth. Today, capital cannot re-engage any major segment of this population in productive enterprise.

The long-term problems of capitalism's tendency to expel living labour from production are thus increasingly revealed; and not only are they manifest through the internal tendency of the organic composition of capital to rise and the rate of profit to fall. They have emerged with a vengeance in the mounting external costs of the mass of labour power which wastes away unvalorized, and which capital can find no way to exploit.

Conclusion

In the contemporary context of capitalist stagnation, the valorization of labour power, the proletariat's only commodity, has become increasingly problematic, in three ways:
(a) Its production cost is soaring–the cost of living and the cost of state social services have both almost doubled in the past decade.
(b) Mass unemployment, underemployment and "over-qualification" signify that this commodity's value in the labour market is not generally being realized.
(c) The shrinking productive base of the developed capitalist economies (relative to their unproductive sectors) reveals an incapacity of private capital to harness labour power sufficiently to the wheel of surplus value, a failure to successfully recapitalize the expanded socialized investment pouring into labour power's production.[34]

These are not three separate problems; they are three facets of the valorization crisis of labour power that directly affect both the bourgeoisie and the working class. The bourgeoisie is intent on pushing governments and top state administrators to take strong steps to ensure that the working class and the poor bear the burden of this crisis and accept a lowering of their living standards, a general devaluation of their only commodity. This offensive is conducted beneath the ideological umbrella of "lowering expectations" and "reviving the work ethic"; because, we are informed, "we have been living beyond our means."

The main features of the capitalist austerity drive in the state sector will undoubtedly be familiar to readers. In the case of each cutback, there are specific economic and social objectives which state administrators are trying to effect, which have been touched on in this article.

Cuts	*Purposes*
Education	Reduce per capita socialized investment in preparing the labour force; reduce qualification claims; stream more rigorously to match training to jobs, intensifying job competition within all sectors of the labour force.
Health Care	Reduce per capita socialized investment in repairing labour power; raise economic disincentives to seeking public health care for "minor" ailments; drive this type of health care back into the private household.
Social Security Transfer Payments	Reduce per capita socialized cost of carrying the reserve army of labour, sharpen its proletarian insecurity to seek work at wage rates which undercut the bargaining power of the employed; raise job insecurity and tighten labour discipline in this process; force dependent sectors of the population to draw more deeply on the private resources of their relatives and friends–to rely, in other words, on private households, and to reduce their demand on state social services; force the poor to fend for themselves, the sick to

> be cared for at home, offspring to look after their parents in old age, parents to mind their pre-school children at home or pay the full cost of private day care, unemployed youth to keep living with their parents, etc.

Clearly the burden of all these measures falls most heavily on women, intensifying domestic work and the double day of labour, and, in many cases, driving women out of the labour market altogether.

How do we fight the cutbacks effectively? There is a tendency for the opponents of cutbacks to be cast, all too readily, as defenders of the status quo before austerity. In the attempt to defend social welfare, we often end up defending the welfare state. Since when did the oppressed have any interest in defending the capitalist state? Of course, we must oppose the closing of a local school, hospital or a welfare office; but, in doing so, we must also mount a critique of the way these services are "delivered"—the fact that they are not staffed or controlled by the people they "serve." There is a great deal of well-placed resentment and hostility towards the welfare state and its bureaucracies that the right is now exploiting to the hilt. We are told that we live in a "mixed economy"—the public sector is "socialist," the private sector is "capitalist" and the growth of the socialist sector is "strangling free enterprise." The real contradiction of the contemporary state in relation to its overall effect on the pace of capitalist accumulation, which has been discussed in this paper, has furnished the forces of reprivatization with a powerful club to beat the left and the oppressed groups generally, who now appear as the uncritical defenders of the welfare state.

We must not let the right manipulate the mass hostility people feel towards the public services they use. We must combine a firm defence of the social gains won through past struggles with a strong criticism of the way these services are presently organized by the state. In this way we can turn the reprivatization sentiments to our advantage. We should demand that community associations, women's organizations, trade unions, cooperative housing corporations, etc., be granted directly the funds now channelled through the state bureaucracies, to spend as their constituencies see fit. We must support the collective self-organization of the oppressed on all fronts and the handing over of state funds to their organizations with no capitalist strings attached. We do not need government women's bureaus and welfare departments as much as we need funds for rape crisis centres, women's hostels and poor people's organizations, based on the principles of self-help and collective accountability. The labour movement must support and sponsor all such initiatives.

These types of independent organizations are not strong enough yet to allow us to place all our eggs in one basket. Existing state services must still be defended because their termination hurts users directly and often there are no alternatives. But we are opposed to the extension of the bureaucratic tentacles of the capitalist state further and further into our communities. We need to project a vision of the future and to act practically to nurture it today. Wherever there is an existing alternative to a state-run service, or one that can be built, we should demand the direct appropriation of public funds for the independent organization of the oppressed. In this way, we can combine people's need for social services with a desire to wrest their control from the state, so that workers and users can administer them collectively.

NOTES

1. Many Marxists confine the operation of the law of value to *capitalist* production, the most developed form of commodity production, but by no means its only form. While Marx himself does not dwell on this question at length in *Capital*, he does comment explicitly on it in Volume III: "The exchange of commodities at their values, or approximately at their values, thus requires a much lower stage than their exchange at their prices of production, which requires a definite level of capitalist development. . . . Apart from the domination of prices and price movement by the law of value, it is quite appropriate to regard the values of commodities as not only theoretically but also historically *prius* to the prices of production." Karl Marx, *Capital*, Vol. III (Moscow: Progress Publishers, 1959), p. 177.

   Engels insisted on the pre-capitalist operation of the law of value (refuting arguments by W. Sombart and C. Schmidt), in an article he wrote after Marx's death; see "The Law of Value and the Rate of Profit," in *Engels on Capital* (New York: International Publishers, 1974), pp. 100-117. More recently, Ernest Mandel in his introduction to a new translation of *Capital*, Volume I, reviews this debate, siding with Engels. See Karl Marx, *Capital*, Vol. I, trans. Ben Fowkes (Harmondsworth: Penguin, 1976), pp. 14-15. The contrary position has been argued by M. Morishima and G. Catephores in "Is There an Historical Transformation Problem," *The Economic Journal* (June 1975).

   One of the most serious consequences of restricting the law of value to capitalist production is that it renders "the value of labour power" incoherent. How can the law of value be said to apply to the production of *this* commodity, when it is not produced capitalistically? Many commentators have stumbled at this point. (See Donald J. Harris, *Capital Accumulation and Income Distribution* (Stanford, California: Stanford University Press, 1978), p. 90: "There are substantive problems in applying the law of value to the commodity labour power which cannot be ignored or dismissed. These are due essentially to the fact that labour power is not itself the outcome of a process of production like other commodities, that is, it is not produced capitalistically.")

   Bortkiewicz, seventy years ago, made a similar critique: "Bringing wages under the law of value, as Marx does, is not permissable since this law, so far as it can be assumed to have validity, rests on competition among producers which, in the case of the commodity labour power, is entirely excluded." Quoted in P.M. Sweezy, *The Theory of Capitalist Development* (New York: Monthly Review Press, 1942), pp. 84-85.

But competition amongst the sellers of labour power is not at all excluded—in fact, it is intense and pervasive in a (labour) market of chronic oversupply. And the sellers of this commodity are personally responsible for its production on a continuous basis. It is therefore quite wrong to say that proletarian households do not compete with one another in the production and sale of their labour power. Merely because they do not compete *in the same way* as firms do is no reason to deny their market competition.

For Marx, the law of value, transformed and expressed through the laws of capital's motion, operates in a really powerful fashion under two conditions: "1) the more mobile the capital, i.e., the more easily it can be shifted from one sphere and from one place to another; 2) the more quickly labour-power can be transferred from one sphere to another and from one production locality to another." He adds: "The second condition implies the abolition of all laws preventing the labourers from transferring from one sphere of production to another and from one local centre of production to another; indifference of the labourer to the nature of his labour; the greatest possible reduction of labour in all spheres of production to simple labour; the elimination of all vocational prejudices among labourers; and last but not least, a subjugation of the labourer to the capitalist mode of production. Further reference to this belongs to a special analysis of competition" (*Capital*, Vol. III, p. 196). The special analysis of competition to which Marx refers here (and which he never completed), must surely refer to competition in the labour market. It seems quite wrong therefore to exclude the production and exchange of the commodity labour power from an overall conception of the operation of the law of value under capitalism. And it seems particularly dubious to argue for this exclusion on the basis of fidelity to Marx's original conception in *Capital*.

For me, proletarian domestic labour is an *unique form* of simple commodity production, upon which the law of value operates in a *particular* way. It tends, in a sluggish fashion, to shape and articulate this labour within the expanded reproduction cycle of labour power, with the other labours which together comprise labour power. Some of these labours are organized directly by capital in Department II. Others are organized in the state sector. All are articulated with one another indirectly and roughly by means of the law of value. Within the labour power cycle, therefore, the law of value operates to equilibrate labours around socially necessary labour times; "in orbit" as it were, around the transmuted form of labour equilibration based on prices of production.

The impact of the law of value upon domestic labour is very much weaker than its impact upon capitalist labour processes. It runs up against an imposing principle of labour organization, based upon the direct use value of domestic labour to proletarians themselves. Its *domination* of this antagonistic logic is a relative one, therefore. In the very way in which the housewife organizes her labour time and manages the household, both principles can be seen to operate. But, ultimately, the law of value dominates. This is because the *sine qua non* of proletarian subsistence remains the capacity to sell labour power on a competitive basis to employers who find it useful for their purposes in capitalist production. Domestic labour in the private household *must* bow to this exchange value imperative.

2. The foregoing treatment may appear to have established nothing more than the operation of Adam Smith's "invisible hand" in the market. And it is true that the phenomenal line of force, which the law of value generates, is *from exchange to production.* But what Marx discovered, which classical political economy did not, was the underlying material conditions, the historically specific and by no means natural circumstances, in which this mysterious inversion took place. How *had* the producers lost control over the products of their labour? How was it that inert products being exchanged came to be invested with an alienated social energy so great that they actually began to lead their producers (and consumers) around by the nose?

   Far from accepting this as a natural process, Marx showed that it was an absurd and socially irrational situation that was the result of an historically specific process—the mass alienation of the producers from the means of production. The dissolution of all manner of collective bonds between producers; their atomization and dispersal in private property units; the expression of their collective interdependency through competition on the market—these were the material conditions that gave rise to the law of value. Marx never divorced impersonal laws of economic motion, which operate with overpowering force ("with the irresistible authority of the law of nature") from the actual social process whereby the mass of producers give up their power and "consent" to play by alien rules. The law of value is, above all, an extraction of the social power of the alienated producers. And its franscendence, in turn, is a measure of the progress of their struggle to establish collective control over their production.

3. Wally Seccombe, "The Housewife and Her Labour Under Capitalism," *New Left Review*, 83 (Jan.-Feb. 1973), p. 9.

4. Some of the problems with ahistorical and logico-deductive treatments of value derive from the first chapter of *Capital,* Volume I. Here it is clear that Marx, in certain passages, gets carried away by the logic of his own exposition of simple commodities exchanging with one another. He does not ground his categories historically. He warns, in the afterword to the second German edition, of exactly this problem, which results from the fact that the "method of presentation must differ from the method of inquiry." The result is that "it may appear as if we had before us a mere *a priori* construction." Such *a priori* construction is particularly evident in his initial treatment of abstract labour, where this is described as a common denominator property of the products of human labour, instead of as a tendential action, a homogenization and abstraction, arising in historically specific circumstances, of widespread commodity exchange. See Karl Marx, *Capital,* Vol. I (Moscow: Progress Publishers, 1954), pp. 45-54. This Hegelian treatment of abstract labour as intrinsic essence is in active tension with a correct materialist discourse that identifies abstract labour as the material result of labour's abstraction. This is the process through which market totalization effects an active indifference on the part of the private, disassociated producers to the immediate conditions of their labour and to the direct use value of their product.
5. Seccombe, p. 16.
6. Margaret Coulson, Branka Magas, Hilary Wainwright, " 'The Housewife and Her Labour Under Capitalism'—a critique," *New Left Review,* 89 (Jan.-Feb. 1975), p. 59.
7. Wally Seccombe, "Domestic Labour: Reply to Critics," *New Left Review,* 94 (Nov.-Dec. 1975), p. 86, fn 2.
8. The way in which this use value/exchange value contradiction is expressed in the management of the housewife's diverse tasks and daily labour time is well captured in Meg Luxton's study, *More Than A Labour of Love* (Toronto: The Women's Press, 1980). I am indebted to her for pointing out how women, in organizing their domestic work day, continuously strive to reconcile these divergent objectives.
9. For a fuller discussion of this trade-off, see Seccombe, "Reply to Critics."
10. Readers may discern here a resemblance to the human capital theories of neo-classical economics. (Cf. Gary Becker, *Human Capital and the Personal Distribution of Income,* Michigan, 1967.) The resemblance is superficial. What we must agree with in Becker's thesis is the proposition that a powerful market rationality governs

the choices household units make concerning how to allocate their time and to gain and spend their income; and that this rationality is open to systematic investigation. But this is as far as the agreement goes. For neo-classical economists regard this rationality as natural, symmetrical and benevolent, when, in fact, it is fetishistic, perverse and enforces a systematic sexist asymmetry upon the economic roles of family members. Secondly, neo-classical economics sees a unitary economic rationality at work here, when, in reality, there is a complex and internally conflicted set of forces at work. In the human capital theory, the fundamental conflict between the household's own use value criteria and capital's disappears from sight. This thesis cannot explain why households systematically *choose* to undervalue the potential of their female "human capital." It cannot explain why wives continue to do the vast majority of housework after they secure external employment. And finally, the assumption that the economic imperatives of profit maximization by capital are similar to the household's subsistence imperatives is erroneous and reactionary, portraying the entire society as a mass of petty capitalists.

11. The food industry is interesting in light of the two tendencies analyzed above. It provides an example of both occurring simultaneously. On the eat-out side, with domestic labour cut almost to zero, we see a big increase at the lower end of the market in fast foods. With the development of mass food production techniques, chains such as MacDonald's have so reduced the labour time embodied in their standard items that it is cheaper to eat these foods out than it is to buy them from supermarkets and prepare them at home. Domestic labour is therefore unable to save money on meals of this type. On the supermarket side, however, where domestic labour does comprise a significant proportion of the total labour time expended, this shift is exactly the opposite. No frills shopping practices, a shift towards basic staples (reflecting less embodied labour time) and an accompanying increase in labour time supplied domestically combine to make up the difference. The family budget enforces capitalism's perverse logic upon the working-class housewife because she can cut costs on these meals (providing the same use value for a decreased exchange value).

12. The ideological enforcement of family norms in the working class is always, to one degree or another, an exercise in myth-making. Extensive working-class diversity in subsistence arrangements is the rule; uniformity is the exception. Intolerance of diversity in living styles within the working class is therefore divisive. Far from homogenizing the large majority, the ostracizing of tiny minorities

suppresses and privatizes the expression of the majority's real diversity. Genuine cultural tolerance is indispensable in forging working-class unity against the state and the bourgeoisie, not only because the working class is originally multinational and multicultural, but also because the autonomy of the subsistence sphere and the structural disjunction between wages and subsistence needs materially cultivates this diversity. The mass media, insofar as it stereotypes this diversity and fosters assimilationist pressures on cultural minorities, acts to forge a conservative ideological bloc of the mythical "mainstream," threatened by minority expression or empathy within its *own* ranks. The gay liberation movement, for example, has understood this dynamic well, and has effectively undercut the perception of homosexuals as an external minority. by calling for repressed gays to come out of the closet.

13. On this, see Mary McIntosh, "The State of the Oppression of Women," in Annette Kuhn and AnnMarie Wolpe, eds., *Feminism and Materialism* (London: Routledge and Kegan Paul, 1978), pp. 254-89 and Jack Wayne and Jim Dickinson, "The Logic of Social Welfare in a Competitive Capitalist Economy." Unpublished paper Dept. of Sociology, University of Toronto, n.d.
14. Cf. H. Land and R. Parker, "Family Policies in Britain: the Hidden Dimension," in J. Kahn and S.B. Kammerman, eds., *Family Policy* (New York: Columbia University Press, 1978).
15. Marx, *Capital,* Vol. I, p. 170.
16. Ibid., p. 486.
17. Ibid., p. 298.
18. Marx, *Capital,* Vol. III, p. 235.
19. Marx, *Capital,* Vol. I, p. 373.
20. On the reproduction of the labour power of semi-proletarian, welfare-dependent people, see Bennett Harrison's study, "Welfare Payments and the Reproduction of Low-Wage Workers and Secondary Jobs," *Review of Radical Political Economists,* Vol. 11, No. 2 (Summer 1979), pp. 1-16.
21. For a valuable overview of this entire process, see Michel Aglietta, *A Theory of Capitalist Regulation* (London: New Left Books, 1979), esp. Ch. 3, "The Transformation of the Wage Earners' Conditions of Life," pp. 151-208.
22. On capitalist technological revolutions and their value dynamics, Ernest Mandel's analysis is unparalleled. See esp. Chs. 3-8 of *Late Capitalism* (London: New Left Books, 1975), pp. 75-273.

23. On this long-term shift see Meg Luxton, op. cit. One of the strengths of her study is its longitudinal base, spanning three generations of housewives in the same community. Beginning with the construction of the first working-class households in Flin Flon in the 1920s, and moving up to the present, she is able to describe the general development of the proletarian household in the twentieth century and the changes which have taken place in women's domestic work.

    For a discussion of these changes in terms of the law of value, see my "Reply to Critics."

24. Marx, *Capital,* Vol. I, p. 373, fn 1.

25. Ian Gough, in *The Political Economy of the Welfare State* (London: MacMillan, 1979), provides a valuable overview of these processes.

26. A comparative statistical breakdown of state sector growth for the developed capitalist countries is provided in an OECD (Organization for Economic Co-operation and Development) Studies in Resource Allocation series: *Expenditure Trends in OECD Countries 1960-1980* (1972), *Public Expenditure on Education* (1976), *Public Expenditure on Income Maintenance Programmes* (1976), *Public Expenditure on Health* (1977).

27. Under capitalism, the socialization of labour runs up against the ultimate barrier of the private appropriation of its product. This is perhaps the most universal contradiction arising within an economy based on generalized commodity production. It should come as no surprise therefore, to find that this contradiction, sooner or later, will manifest itself in the case of the commodity labour power.

28. In his analysis of the English Factory Acts, Marx clearly recognizes the long-term tendency towards increased state intervention in and regulation of the economy. He predicts "the general extension of factory legislation to all trades" and sees in this "the existence of an irresistible tendency towards the general application of those [regulatory] principles" (*Capital,* Vol. I, p. 472).

29. Marx, *Capital,* Vol. I, p. 603.

30. Additional education should enable the worker to realize a higher price for his labour power as well. Thus, the employer and the employee divide up the fruits of the educational investment according to the balance of class forces. In the current period, state investment in education is failing both capitalists, who are unable to take full advantage of labour power's upgrading, and workers, whose educational attainment makes very little difference to their eventual incomes.

31. Harry Braverman, *Labor and Monopoly Capital* (New York: Monthly Review Press, 1974).

32. For a fuller discussion of the deskilling controversy, see Tony Elger, "Valorization and 'Deskilling': A Critique of Braverman," *Capital and Class,* 7 (Spring 1979).

33. Marx, *Capital,* Vol. I, p. 458.

34. I have not developed an adequate analysis of this factor here. See David Yaffe, "The Crisis of Profitability," *New Left Review,* 80 (1973).

DOMESTIC LABOUR AND THE REPRODUCTION OF LABOUR POWER: TOWARDS AN ANALYSIS OF WOMEN, THE FAMILY AND CLASS

Emily Blumenfeld and Susan Mann

As Emily Blumenfeld and Susan Mann point out, the privatization of domestic labour is the fundamental basis for women's oppression under capitalism. The crucial strategic question is, then, whether or not the work carried out in the privatized household can be socialized under capitalism. Blumenfeld and Mann address this question at some length and in doing so present a strong critique of a number of positions held by radical feminists.

Blumenfeld and Mann maintain that the primary role of domestic labour under capitalism is the production and reproduction of the commodity labour power. They argue that domestic labour constitutes a form of simple commodity production that structurally links the privatized household to the larger capitalist economy. In making their case, the authors implicitly contest a number of assumptions made by BRISKIN *and* FOX *and thus contribute to the ongoing debate over the nature of women's domestic labour under capitalism.*

Through their analysis they illuminate the intersection of sexual oppression and class oppression and reject the notion that the oppression of women can be discussed irrespective of social class. In turn, these authors point out a number of frequently overlooked, but important technical obstacles to the socialization of domestic labour within a capitalist social formation.

To date, there are two major political currents in the more radical analyses of women's oppression. On the one hand, Marxist feminists argue that socialism and the abolition of private property provide the necessary preconditions for the emancipation of women, requiring a revolutionary alliance between feminists and the working class. On the other hand, radical feminists maintain that the oppression of women is the most fundamental and deep-rooted form of oppression, and that the struggle for sexual liberation must not be subordinated to any other. While both of these theories entail a radical attack on the institution of the family and a demand for the socialization of domestic labour, their political implications and strategies are very different.

A number of significant issues separate radical feminists from Marxist feminists but the question of the origins of women's oppression has perhaps received the most attention in recent years. This debate has centred on the validity of the Marxist theory of the origins of patriarchy as elaborated by Engels in *The Origin of the Family, Private Property and the State,* which was largely based on Marx's *Ethnological Notebooks.*

Engels understood the "overthrow of mother right" to have been historically grounded in the growth of a controlled surplus following the First Agricultural Revolution. He argued that the subsequent need for control over women functioned to ensure the patrilineal transmission of private property from generation to generation. By linking the origins of patriarchy with the origins of private property Engels established the integral relationship between women's liberation and socialism. Radical feminists, who view the sexual struggle as the primary struggle and the transcendence of women's oppression as separate from the question of the abolition of private property, have sought an alternate theory of the origins of patriarchy. This has been attempted with varying degrees of sophistication.[1]

Undeniably, there is a need for further research on the transition to patriarchy as a prerequisite to a complete theory of women's oppression. However, we shall enter the debate with the radical feminists on a somewhat different level. Rather than seeking the origins of women's oppression we shall focus on the possibilities for the transcendence of women's oppression within bourgeois society. Specifically, we intend to examine the barriers to the socialization of domestic labour within a capitalist social formation.

Both radical feminists and Marxist feminists call for the socialization of domestic labour as a necessary prerequisite to women's liberation. This would require the negation of the present privatization of the tasks subsumed under domestic labour, making these tasks collective or community responsibilities rather than having them fall primarily on the shoulders of women, as they do now. However, while in agreement on this fundamental precondition of women's liberation, Marxist and radical feminists remain divided over whether or not it is possible to socialize domestic labour under capitalism. The political implication that follows from this question is clear: if the socialization of the household is incompatible with the requirements of capitalist production and reproduction, then socialism is the necessary prerequisite for women's liberation. The resolution of this problem requires a comprehensive understanding of the role of domestic labour under capitalism—hence a political economy of the household.

In this article, we consider the significance of the socialization of domestic labour as a fundamental precondition of women's liberation and question whether or not domestic labour can be socialized under capitalism. We address aspects of the current debate over domestic labour, primarily through an analysis of Marx's writings, and secondarily through a critique of some of the major contemporary feminist writings. Specifically, we examine the role of domestic labour in the production and reproduction of the "peculiar" commodity labour power as the primary structural link between the household and the larger capitalist economy. We argue, in contrast to radical feminists, who view sexual oppression and class oppression as two separate and distinct issues, that an adequate understanding of women's role in domestic labour cannot be discussed irrespective of social class. Finally, we examine some of the obstacles to the socialization of domestic labour under capitalism. In particular, we discuss how the unique nature of the domestic labour process—the large gaps between production time and labour time, the sporadic aspect of housework and the absence of a specialized and non-overlapping division of labour—presents a number of problems that make domestic labour unamenable to socialization under capitalism.

The Issue of the Socialization of Domestic Labour

There are three fundamental aspects to sexual equality in a Marxist analysis of the so-called "woman question." The first is political or legal equality—"equal rights"—as a necessary condition for sexual equality. The second is economic equality in that women's full and equal participation in social production is necessary for sexual equality. Economic equality is only formally realized through such measures as equal pay for equal work and the removal of sex-typed restrictions on equal access to all jobs and occupations. The substantive realization of women's full and equal participation in social production is further predicated on a third condition—the socialization of domestic labour—meaning the collective (as opposed to private) responsibility for such tasks as child care, housekeeping and cooking. Only in the face of prolonged and intense struggle has capitalism variably approached the first and second conditions. Yet even where capitalist systems allow for the formally "equal" political and economic participation of women in the larger society, this occurs only insofar as the private servitude of wives and mothers is maintained—only insofar as the third condition, the socialization of domestic labour, remains unrealized.

Given these contradictions, it is not surprising that writers in the feminist tradition have long argued that one of the major barriers to the transcendence of women's oppression is the fact that women as a group are relegated to the necessary but subordinate work in the home. The household or family constitutes the major institution of social control over women because the tasks subsumed under domestic labour—procreation, childrearing, household maintenance and the provision of immediate sustenance—clearly delimit women's social role. For those women who by necessity or choice do participate in the larger society, the absence of universal day care and the demands of petty housework preclude their actual full and equal participation in social production.[2] Below we argue that the contradictions between home responsibilities and work demands that comprise the "double burden" are just concrete manifestations of a larger contradiction that exists within every capitalist system between the capitalistic production of commodities in general and the non-capitalistic production of the commodity labour power.

Under a capitalist mode of production, capitalists control the production and reproduction of all factors of production with few exceptions. One major exception is the absence of direct capitalist control over the production and reproduction of the commodity labour power. As paradoxical as it seems, the very commodity which provides the basis for capitalist accumulation—value-creating labour power—continues to be produced non-capitalistically, outside of the capitalist economy proper.

The production and reproduction of labour power has four distinct moments. At the individual level there is the generational replacement of individuals through procreation, childrearing and socialization, as well as the day-to-day renewal of the labouring capacity of existing workers. This long and short-run reproduction of labour power takes place largely within the confines of the isolated and privatized household. In contrast, reproduction at the collective or class level is usually the responsibility of the state and is undertaken through a mixture of hegemony and force. This includes, on the one hand, the reproduction and maintenance of the family or household as a social institution, which is secured by state policies such as redistributional income programs, child benefits, various unemployment, accident and health schemes, and state control over access to birth control and abortion. On the other hand, in order to standardize the quality of individual labour power in the face of the variable particularities of individual families, the state has also historically taken over a number of former household tasks, through the imposition of compulsory social services such as education, or, in the case of social "deviants," mental institutions and prisons.[3] While this triumvirate of household, economy and state constitutes the productive and reproductive moments of capitalist society as a totality, our interests in this paper are primarily the intersection between household and economy and in particular the relationship between domestic labour and capitalist production. Moreover, of these three spheres–household, economy and state–the household is the only sphere that remains unsocialized. What does this mean and why is it important?

The socialization of production refers merely to the cooperative nature of work, wherein workers work together and alongside one another in the same or in a related production process. As Marx pointed out, this collective nature of work, even when it takes place under the control of a capitalist entrepreneur (e.g. the modern factory), leads to a greater efficiency of production as well as to a greater development of cooperation and class identity among workers.[4] Socialization in the work place is thus the opposite of privatization. Unlike most other forms of work in contemporary society, domestic labour remains a privatized form of production where there is no general extension of the cooperative relations between those persons (namely housewives) who engage in household tasks. Rather, cooking, cleaning and childrearing take place within the confines of individual household units.

That privatization places constraints on the efficiency of household units is evident in the wastefulness which occurs when each individual household owns its own vacuum cleaner, dishwasher and so forth. But even more important, in Marxist theory, privatization is understood to result in several distortions of human relations. As the "sanctity" of privacy allows the household to close its doors to public scrutiny and supervision, it is not surprising that the household in modern society remains the major arena of personal violence: wife battering and child abuse are the very products of privatization. In addition, privatization places real constraints on the development of the political consciousness and the activity of the labourers who work within these individualized settings. Not only are housewives difficult to organize and mobilize because they are scattered in their individual households, but the isolated structure of the household places limitations on their interactions with each other. These conditions inhibit the development of a common identity and shared political aims and goals and result instead in the identification of social problems as personal ones.

Moreover, to say that domestic labour remains outside the capitalist economy proper is to say that one of the most basic and fundamental institutions in bourgeois society—the household—is precluded from bourgeois relations of production. As such, the privatized household stands juxtaposed to the capitalist factory and the labour performed within the household, domestic labour, has no market value in a society where virtually everything else is commoditized. In short, we are confronted with a stark example of the uneven nature of capitalist development—*capital's inability to penetrate the sphere of the production and reproduction of the commodity labour power.* Why is this the case? Why does capital leave the production and reproduction of its most vital commodity in the hands of non-capitalists? Finally, what implications does this uneven development have for the position of women in capitalist society?

While numerous writers on women and the family have recognized these contradictions, they have failed to ascertain why capitalism necessitates this privatized sphere of reproduction. The Frankfurt School, in one of the few "Marxist" attempts to analyze the relationship between capitalism and the family, advanced an essentially psychoanalytical thesis, wherein the repressive reproduction of capitalist authority relations was seen as being autonomously generated by the relations that exist between family members. This line of reasoning, with its emphasis on the autonomous nature of reproduction, suffers from idealism, an idealism that follows directly from its reliance on Freudian categories.[5]

In contrast, we would suggest that the relationship between the privatized family and the capitalist economy is not merely a subjective one, whereby the subjectivity generated in one sphere is appropriate for use in attaining the ends of another sphere. Rather, the family is structurally linked to capitalism because of its fundamental role in the reproduction of the working class. Hence we see the link between household and economy primarily as institutionally or structurally rather than psychologically maintained. The Frankfurt School lacked a political economy of the reproduction of labour power—a materialist analysis of the relationship between capitalist production and the production that takes place in the household—it is to this analysis that we now turn.

The Class Nature of Privatized Domestic Labour

In Marxist theory the primary locus of sexual inequality is the familial household—hence the concept of domestic slavery.[6] But the source of that inequality lies outside the relations between the sexes, in the relations of production. That is, the relations of production demarcate periods of history, and this mode of producing life determines a corresponding family form. Thus an historical understanding of women's position requires an analysis of patriarchy in a particular social formation, in this case, within the capitalist formation.

Domestic slavery, or the relation between the sexes and the generations through which men exercise dominion over women and children, is premised in Marxist theory on the rise of private property. As mentioned earlier, the intergenerational assurance of patrilineal property transmission (in the face of uncertainty with respect to paternity) necessitated private control of women's childbearing capacity.

This control is as necessary to ensure dynastic continuity as to transfer small plots of landed property. Thus it holds for the ruling classes in history as well as for peasant-proprietors. But capitalism marks an historical turning point in this respect, for it is premised on the existence of a proletariat which is separated from property and has nothing to sell but its labour power. If property transmission is a basis for sexual inequality, we should expect, then, that under capitalism, this inequality will vary according to social class.

Bourgeois women in this society are preeminently controlled as childbearers and their children restricted by a paternal dominion that is exercised in the strong familial pressure on intra-class marriage (i.e., strict rules of class endogamy).[7] However, this control includes, by virtue of wealth, a great amount of freedom in lifestyle for bourgeois women and children. For example, birth control and abortion are not financially restricted for bourgeois women. As Clara Zetkin noted of the woman "of the Upper Ten Thousand," by virtue of her possession of property, she "can freely develop her individuality; she can live in accordance with her inclinations. As a wife, however, she is still always dependent on the man."[8]

There is no similar basis of domestic slavery for the propertyless proletariat.[9] Intra-class marriage restrictions also exert control over the proletariat, but only by virtue of the generational demands of private property transmission in the property-holding class. That is, there is no intrinsic basis for domestic slavery based on considerations of property transmission within the proletariat. Consequently as capitalism extends its domain, ever separating more workers from their means of production, a greater proportion of the population is removed from this basis. In turn, the complete abolition of private property, the transcendence of capitalist society, would entirely remove this basis of domestic slavery.

There is control over proletarian women's childbearing capacity, a control that is increasingly being exercised by the bourgeois state rather than by the privatized family. Related to the necessity of assuring an adequate supply of labour power, it is a concern of capital rather than a personal relation of oppression and is reflected in the state's control over working-class access to birth control, abortion, etc.[10] Thus the control over the proletarian women's childbearing capacity is an inter-class relation. This inter-class control produces sexism, which is a capitalist rather than a patriarchal form.

Nevertheless, sex oppression still exists within the proletariat. What, then, is the basis of domestic slavery in the proletariat? We will argue that an analysis of the intersection of domestic slavery and capitalism must turn to an analysis of privatized domestic labour. Because domestic slavery both predates and is maintained throughout capitalism it cannot provide the *differentia specifica* of women's position under capitalism.[11] What does provide this distinguishing feature in capitalist society is the privatization of domestic labour. If the crux of domestic slavery is control over the childbearing capacity of women, the crux of domestic labour in contemporary society is privatization.

The privatization of women's existence as domestic labourers prior to capitalism was mediated by collectivity in production, whereby much of women's labour took place in a collective setting with other women. This itself presupposed some communal property—for example, wood and water for cooking and cleaning. But capitalism presupposes the appropriation of communal property through the process of primitive accumulation, by which Marx meant the "historical process of divorcing the producer from the means of production."[12] Primitive accumulation, which formed the basis for the very origins of capitalism, not only separated the labourer from his/her means of production, but it separated the individual from the community. In Marxist theory, the privatization of women's existence is accentuated under capitalism by (a) the breakdown of community (we understand "community" to derive from collective relations to varying combinations of communal and private property),[13] and (b) the subordination of the family as a production unit to capitalist units of production.

The process of the privatization of domestic labour is reflected in the various discussions of the separation of industry from the household with the growth of modern industrial capitalism. For example, bourgeois social theorists argue that as "modernization" proceeds, more and more family functions are taken over by other institutions. In particular, these theorists focus on the separation of the household from its productive function, whereby the household or family is left merely as a unit of consumption. However, this analysis concerns itself exclusively with the level of appearances in bourgeois society. And indeed to capitalist production, the household appears merely as a consumption unit—a purchaser of the commodities produced by capitalist enterprise.

While it is true that the household has been separated from capitalist industry and from capitalist production, it nevertheless remains a sphere of production. Labour takes place within the household even though that labour is unremunerated and frequently not recognized as "work." And indeed, it is this work—domestic labour—that is ignored by bourgeois social theory. While domestic labour is not a capitalist form of production because it does not involve wage labour, it is a form of production.

Household production or domestic labour is a non-capitalist form of production that is linked to capitalist forms of production through exchange or circulation. We argue that the exchange which takes place between these two spheres of production (non-capitalist household production and capitalist production proper) is an exchange (or circulation) of commodities. That is, the household can only purchase commodities produced by capitalist enterprise through the value it receives from the production and sale of its own commodity—labour power. Consequently, there is an integral relation between consumption and production. Moreover, in a market economy, one must produce commodities, or like the capitalist, exercise ownership over the commodities produced by others, in order to consume commodities. We argue, then, that household production is a non-capitalist form of commodity production.

Under capitalism, the products of the household are increasingly reduced to one–labour power. The commodities purchased by the household (food, clothing, refrigerators, etc.) become the "domestic means of production" upon which domestic labourers labour. It is through this labour that the household reproduces the labouring capacity of the individual–the commodity labour power, which in turn allows the process of household production to be renewed. Reproduction of all productive forms refers to the renewal of a prior process of production, hence the re-creation from one round of production to another of all the factors of production, which includes both the means of production and the social relations of production in a given productive unit. And it is in this sense that we speak of the production and reproduction of labour power as the primary task of domestic labour under capitalism.

That it is labour power and not just individuals that are produced and reproduced is significant. Prior to capitalism, domestic labour would only produce and reproduce the labouring capacity of individuals, a capacity inseparable from the individual him or herself, since the ability to self-consciously act upon and transform nature is an intrinsic characteristic of the human species. However, for those who do not labour, but rather live off of the labour of others (as the slaveowners of antiquity or the feudal lords under feudalism) this labouring capacity is separated out because it is unrealized. This separation of "labouring capacity" from the individual distorts the individual as human being.[14] Only in capitalist society can these two moments be analytically separated out for the labouring population, because under this mode of production the capacity to labour–labour power–becomes commoditized for large segments of the population. The individual likewise becomes distorted, becoming an appendage of capitalist production. While it is only the individual's labour power that is bought and sold on the market, the individual can in no way separate him or herself from his/her labouring capacity. Hence the illusory nature of the wage slave's "freedom."[15]

It follows that because in capitalist society most but not all individuals are divorced from their means of production and thereby forced to sell their labour power on the market, domestic labour is a form of commodity production only in certain classes. Domestic labour, like domestic slavery, cannot be discussed without reference to class differences.

The class specific nature of the domestic labour question is frequently overlooked. Consequently women's liberation is often viewed as uniformly problematic for all women. Yet, although the privatization of domestic labour is the primary basis for women's oppression in capitalist society, not all women are potential or actual domestic labourers. It is only in the propertyless classes that family members (primarily women) are relegated the unremunerated tasks of domestic labour in the production and reproduction of the commodity labour power. In bourgeois households the tasks subsumed under the category of domestic labour are generally performed by paid employees–maids, butlers, cooks and so forth–and not by family members.[16] Moreover, in bourgeois households there is no production and reproduction of the commodity labour power because bourgeois households live off the surplus value produced by others.

Only in the propertyless labouring classes does domestic labour have this commodity-producing function. In capitalist society this characteristic is shared by two classes: the proletariat and what has come to be called the "new middle classes." These two classes are analytically distinct: the "new middle classes," unlike the proletariat, do not produce surplus value but constitute the necessary, but "unproductive of value" labour force required by the capitalist system (Marx's "unproductive labourers," e.g., public employees, etc.).[17] Nevertheless, since in both classes labourers are divorced from their means of production and hence compelled to sell their labour power on the market, domestic labour has a similar commodity-producing role. That is, in both classes, all of the tasks subsumed under domestic labour—the provision of sustenance, the maintenance of the household environment, procreation and socialization—are primarily directed towards reproducing the next day's and the next generation's wage labour force.

The household or family, as well as women, are thus differentiated by class. Although all households produce individuals, not all households produce the commodity labour power. The following analysis, then, is confined exclusively to the domestic labour process in the households of the propertyless, labouring classes.

Domestic Labour as a Form of Petty Commodity Production

In Volume I of *Capital,* Marx describes petty commodity production as follows:

> The private property of the labourer in his means of production is the foundation of petty industry, whether agricultural, manufacturing, or both. . . . [It] *attains its adequate classical form, only where the labourer is the private owner of his own means of labour set in action by himself.* . . . This mode of production presupposes . . . scattering of the means of production. As it excludes the concentration of these means of production, so also it *excludes co-operation,* division of labour within each separate process of production [emphasis added].[18]

For Marx, the essence of petty commodity production lies in the fact that it is a privatized form of production for exchange characterized by the unity of labour and capital. That is, the petty producer owns the means of production, and along with other family members provides the labour force for this economic unit. Under such conditions, there is no class exploitation in the strict sense of the concept because the petty producer is not engaged in the hiring of wage labour and hence the extraction of surplus value. Moreover, the absence of surplus value in petty commodity producing units precludes the possibility of accumulation. All forms of petty commodity production operate at the level of simple circulation, whereby the realization of the value of the commodities produced returns an equivalent value in terms of the socially necessary labour time required to produce them.[19] Following Marx's analysis, then, we argue that domestic labour as a form of production in the households of the propertyless labouring classes falls into the category of petty commodity production.

Like any other form of petty commodity production, the domestic labour process is characterized by the unity of labour and capital. That is, those who "own" the means of production also act as direct producers. Historically, petty commodity production has included production by isolated individuals, by families or by households whose composition is not identical to familial composition. Thus there is an empirical variability to units of petty commodity production. Nevertheless, in each case, the direct producers also owned their means of production. This is true as well for the domestic labour process. Not only do domestic labourers own or "possess" their domestic means of production (e.g., stoves, refrigerators, etc.) but also, whether the household is composed of one individual (e.g., a single man) or a family, the labour is performed by those in possession of their means of production.

In the case where the unit of household production is a family, the familial nature of the domestic labour process is often obscured. For instance, by highlighting how domestic labour circumscribes and conditions women's role in society, many feminists have failed to recognize or have ignored completely the role in domestic labour of other family members, particularly children. While undoubtedly the woman is primarily responsible for the care of the young, one cannot ignore the role of the father or the role of siblings in this process. Moreover, a number of tasks subsumed under domestic labour are characterized by a "sexual" division of labour; this is true of tasks such as taking out the garbage, mowing the lawn or repairing household appliances, which generally fall into the domain of male family members. We are not implying here that domestic labour is collective production, nor are we denying that women are primarily responsible for these tasks. We are merely pointing out that all family members make some contribution, however unequal. That is, the social organization of domestic labour is familial.[20]

The second feature that domestic labour shares with all other forms of petty commodity production is that it operates only at the level of simple circulation. In sharp contrast, capitalist production involves an increment of value, because the labour power purchased by the capitalist produces not only its equivalent (exchange value) but also surplus value, which is the source of profit for capital.

However, for the seller of labour power–the worker–it is only the exchange of his or her labour power that is significant, and that is confined to the level of circulation. And as Marx points out, the exchange between labour and capital from the point of view of labour is only an exchange of equivalents. Wages (the price of labour power) bring the worker "only subsistence, the satisfaction of individual needs, more or less–never the general form of wealth" (capital accumulation).[21] The value of the commodity that the worker sells (labour power, in part the product of domestic labour) is returned to him, then, only as an equivalent. This has important implications for the domestic labour process under capitalism.

If we agree that the production and sale of the commodity labour power operates only on the level of simple circulation, this production process precludes accumulation. This is true for all forms of petty commodity production, since by definition there is no exploitation of wage labour and hence no extraction of surplus value. Simple commodity circulation or the exchange of equivalents means that the accretion of wealth does not occur for the proletariat. The institutional significance of this includes the restriction of family savings to the sphere of circulation.[22] Household savings for the proletariat are simply intertemporal transfer savings, popularly called "savings for a rainy day," whereas for the bourgeoisie and bourgeois families, savings banks are capital-holding institutions.

Another consequence of simple circulation is the indebtedness of forms of petty commodity production. In order to purchase additional "means of production" to increase labour productivity, petty commodity production must rely on a source of revenue outside of production—namely credit. For instance, the family farmer must first borrow in order to purchase additional means of production. Similarly, in order to increase domestic labour productivity and thereby its standard of living (e.g., by purchasing washing machines, refrigerators, etc.), the household must go into debt. It is in this sense that we speak merely of the "possession" of domestic means of production, which are often only becoming "owned" as a consequence of the credit relation. It is precisely through this relation of indebtedness that petty commodity producers in capitalist society remain subordinated to merchant capital.

The third feature of domestic labour, which is similar to all other forms of petty commodity production, is that it is a non-capitalist form of production for exchange. We argue that the time expended in domestic labour, like the labour time expended by any other petty producer, enters into and thus contributes to the value of a commodity—in the case of domestic labour, the commodity labour power. As this appears to be one of the most controversial aspects of our political economy of the household, we shall outline it at some length below.

With few exceptions, most writers in the feminist tradition have assumed that domestic labour is production that lies outside the sphere of commodity production (both capitalist and non-capitalist commodity production). Thus even the more astute writers within the Marxist tradition have viewed domestic labour as merely engaged in production for use.[23] Like the bourgeois theorists, these feminists envision a radical separation between the activities and products of the household and the activities and products of the larger market economy. The household is viewed merely as a consumer of commodities, not as a producer of commodities.

If we follow Marx's discussion of the value of the commodity labour power, we find three moments to his analysis: (a) the reproduction of labour power refers to the means of subsistence necessary for the reproduction of the proletariat; (b) there is an historical and moral element that enters into the determination of the value of labour power; and (c) more than individual labour power must be produced—the value of labour power refers to the reproduction of a class.[24] Let us examine each of these moments to see how domestic labour contributes to the value of labour power.

We begin with the most visible part of this process, the exchange between labour and capital—the sale and purchase of the commodity labour power. Like any other commodity, labour power has both a use value and an exchange value. The worker receives from the sale of his/her commodity an equivalent (the exchange value of labour power), while the capitalist receives the use value of labour power for a given period of time, the working day. While the exchange value of labour power is realized in the sphere of circulation, its use value is realized in the sphere of capitalist production, where this "peculiar" commodity produces not only the equivalent of its exchange value but an increment of value—surplus value. During this productive consumption of labour power by capital, the worker "*divests* himself of labour as the force productive of wealth."[25] In addition to being cut off from the possibility of accumulation, the worker's labour power is worn down, and at the end of the working day it must be replenished so that the exchange between capital and labour can begin anew the next day. As Marx writes, labour power "becomes a reality only by its exercise," only by working. "But thereby a definite quantity of human muscle, nerve, brain, etc. is wasted" and must be restored.[26]

According to Marx, the labour time necessary for the production of labour power "reduces itself to that necessary for the production of the means of subsistence; in other words, the value of labour power is the value of the means of subsistence necessary for the maintenance of the labourer."[27] A central issue of debate has been an understanding compatible with the labour theory of value of domestic labour's role in the determination of the value of labour power. Because it is a question of the determination of the value of equivalents, it has been argued by others that domestic labour cannot contribute to the value of labour power. The understanding that means of subsistence alone (e.g., commodities purchased by the household) enter into the value of labour power has led to a conceptualization of domestic labour as something other than commodity production. Let us consider the question of whether the household is not just a consumer of commodities, but also a producer of the commodity labour power.

We know that the labourer uses his/her wage to purchase commodities produced by capitalist production (e.g., food and clothing) as the domestic means of production that are needed to replenish his/her labour power. This purchase of commodities takes place in the sphere of circulation. The commodities do not automatically reproduce the labourer in the sphere of exchange—for example, food must generally be prepared before it is eaten. Therefore, the commodities purchased by the wage are taken home, to another sphere of production (a non-capitalist sphere of production) where additional labour time—domestic labour time—is expended in transforming them into finished products (e.g., cooked meals).

Moreover, the commodities purchased on the market as well as the "finished products" to which domestic labour time has been added are consumed by all members of the family regardless of whether or not they are themselves wage labourers contributing to household income. That is, the wage, according to Marx, is a family wage.[28] Those writers who mechanically equate the wage labourer's exchange value to the value he or she consumes frequently overlook the familial nature of wage consumption. Consequently, they also overlook the contribution of domestic labour (which as we mentioned above was familial or joint production) and in doing so, ignore the integral relation between consumption and production.[29]

Yet everyone can see the expenditure of domestic labour time in the drudgery of housework. However, its translation into economic terms is problematic. Because domestic labour is unpaid, unremunerated, it does not have a market value (a price) and therefore cannot be translated into monetary terms. Thus others argue that if the value of domestic labour cannot be computed, how can it enter into the value of labour power?

In part this seeming paradox is a result of the mystification of commodities under capitalism. Marx used the term "commodity fetishism" to describe how in capitalist society commodities (especially the money commodity) are often thought to hold properties which they do not have. In particular, Marx exposed the fallacy of viewing money and prices as the determiners or rulers of value.[30] This mystification is the very product of the fact that under capitalism, "value" increasingly takes on a monetary form (e.g., prices, wages, etc.). Yet, if we penetrate this mystification, we see that what really constitutes the value of a commodity is the socially necessary labour time needed to produce it, not its monetary value or price.[31] Prices, including the price of the commodity labour power (the wage) are not necessarily synonymous with value. And, as Marx makes clear, oscillations in the market price of labour power conceal the economic bondage of the wage labourer.[32]

Moreover, Marx goes on to alert us to the fact that "the whole mystery of commodities, all the magic and necromancy that surrounds the products of labour as long as they take the form of commodities, vanishes therefore, so soon as we come to other forms of production."[33] And indeed, it is clear when we examine non-capitalist forms of production that non-commoditized forms of labour (labour that has no market price) still contribute to the value of commodities. Consider, for example, the family farmer–a classic example of a non-capitalist petty commodity producer. The family farmer's labour power, like the housewife's labour power, is not commoditized (it has no market price); yet few would argue that the farmer's labour time does not contribute to the value of the agricultural commodities he produces. While this feature of labour time expended by non-capitalist commodity producers was discussed by Marx over a century ago, it continues to be ignored for the case of domestic labour.

In turn, the case of domestic labour is further obscured by the fact that wages, the monetary price of labour power, is all that the individual household receives. Yet we know that wages can rise or fall above or below the "exchange value of labour power." As Marx writes, "if the price of labour power falls to this minimum, it falls below its value, since under such circumstances it can be maintained and developed only in a crippled state." That is, the value of every commodity–including labour power–is determined by "the labour time requisite to turn it out so as to be of 'normal quality.' "[34] It is in the context of considering "normal labouring capacity" that Marx points out in *Capital,* Volume I, that there enters into the determination of the value of labour power an historical and moral element. That is, the necessary wants and the necessary means of satisfying them depend on sociohistorical conditions.[35]

Labour power, like any other commodity, has to be of "normal quality" to compete successfully on the labour market. But not all labour power is of normal quality. While the wage is a family wage, it does not necessarily follow that this wage allows all proletarian families to be reproduced at "normal labouring capacity." This contradiction rests on the fact that although a proletarian standard of living refers to the proletariat as a class, the proletariat is not concretely reproduced as a class; rather, individual labour power is compelled to seek its reproduction primarily in the context of the privatized family. The gross inequalities in the distribution of goods in capitalist society lead not only to the division of society into classes, but also, within the propertyless classes, to further divisions, causing some individuals' labour power to be reproduced in a visibly crippled state. The appalling statistics on malnourished children in the urban ghettos of the advanced capitalist nations is a stark example of labour power which is not produced and reproduced so as to be of "normal quality."

We follow Marx in viewing the total wage paid to the working class as equivalent to or tending towards the total means of subsistence (including the historical and moral component) required to reproduce that class. And we recognize that individual households vary in their income and hence their concrete wage levels may fall above or below the exchange value of labour power.[36]

The historical and moral element in the determination of the value of labour power is the "traditional standard of life."[37] This also includes a number of factors which are not easily calculable in monetary terms. Take, for instance, the role of class struggle. Successful strikes, by directly raising the standard of living, clearly contribute to the historical and moral element that enters into the value of labour power. Even unsuccessful strikes, although they do not result in an increment of wages, add to the value of labour power. The lessons learned in the bloody history of class struggle, while not commoditized directly, nevertheless contribute to the historical and moral element which determines the value of labour power.

Thus far we have the value of labour power equal to commodities as a quantity of means of subsistence sufficient to produce labour power of "normal quality" at a historically determined standard of living. Let us now clarify the family nature of the value of labour power, and consider the reproduction of the class.

Marx points out that the reproduction of labour power refers to the reproduction of the whole of the working class. The value of labour power refers to reproduction and multiplying as well as to maintenance and living. The proletariat is temporally reproduced across generations in proletarian households. This is imperative because the owner of labour power—the worker—is mortal.[38] The worker exchanges with capital "his entire labouring capacity, which he spends, say, in 20 years."[39] Sooner or later the worker is no longer capable of working. The continuity of his appearance on the market requires that the "seller of labour power must perpetuate himself"—by procreation. "The labour-power withdrawn from the market by wear and tear and *death* must be continually replaced by, at the very least an equal amount of fresh labour power."[40] Thus Marx cites the bourgeois Torrens' recognition that the labourer must be enabled "to rear such a family as may preserve in the market an undiminished supply of labour power."[41] The value of the means of subsistence necessary for the reproduction of labour power must include the "means necessary for the labourer's substitutes, i.e., his children," in order that the bearers of this peculiar commodity may perpetuate their appearance in the market.[42] The reproduction of the proletariat is also, then, a generational phenomenon: classes perpetuate themselves across generations.

Domestic labour solves this generational problem for capital due to its amenability to familial organization. Moreover, privatized domestic labour allows capital to shift the burden of the costs of reproducing the proletariat as a class onto individual working-class households. For as we have argued above, domestic labour is indirectly remunerated out of wages (exchange value) rather than profits (surplus value). If, on the other hand, domestic labour were socialized under capitalism, this would no longer be the case.

Socialized domestic labour would be a public rather than a private responsibility, funded primarily through taxation (which includes property taxes as well as more regressive forms). This different basis of funding is visible if one compares domestic labour with other existing socialized extensions of the household, such as primary education. However, if by socializing domestic labour capital could significantly reduce the socially necessary labour time needed to reproduce labour power, as it has done in other branches of production, then the advantages to capital as a whole would far outweigh the costs incurred.

This brings us to the question of obstacles to the socialization of domestic labour under capitalism. This question has not been adequately pursued by any contributors to the domestic labour debate. Most writers who *have* addressed the question maintain that there is nothing inherent in the domestic labour process that would prevent it from being socialized under capitalism.[43] In contrast, we aim to show that the domestic labour process embodies certain peculiar features which are antithetical to capitalist production. Hence, capitalism tends to shy away from this sphere of production, leaving it in the hands of the privatized, petty-producing household.

Obstacles to the Socialization of Domestic Labour under Capitalism

In Marxist theory, there are two aspects to the mode of production which demarcates historical periods: on the one side, the production of means of subsistence, food, clothing, shelter and the tools required for their production; and on the other side, the production of human beings themselves. The stage of development of labour and the stage of development of the family are both kinds of production.[44] We have argued that the production of labour power occurs through privatized domestic labour and that this family form corresponds to capitalism. But we also know that capitalist forms of production are not antithetical to the socialization of the workplace. In fact, they operate more profitably through the greater efficiency of cooperative labour processes. Why then is domestic labour one of the few spheres of production that capitalism has failed to conquer? What are the objective reasons for capital's inability to penetrate the production and reproduction of its most vital commodity–labour power?

Marx recognized that the contradictions between the privatized household and the larger capitalist economy would become heightened with the increased participation of women in wage labour. Thus his well-known comment:

> . . . modern industry, by assigning as it does an important part in the process of production, outside the domestic sphere, to women, to young persons, and to children of both sexes, creates a new economic foundation for a higher form of the family and of the relations between the sexes.[45]

Yet he also realized that certain features of the capitalist mode of production could act as fetters on social development and even on capital's ability to penetrate and conquer certain spheres of production. In particular, Marx provides some insights about why certain privatized and "backward" spheres of production are maintained and reproduced within a capitalist social formation.

In Volume II of *Capital*, Marx identifies a number of features of certain spheres of commodity production which make them less amenable to capitalist forms of production. Two of these features are of particular importance to our argument. First, Marx notes how certain spheres are characterized by a relatively lengthy production time. Production time refers to the total time it takes to produce a finished (i.e., marketable) commodity.[46] While production time varies for different commodities, a lengthy production time can be particularly problematic to capitalist forms of production when natural constraints operate to minimize the ability to socially modify or reduce it. Consider cereal grain production, for example, where only annual harvests are possible, or the growth of livestock to "economic maturity," which can take a number of years. As Marx points out, a lengthy production time often has an adverse effect on the rate of profit. That is, with all other conditions held constant (e.g., rate of exploitation, etc.) the rate of profit can be enhanced simply by reducing the total production time.[47] However, in some spheres, natural limitations preclude the manipulation of production time, making profit maximization difficult.

Second, some spheres of commodity production are characterized not only by a relatively lengthy total production time, but labour is used only sporadically within this production time. As Marx explains, total production time consists of two parts: one period when labour is engaged in production, and a second period during which the unfinished commodity is "abandoned to the sway of natural processes without being at that time in the labour-process."[48] Instances of the latter would include such natural, chemical and physiological processes as the gestation period of livestock, the drying stage of pottery, bleaching, fermenting and so forth. While labour may and generally does initiate these processes, after this input, the process continues on its own.

Moreover, Marx states explicitly that during the intervals when production time and labour time do not coincide, no value is created. These intervals may be necessary to the production and completion of a finished commodity; however, since they do not absorb labour, they do not create value.[49] Hence it follows logically that the more production time and labour time coincide, the greater the productivity and self-expansion of capital within a given period of time. Some spheres of production involve long intervals when labour is temporarily suspended, which mitigates against continuous "value-creating" production. This is best illustrated by production processes that entail highly seasonal labour requirements. For example, in wheat production there is a lengthy period, when the seed is maturing in the earth, when labour is almost completely suspended. In this case, the reduction of "excess" production time over labour time is severely restricted by natural factors and cannot easily be socially modified or manipulated.

While the length of production time can have adverse effects on the rate of profit, the non-identity of production time and labour time can result in the underutilization of both constant and variable capital. For instance, constant capital lying idle during the excess of production time over labour time finds its value whittled away by physical depreciation and social obsolescence. Thus it is always in the interests of capital to keep the machines running and therefore to invest in the production of those commodities which are amenable to more continuous production.[50]

It is for reasons such as these that Marx argues that capitalism tends to leave risky and less profitable spheres of production in the hands of non-capitalist producers.[51] Uneven capitalist development and the persistence of non-capitalist and "backward" economic sectors are thus products of the logic and nature of a system based on the maximization of private profit. Let us now look at some of the specific features of the domestic labour process that similarly act to place barriers in the path of capitalist development.

Production Time and Labour Time in Domestic Labour

Domestic labour reproduces everyday life and can be analytically separated into four aspects. The restoration and renewal of the labouring capacity of potential and actual workers includes both the preparation of immediate sustenance—food preparation—and the maintenance of the household environment—housekeeping. The intergenerational reproduction of labour power also has two moments which are analytically distinct—childbearing and childrearing.

The case of food preparation illustrates one obstacle to the socialization of domestic labour under capitalism. The provision of immediate sustenance, the preparation of food for the living organism, is clearly a necessity. Equally obvious (although of no necessity) is the fact that it is generally the woman who prepares the food and feeds the family within the context of the privatized household. If one carefully considers the actual production process involved in the preparation of "daily bread" a number of features of this process inhibit its incorporation into capitalist commodity production. For instance, the transformation of raw food into cooked meals involves a noticeable gap between production time and labour time. The attraction of the new self-regulating cooking devices which reduce heat or turn off automatically reflects the normal inconvenience of waiting for or constantly supervising the cooking of foods that require a relatively lengthy production time (e.g., stews, roast beef, etc.). Without such recent technological advances, cooking as a production process clearly involves an under-utilization of labour.

The continuous use of both labour and cooking "machinery" is also precluded by the social and physiological rhythms of the human eating cycle. Unlike in commercial stock production, there are no short-cuts such as forced feeding or fast fattening processes developed for the human species. Rather, our eating habits are temporally structured, both by our physiology and by social factors such as work and culture. The intervals between meals introduce a sporadic and non-continuous nature to the production process, which therefore does not encourage capitalist penetration.

That these problems are real is reflected in the fact that only in certain instances has capital overcome these obstacles. The greatest concentration and centralization of the fast food preparation industry has occurred in such instances as MacDonald's and Burger King. Not only have these food giants minimized the gap between labour time and production time by producing "fast foods" which require a relatively short production time, but they also produce only certain foods such as eggs, hamburgers and french fries, which are amenable to "all day eating." In short, what MacDonald's has accomplished under the guise of "doing it all for you" is reducing the unproductive gaps which the normal housewife experiences in the intervals within and between meal production.

While technological advances such as self-regulating cooking devices, TV dinners and microwave ovens significantly reduce the gaps between production time and labour time in the preparation of foods, they fail to entirely resolve the problem of continuous production because humans do not eat the entire day through. MacDonald's and its competitors resolved this problem by only producing foods amenable to all-day eating. However, the alternative, which entails the organization and synchronization of the meal times of large groups of people, requires social planning–the antithesis of the anarchy of the free market. While school cafeterias, hospital canteens and military institutions manage more or less successfully on these dimensions, they are, of course, not governed by profit maximization.

Only in the last two decades have we witnessed a rapid proliferation of capitalist restaurants directed towards mass consumption. Hence, only very recently have capitalist enterprises provided a practical alternative (in terms of costs of production) to privatized household food preparation. These rapid developments have accompanied the introduction of advanced technology, mitigating some of the problems associated with the non-identity of production time and labour time and the increased participation of women in the labour force. Future projections suggest both a widening and a deepening in the capitalist development of the fast foods industry, namely increased capital investments in fast food operations; competitive advertising shifting its focus to the "ostensible" nutritional quality of fast foods; and branching out into areas such as Chinese or Indian ethnic specialities.[52] From these projections it would appear that capital has surmounted a number of obstacles to socializing food preparation. However, the very lateness of these developments in terms of the history of modern capitalism is testimony to the problematic nature of this sphere.

Moreover, food preparation is merely one of the aspects which occupies the woman *qua* housewife. Another moment in the reproduction of everyday life finds the domestic labourer as procreator and childrearer, and these tasks of domestic labour prove much more resilient to capitalist penetration. To become a labourer who can alienate his/her labour power during his/her lifetime requires a period of becoming "economically mature." This raises the question of whether or not child care can be incorporated into capitalist commodity production. There are two considerations in answering this question: one concerns the nature of the child as a human being and the other, the inherent characteristics of childrearing as a form of production. Let us first examine some of the problematic features of the production process itself.

On the one hand, the reproduction of the species is prescribed by definite natural processes. Neither the period of gestation nor the growth to "economic maturity" can be easily shortened. While nine months of gestation is not synonymous with nine months of incapacity for the mother, it does involve a relatively lengthy production time for the commodity labour power. On the other hand, production time does not end with the birth of the child, who remains in a dependent state until both physiological development and social development allow her or him to become physically, cognitively and economically mature. The production time required in the development of the "economically mature" person varies historically, culturally and in accordance with the dominant form of production. For instance, even a four-year-old child is "economically useful" on coffee plantations in Brazil. However, whether it is four years or the often accepted seven years required for physical and cognitive development, there is a lengthy minimum production time before a child can actualize a labouring capacity–before he or she can alienate him or herself to capital.[53] This lengthy production time is an obstacle to childrearing premised on profit maximization.

There is also a qualitative and inalienable aspect to childrearing, which is part of the process of becoming human, even within capitalist society, where the process is distorted. This inalienable and qualitative aspect of childrearing involves the affective relations between adult and child.

On the one side, the necessity of affective relations for

human development precludes substituting machinery for the human agent in the childrearing process. Yet the very process of substituting constant capital for variable capital has been a hallmark of capitalist development. Indeed, as Marx pointed out, the increasing organic composition of capital (the increasing ratio of machinery to labour) was a major tendency which accompanied the concentration and centralization of capitalist production and provided the basis by which capitalist forms of production succeeded in the competitive struggle against "backward" and less efficient units of production. However, childrearing is an immutably "labour intensive" process and, as such, is not likely to attract large-scale capital investment.[54]

On the other side, affective relations are incompatible with the impersonal and instrumental social relations necessitated by capitalist relations of production. Instrumentality, the use of others for specific goals and purposes, by its very nature implies a separation of the person from his or her ability to perform certain tasks and services. In this sense, people are interchangeable because it is the performance of the task—not the specific person—that is important. Under capitalism, free market hiring and firing of employees is predicated on the separation of the person from the role he or she performs. In sharp contrast, affectivity involves an emotional attachment to the "other" wherein the "other" becomes integrally related to one's own self-identification. This negates relating to the "other" merely as a performer of certain tasks and requires interaction in which the "other" is viewed as a "unique totality." Consequently, in an affective relationship there can be no interchangeability of persons without emotional repercussions to both parties.

In recognition of this inalienable aspect of childrearing, numerous feminists have voiced their reservations regarding the incorporation of domestic labour into capitalist commodity production. Margaret Benston has noted that the "fear of the barracks-like result of introducing housekeeping into the public economy is most realistic under capitalism," for this "would have the unpleasant consequence of including all human relations in the cash nexus," that is, "complete psychic isolation."[55] In a similar vein, Rowbotham argues that the capitalist penetration of domestic labour would "turn the family into a rationalized part of commodity production, a baby farm with paid employees and no sentiment."[56]

Both Benston and Rowbotham view domestic labour as lying outside of commodity production.[57] Logically, it is a short step to counterpose the household as the private, non-commodity producing sphere with the work place, the public, commodity producing sphere and to posit the former as compatible with the essential nature of childrearing. While we agree that affectivity is an essential dimension of human development, it does not necessarily follow that the privatized household is the only place in which such significant human relations can be established. In fact, the horrifying statistics on child battering and violence in the family indicate that the choice between privatized and socialized brutalization is a false one. Moreover, such a counterposition ignores the alternative of the public, non-commodity producing sphere of community and state-sponsored child care, for example.

However, it is interesting to note that in capitalist societies the only systematic, collectively organized child care that has any stability or continuity over time appears to remain the prerogative of relatively small, self-contained communities such as the Hutterites. In these cases, however, the communal organization of property provides the material foundation for these "superstructural" developments. Moreover, these communities only constitute a peripheral form of social organization in capitalist societies, usually existing relatively self-sufficiently due to their largely agrarian bases and in no way threatening to the major economic institutions.[58]

On a societal level, as contrasted with a community level, a systematic and stable program of collectively organized state-sponsored child care has only occurred in socialist societies. This would seem to indicate certain limitations on the role of the state sector in capitalist societies. Indeed, where state-sponsored day care does exist in the advanced capitalist nations it is at best minimal and remains forever vulnerable to changes in the priorities of national budgets. State-funded day care systems are one of the first to go when fiscal crises require cutbacks in government spending. Consequently, while twenty-four-hour state-sponsored day care has been a demand of feminists in the advanced capitalist nations, we would argue that this alternative cannot be realized under capitalism precisely because the capitalist state has no source of revenue independent of variable capital (e.g., "sales taxes" and taxation of wages) and surplus value (e.g., "property taxes" and taxation of the profits of capital).[59] As such, capitalist state expenditures for labour which is unproductive of value (e.g., that of civil servants and state employees) impinges on the profit maximization of "free" enterprise. This problematic is reflected in the fact that state expenditures remain circumscribed by the vicissitudes of the market and hence expand and contract with the ups and downs of the business cycle. The actualization of this alternative, then, is perennially unstable, for under capitalism, the reproductive expenditures of the state are never entirely removed from the dictates of private accumulation.

Above we examined some of the features of the domestic labour process that inhibit its incorporation into capitalist commodity production proper. To do this, it was necessary to separate out some of the disparate tasks that make up the totality of household production. However, the very fact that domestic labour is characterized by the absence of a clearly defined and non-overlapping division of labour serves to compound the difficulties of socializing domestic labour under capitalism.

The housewife must perform, and sometimes simultaneously, innumerable tasks—chef, nurse, maid, psychiatrist, mother and lover. Moreover, the fact that housework is interwoven with work that relates directly to human beings introduces an emotional strain that does not characterize the "normal" job routine. Crying children and demanding husbands force the housewife to stop what she's doing, sort out the chaos and only then return to complete her prior task. Such easily interruptable work must of necessity require little concentration. Hence the monotony and meaninglessness of housework is part and parcel of its nature and requirements.

The specialization of tasks is not in itself antithetical to monotony. Indeed, capitalist production is notorious for the meaningless, repetitive and tedious nature of its highly specialized division of labour. What is problematic to capitalism, however, is the synchronization of the disparate tasks now subsumed under domestic labour to the requirements of continuous production. Eli Zaretsky recognized this when he wrote, "The family, attuned to the "natural' rhythms of eating, sleeping and childcare can never be wholly synchronized with the mechanized tempo of industrial capitalism."[60] To do so would be a feat that would put Taylorism to shame.

The situation is further compounded by the fact that the tasks which make up domestic labour are both in contradiction to and necessary to one another. The following description by one anguished housewife captures well these contradictions:

> "[A]ny inclination I might have to take my work seriously is comically scotched by Carl (her son) in his constructive moments as much as in his destructive ones. Anything I do attracts his attention, so if I tidy a room he picks up the object as I put it down. Or if I clean the windows . . . he comes after me, imitating my movements with his hands, and smearing what I have just done. . . . I begin to feel hilariously unreal."[61]

Indeed, what is required of the housewife faced with such contradictions is almost superhuman. Relations with people interrupt relations with things, and each requires a different mode of reaction. A plate can be smashed to the floor in a moment of frustration and anger with little consequence—but not so a child. As Rowbotham points out, "it is not surprising that violence breaks out in the family, or that people are made victims of families, that children are devoured, and smothered, and hurt and battered in families. The family under capitalism carries an intolerable weight: all the rags and bones and bits of old iron the capitalist commodity system can't use."[62]

However, what Rowbotham and other feminists fail to recognize when they still maintain that domestic labour can be socialized under capitalism[63] is that these "rags and bones and bits of old iron" cannot be used by capitalism for particular reasons. The very nature of the domestic labour process is antithetical to the requirements of capitalist production. The large gaps between production time and labour time, the petty and sporadic nature of the work, the absence of a specialized and non-overlapping division of labour, and the interruption of emotions and human relations at every turn, all create innumerable obstacles to the incorporation of domestic labour into capitalist commodity production.

Whereas capitalism has successfully penetrated many spheres of production in modern society, leaving in its path the ruination and subsequent elimination of most forms of petty commodity production, it has failed to significantly penetrate the petty production involved in housework. While it has successfully conquered many types of commodity production, by reducing the labour time needed to produce these commodities, it has not successfully reduced the socially necessary labour time required in certain spheres of domestic labour production. To socialize these spheres under capitalism would be a cost few capitalists are willing to bear.

Nor can the capitalist state undertake these problematic spheres of production. To do so would mean replacing domestic labour with commoditized forms of labour (e.g., paid day care workers, etc.). This would require a substantial increase in the expenditures required to reproduce labour power, indirectly raising the "subsistence level of the proletariat as a class," and hence directly cutting into the profits of capital.

Capital, then, has a real economic interest in the maintenance of privatized domestic labour, and thus the maintenance of the privatized family. On the one hand, this leaves capital with a profound contradiction because the very commodity upon which capitalist accumulation is predicated—value-creating labour power—must continue to be produced non-capitalistically, within the confines of the privatized household. On the other hand, this leaves women in capitalist society with no other alternative than the transcendence of capitalist society itself as the path to their liberation.

NOTES

1. For the "classic" radical feminist analysis, see Shulamith Firestone, *The Dialectic of Sex: The Case for Feminist Revolution* (New York: Bantam, 1970).
2. V.I. Lenin, *The Emancipation of Women* (New York: International Publishers, 1966), pp. 63-64. See also Charnie Guettel, *Marxism and Feminism* (Toronto: The Women's Press, 1974), pp. 49-60.
3. For a more detailed discussion of the intersection between the household, the economy and the state in the reproduction of the working class, see James M. Dickinson, "Theory of Reproduction" (Mimeo., University of Toronto, Toronto, 1979).
4. Karl Marx, *Capital,* Vol. I (Moscow: Progress Publishers, 1954), Chap. XIII. See also Frederick Engels, *Engels on Capital* (New York: International Publishers, 1974), pp. 80-81.
5. See, for example, Theodore Adorno, "Types and Syndromes," *The Authoritarian Personality* (New York: Norton, 1969); Max Horkeimer, "Authority and the Family," *Critical Theory* (New York: Seabury Press, 1972); and Herbert Marcuse, "A Study in Authority," *Studies in Critical Philosophy* (Boston: Beacon Press, 1973).

6. Frederick Engels, *The Origin of the Family, Private Property and the State* in Karl Marx and Frederick Engels, *Selected Works* (Moscow: Progress, 1968).
7. Ibid., p. 500.
8. Clara Zetkin, "Proletarian Women and Socialist Revolution," reprinted in Hal Draper and Anne G. Lipow, "Marxist Women Versus Bourgeois Feminism," *Socialist Register* (1976), pp. 193-94.
9. Engels, *Origin of the Family*, p. 499.
10. Cf. Gordon Welty, "Bureaucracies and Professions," *Southern Journal of Criminal Justice*, 3 (1978), p. 9.
11. Thus Zetkin argues that the demand of bourgeois women is for "free and independent control over their property" which is "the last stage in the emancipation of private property." Zetkin, "Proletarian Women," pp. 193-94.
12. Marx, *Capital*, Vol. I, p. 714.
13. Karl Marx, *Grundrisse* (Harmondsworth: Penguin, 1973), p. 471.
14. In the ruling classes this distortion is reflected in various forms of parasitism (e.g., gluttony, debauchery, etc.).
15. Marx, *Capital*, Vol. I, p. 668.
16. The class specific nature of domestic labour is even recognized by bourgeois writers. See, for example, J.R. Eshleman, *The Family: An Introduction* (Toronto: Allyn and Bacon, Inc., 1978), pp. 273, 276.
17. Welty, "Bureaucracies and Professions," p. 6.
18. Marx, *Capital*, Vol. I, p. 713.
19. Ibid., p. 150.
20. To formulate the question of domestic labour as the family labour of joint production means that the woman cannot be seen as the analogue of the wage labourer. Thus we take exception to this point in Wally Seccombe's otherwise admirable early piece, "The Housewife and Her Labour Under Capitalism," *New Left Review*, 83 (1974), pp. 12-13.
21. Marx, *Grundrisse*, p. 294.
22. Ibid., p. 285.
23. Margaret Benston, "The Political Economy of Women's Liberation," *Monthly Review* (Sept. 1969), p. 16; Sheila Rowbotham, *Woman's Consciousness, Man's World* (Harmondsworth: Penguin, 1973), p. 61.

24. Marx, *Capital,* Vol. I, pp. 168-69.

25. Marx, *Grundrisse,* p. 307.

26. Marx, *Capital,* Vol. I, p. 167.

27. Ibid.

28. Ibid., p. 168.

29. Consumption refers on the one side to productive consumption and on the other to individual consumption. The former occurs at the point of capitalist production, and as capital and labour power are consumed (materialized) in the labour process, the product is surplus value. Labour power is productively consumed in the sphere of capitalist production. On the other side is individual consumption of the means of subsistence. This individual consumption is what is at issue in the production and reproduction of labour power. Marx emphasizes that for the workers, individual consumption is "money expressed in the form of articles of consumption, use values, which they obtain from the capitalist in the act of exchange between the two of them" (Marx, *Grundrisse,* p. 300). Individual consumption is not an autonomous sphere of activity. As Marx makes clear, "in production based on capital, consumption is mediated at all points by exchange" (ibid., p. 419).

30. Marx, *Capital,* Vol. I, pp. 80-81.

31. Ibid., p. 81.

32. Ibid., p. 571.

33. Ibid., pp. 80-81.

34. Ibid., p. 169.

35. Ibid., p. 168.

36. For a more detailed and alternative approach to this question of how individual household income falls above or below the exchange value of labour power, see Jack Wayne and James Dickinson, "The Logic of Social Welfare in a Competitive Capitalist Economy," Third Annual Conference on Blue Collar Workers and their Communities, Windsor, Ontario, May 1979.

37. Karl Marx, "Wages, Prices and Profits" in Karl Marx and Frederick Engels, *Selected Works in Two Volumes,* Vol. I (Moscow: Foreign Languages Press, 1962), p. 443.

38. Marx, *Capital,* Vol. I, p. 168.

39. Marx, *Grundrisse*, pp. 293-94. Marx makes clear that this, "the fact that labour is a constant new source of exchange with capital," is inherent in wage slavery. That is, the worker "only sells a temporary disposition over his labouring capacity, and hence can always begin the exchange anew as soon as he has taken in the quantity of substances required in order to reproduce the externalization of his life."

40. Marx, *Capital*, Vol. I, p. 168.

41. Ibid.

42. Ibid.; Marx, "Wages, Prices and Profits," p. 426.

43. See, for example, Jean Gardiner, "Women's Domestic Labour," in *Capitalist Patriarchy and the Case for Socialist Feminism*, Zillah Eisenstein, ed. (New York: Monthly Review, 1979), p. 178; Rowbotham, *Women's Consciousness, Man's World*, p. 67; Seccombe, "Housewife and Her Labour," p. 17.

44. Engels, *Origin of the Family*, p. 449.

45. Marx, *Capital*, Vol. I, p. 460.

46. Karl Marx, *Capital*, Vol. II (Moscow: Progress Publishers, 1956), pp. 242-43. See also Marx, *Grundrisse*, pp. 668-69.

47. Marx, *Capital*, Vol. II, pp. 233, 317; Karl Marx, *Capital*, Vol. III (Moscow: Progress Publishers, 1959), p. 70.

48. Marx, *Capital*, Vol. II, p. 243.

49. Ibid., p. 127. See also Marx, *Grundrisse*, p. 669, where Marx writes: "Value, hence also surplus value, is not equal to the time which the production phase lasts; but rather to the labour time, objectified and living, employed during this production phase."

50. Marx, *Capital*, Vol. II, pp. 176, 246.

51. For a more detailed discussion of the way in which the non-identity of production time and labour time places impediments in the path of capitalist development, see S.A. Mann and J.M. Dickinson, "Obstacles to the Development of a Capitalist Agriculture," *The Journal of Peasant Studies* 5 (1978), pp. 466-81.

52. For a discussion of these future projections see *Dayton Daily News*, Oct. 1, 1979, where it is reported that in the 1980s there will be "increased reliance on the surrogate cook." This is related to the increased participation of married women in the work force and a decline in family size (smaller households are inclined to eat out more often). Increased foreign investments in fast food franchising is also reported.

53. Piaget's discoveries in genetic psychology support the above points on the nature of human development. Piaget's theory stresses the segmental, stage-like evolution of child development wherein each stage is necessary and integrative in the sense that what is acquired at a given stage becomes an integral part of what is acquired later. See Jean Piaget, *The Child and Reality* (Harmondsworth: Penguin, 1976). See in particular, "Time and Intellectual Development," where he concludes that the acceleration of child development has definite limits, due to the nature of development as a series of equilibrium stages.

54. A recent example of the unsuitability of childrearing or even child-minding to capitalist forms is evident in the failure of Mini-Skools Ltd., a private day care company, to meet Ontario staffing requirements for such institutions. Among the charges levelled against Mini-Skools was that their staffing ratio was 18 to 1 whereas the province called for a ratio of 3 to 1; that unsanitary conditions existed in their buildings; and that there was a shortage of food. See the *Toronto Star,* Apr. 18, 1979.

55. Benston, "Political Economy of Women's Liberation," pp. 23-24.

56. Rowbotham, *Woman's Consciousness, Man's World,* p. 104.

57. Ibid., p. 61 and Benston, "Political Economy of Women's Liberation," p. 16.

58. See, for example, Karl Peter, "The Dialectic of Family and Community in the Social History of the Hutterites," in *The Canadian Family in Comparative Perspective* L. Larson, ed. (Scarborough: Prentice-Hall, 1976), pp. 337-51; William Kephart, *Extraordinary Groups* (New York: St. Martin's, 1976), pp. 91-93 (on the Oneida Community), and p. 267 (on the Hutterite *Kleinschul*). On Owenism, see Robert Owen, *Report to the County of Lanark,* V. Gatrell, ed. (Harmondsworth: Penguin, 1970), pp. 134ff. On the Fourierist *Phalanx,* see Charles Fourier, *Design for Utopia,* Charles Gide, ed. (New York: Schocken, 1971), Chap. IV.

59. Since the wage fund (total variable capital) tends toward the level necessary for the reproduction of the working class, this wage fund is more properly identified with *disposable* personal income, not with (pre-tax) personal income. Thus variable capital is to be identified with "take-home pay," and the witholding of tax from "gross" personal income as an implicit tax on surplus value.

60. Eli Zaretsky, *Capitalism, the Family and Personal Life* (New York: Harper and Row, 1976), p. 49. He follows here E.P. Thompson, "Crime, Work-Discipline and Industrial Capitalism," *Past and Present,* 38.

61. Rowbotham, *Woman's Consciousness, Man's World*, p. 73.

62. Ibid., p. 77.

63. Ibid., p. 67. See also Gardiner, "Women's Domestic Labour," p. 177; Seccombe, "Housewife and Her Labour," p. 17.

AN ANNOTATED BIBLIOGRAPHY ON WOMEN AND THE FAMILY

Bonnie Fox

This bibliography is intended for those beginning the search for an understanding of women's oppression. It includes a thorough listing of theoretical and empirical work on women's domestic labour, as well as some of the most useful material on the general issue of women's oppression, historical changes in women's productive role, early working-class household budget studies and social-historical descriptions of changes in family and household structure. The annotations attempt to outline briefly the material discussed rather than to evaluate the work—although evaluation is expressed both indirectly in the choice of books and articles listed and directly in many of the descriptions. Because the important work on domestic labour is both summarized and evaluated throughout the book, the annotations on that material are very brief. Small capital letters within an annotation indicate that an author is mentioned elsewhere in the bibliography.

Abbott, Edith. *Women in Industry: A Study in American Economic History.* New York: D. Appleton and Co., 1910.

An examination of the changing sexual division of labour, especially in industries employing women, from the early days of American manufacturing.

Acton, Janice, Penny Goldsmith and Bonnie Shepard, eds. *Women at Work: Ontario, 1850-1930.* Toronto: The Women's Press, 1974.

A useful Canadian anthology containing both descriptions and analyses of the key occupations available to women during the period.

Anderson, Michael. *Family Structure in Nineteenth Century Lancashire.* Cambridge: Cambridge University Press, 1971.

A study that reports on household and family structure from an analysis of census returns from mid-nineteenth century England; compares an industrial town, agricultural villages and villages with non-agricultural bases.

Ariés, Philippe. *Centuries of Childhood: A Social History of Family Life.* New York: Vintage Books, 1962.

A study of the historical development, in Europe, of ideas about childhood and the family. A fascinating book, but because the chief sources were family portraits, generalizations do not necessarily extend to the situations of proletarian and peasant families.

Baker, Elizabeth. *Technology and Women's Work.* New York: Columbia University Press, 1964.

A detailed discussion of changes in women's work outside the home in the United States, from the eighteenth century through much of the twentieth century.

Banks, J.A. and Olive Banks. *Feminism and Family Planning in Victorian England.* Liverpool: Liverpool University Press, 1964.

A study, using primary sources, of changes in the household role, legal rights and career opportunities of middle-class and bourgeois women, with a focus on the changing attitudes towards and use of birth control.

Barker, Diana and Sheila Allen, eds. *Dependence and Exploitation in Work and Marriage.* Essex: Longman, 1976.

A sociological anthology on women and the family, with a provocative article on housework by Lenore Davidoff.

________. *Sexual Divisions and Society: Process and Change.* London: Tavistock, 1976.

A wide-ranging anthology of articles on women and gender roles.

Baxandall, Rosalyn, Elizabeth Ewen and Linda Gordon. "The Working Class Has Two Sexes," *Monthly Review,* 28 (July-Aug. 1976), pp. 1-10.

A discussion of the changes in domestic labour due to monopoly capitalism.

Bebel, August. *Women Under Socialism.* New York: Schocken Books, 1971.

Written in the latter part of the nineteenth century, the book is a discussion by a classical Marxist of women's situation in the past, present and future; demonstrates women's oppression in the nineteenth century.

Beechey, Veronica. "Some Notes on Female Wage Labour in Capitalist Production," *Capital and Class,* 3 (Autumn 1977), pp. 45-67.

A theoretical discussion of why married women may have become a preferred reserve army of labour.

Benston, Margaret. "The Political Economy of Women's Liberation," *Monthly Review,* 21 (Sept. 1969), pp. 13-27.

A Marxist theory of domestic labour as use value production.

Blumberg, Rae Lesser. *Stratification: Socioeconomic and Sexual Inequality.* Dubuque: Wm. C. Brown Co., 1978.

A useful introductory sociology textbook, which adopts a framework different from those usually employed by bourgeois sociologists and uses it to describe women's position through human history and today.

Boserup, Ester. *Woman's Role in Economic Development.* London: George Allen and Unwin, 1970.

An examination of women's productive role and their social status under different modes of production, with a focus on the deterioration in women's position due to changes accompanying economic development.

Branca, Patricia. *Silent Sisterhood: Middle-Class Women in the Victorian Home.* London: Croom Helm, 1975.

An examination of the life of the middle-class Victorian housewife that relies on a range of primary sources.

Braverman, Harry. *Labor and Monopoly Capital: The Degradation of Work in the Twentieth Century.* New York: Monthly Review Press, 1974.

An important and eminently readable book that discusses changes in the conditions of white collar wage work, the significance of women's increased involvement in paid employment and changes in the household and its relation to capitalist production in the twentieth century.

Bridenthal, Renate. "The Dialectics of Production and Reproduction in History," *Radical America,* 10 (Mar.-Apr. 1976), pp. 3-14.

A brief theoretical discussion of the labour involved in the reproduction of labour power—and where that reproduction occurs.

Bridenthal, Renate and Claudia Koonz, eds. *Becoming Visible: Women in European History.* Boston: Houghton Mifflin, 1977.

A serious anthology of social-historical work on women; includes Eleanor LEACOCK's fine article on women in egalitarian societies.

Buhle, Mari Jo, Ann Gordon and Nancy Schrom. "Women in American Society: An Historical Contribution," *Radical America,* 5 (July-Aug. 1971), pp. 3-67.

A social history of changes in women's work and their social position from colonial times to the early twentieth century in the United States.

Byington, Margaret. *Homestead: The Households of a Mill Town.* New York: Charities Publication, 1910.

A study of working-class households in an early twentieth-century American steel mill town that discusses women's contribution to household maintenance.

Carter, Mary. "Review—Housework Under Capitalism—Wally Seccombe," *Revolutionary Communist,* 2 (May 1975), pp. 45-50.

A critique of SECCOMBE's early work.

Caulfield, Mina Davis. "Universal Sex Oppression? A Critique from Marxist Anthropology," *Catalyst,* Nos. 10-11 (Summer 1977), pp. 6-78.

An intelligent and incisive discussion of a key question facing feminists.

Chapin, Robert C. *The Standard of Living Among Workingmen's Families in New York City.* New York: The Russell Sage Foundation, 1909.

An early working-class household budget study.

Clark, Alice. *Working Life of Women in the Seventeenth Century.* London: Frank Cass and Co., 1919.

A description of the changes in women's work that accompanied the development of the capitalist mode of production in England; uses mostly primary sources.

Connelly, Patricia. *Last Hired, First Fired: Women and the Canadian Work Force.* Toronto: The Women's Press, 1978.

A short book that sets out, in a straightforward way, the argument that women are a reserve army of labour, using Canadian data as evidence.

Coulson, Margaret, Branka Magas and Hilary Wainwright. "The Housewife and Her Labour Under Capitalism—a Critique," *New Left Review,* 89 (Jan.-Feb. 1975), pp. 59-71.

A Marxist critique of SECCOMBE's early theory of domestic labour.

Cowl, Margaret. "The Economic Role of the Housewife," *Political Affairs,* 51 (Aug. 1972), pp. 52-62.

A response to LUMER that emphasizes the importance of men's and women's exploitation under wage labour to women's oppression in the household.

Dalla Costa, Mariarosa. *Women and the Subversion of the Community.* Bristol: Falling Wall Press, 1972.

An important early attempt to analyze the relation between domestic labour and capitalist production; more polemical than analytical.

de Beauvoir, Simone. *The Second Sex.* New York: Alfred A. Knopf, Inc., 1952.

A classic work with a review of biological facts on sex differences, an historical sketch of women's changing position, a review of mythology about women, a discussion of women's life cycle and their social position today and a non-materialist explanation of women's oppression.

Denis, N., F. Henriques and C. Slaughter. *Coal Is Our Life: An Analysis of a Yorkshire Mining Community.* London: Tavistock, 1956.

A community study that examines sex roles.

Dexter, Elizabeth. *Career Women of America, 1776-1840.* New Hampshire: Marshall Jones Co., 1950.

An examination, using primary sources, of women's careers and changes in women's status during this period in America.

————. *Colonial Women of Affairs.* Boston: Houghton Mifflin Co., 1924.

An examination of evidence (mostly contemporary newspapers) on women's occupations in the colonial United States, with an appraisal of the changes that led to a narrowing of career opportunities for women.

Dixon, Marlene. *Women in Class Struggle.* San Francisco: Synthesis Publications, 1978.

A collection of essays ranging from theoretical analyses of domestic labour to political analyses of the women's movement.

Earle, Alice Morse. *Home Life in Colonial Days.* Stockbridge, Mass.: The Berkshire Traveller Press, 1974.

Written in 1898, this book provides detailed descriptions of household technology and women's housework in colonial days.

Edwards, Hodee. "Housework and Exploitation—a Marxist Analysis," *No More Fun and Games,* 5 (July 1971), pp. 92-100.

An early discussion of domestic labour as the reproduction of labour power.

Ehrenreich, Barbara and Deirdre English. *For Her Own Good: 150 Years of the Experts' Advice to Women.* Garden City: Anchor Press/Doubleday, 1978.

A provocative history that discusses changes in the housewife and mother roles.

______. "The Manufacture of Housework," *Socialist Revolution,* 5 (Oct.-Dec. 1975), pp. 5-41.

A description and analysis of changes in household technology.

Eisenstein, Zillah, ed. *Capitalist Patriarchy and the Case for Socialist Feminism.* New York: Monthly Review Press, 1979.

An anthology that attempts to unite Marxist theory and feminist notions of patriarchy; articles by Nancy Chodorow, Lindon Gordon and Mary Ryan are worth reading.

Engels, Frederick. *The Condition of the Working Class in England.* Oxford: Basil Blackwell, 1958.

The important study of working-class households in industrializing England.

______. *The Origin of the Family, Private Property and the State,* ed., with an introduction by Eleanor Burke LEACOCK. New York: International Publishers, 1942.

The classical Marxist theory of the origins of women's oppression.

Fee, Terry. "Domestic Labour: An Analysis of Housework and its Relation to the Productive Forces," *Review of Radical Political Economics,* 8 (Spring 1976), pp. 1-9.

A critique of Marxist theories of domestic labour.

Feminist Theory Collective. "Comment on Szymanski," *Insurgent Sociologist,* 6 (Spring 1976), pp. 35-40.

A good comment on a weak article (see SZYMANSKI, "The Socialization of Women's Oppression").

Ferneyhough, Beatrice. "On 'Confinement of Women to Housework as an Exclusion from Social Production,' " *Political Affairs,* 53 (Mar. 1974), pp. 50-55.

A discussion of the class nature of the family, whose members are seen as "chattel slaves."

Firestone, Shulamith. *The Dialectic of Sex.* New York: Bantam, 1970.

The chief radical feminist analysis of women's oppression and its sources.

Fisher, Elizabeth. *Woman's Creation: Sexual Evolution and the Shaping of Society.* Garden City: Anchor Press/Doubleday, 1979.

A thorough discussion, drawing on a wide diversity of sources, of the fundamental issue for feminists—how men came to dominate women. The book assumes sexuality is a key material force in society and examines the evolution of sexual behaviour.

Foner, Philip. *Women and the American Labor Movement: From Colonial Times to the Eve of World War I.* New York: The Free Press, 1979.

A thorough and sensitive history of the struggles of working women and their treatment by the male-dominated trade union movement in the United States.

Friedan, Betty. *The Feminine Mystique.* New York: Dell, 1963.
A North American classic, which considers women's oppression from a middle-class perspective, but which vividly captures the personal experience of privatized domestic labour.

Gardiner, Jean. "The Political Economy of Domestic Labour in Capitalist Society," in *Dependence and Exploitation in Work and Marriage,* eds. Diana Barker and Sheila Allen. London: Longman, 1976, pp. 109-21.
A discussion of domestic labour that emphasizes the issue of women's class.

———. "Women's Domestic Labour," *New Left Review,* 89 (Jan.-Feb. 1975), pp. 47-59.
A Marxist critique of SECCOMBE's early theory of domestic labour and an alternative theory of domestic labour as use value production.

———, Susan Himmelweit and Maureen Mackintosh. "Women's Domestic Labour," *Bulletin of the Conference of Socialist Economists,* 4 (June 1975), pp. 1-11.
A critique of Marxist analyses of domestic labour.

Gavron, Hannah. *The Captive Wife: Conflicts of Housebound Mothers.* London: Routledge and Kegan Paul, 1966.
An empirical study of the conditions and social relations of domestic labour for working-class and middle-class housewives in Britain; methodologically problematic.

Gerstein, Ira. "Domestic Work and Capitalism," *Radical America,* 7 (July-Oct. 1973), pp. 101-31.
A Marxist theory of domestic labour as a unique kind of labour.

Giedion, Siegfried. *Mechanization Takes Command.* New York: Norton and Co., 1948.
A history of changes in housing designs and household equipment.

Gordon, Linda. *Woman's Body, Woman's Right: A Social History of Birth Control in America.* New York: Grossman Publishers, 1976.
A thorough history of state control of the means of birth control, with a class analysis of the struggle for access to them.

Gordon, Michael, ed. *The American Family in Social-Historical Perspective.* New York: St. Martin's Press, 1973.
An excellent anthology of social historical work on changing family

and household structures, changes in the experience of "youth" as a stage in the life cycle, changes in ideas of "womanhood" and changes in sexual practice.

Gough, Ian and John Harrison. "Unproductive Labour and Housework Again," *Bulletin of the Conference of Socialist Economists*, 4 (1975).
A Marxist theoretical analysis of domestic labour.

Guettel, Charnie. *Marxism and Feminism.* Toronto: The Women's Press, 1974.
A critical examination of feminist theories of women's oppression.

Harrison, John. "The Political Economy of Housework," *Bulletin of the Conference of Socialist Economists* (Winter 1973), pp. 35-52.
A Marxist theory of domestic labour.

Hartman, Mary and Lois Banner, eds. *Clio's Consciousness Raised.* New York: Harper and Row, 1974.
A fine anthology on women's social history, with an article by Laura Oren that examines household budgets (from the late nineteenth century in England) to reveal the housewife's status and material welfare, and an article by Ruth Swartz Cowan on the mechanization of the North American household.

Hewitt, Margaret. *Wives and Mothers in Victorian Industry.* London: Rockliff, 1958.
An examination, using primary sources, of the effects of women's employment in nineteenth-century English factories, on family life, housekeeping standards, fertility, etc.; involves a description of working-class households and bourgeois ideology about them.

Himmelweit, Susan and Simon Mohun. "Domestic Labour and Capital," *Cambridge Journal of Economics,* 1 (Mar. 1977), pp. 15-31.
A review and critique of the domestic labour debate.

Holcombe, Lee. *Victorian Ladies at Work: Middle-Class Working Women in England and Wales, 1850-1914.* Hamden, Conn.: Archon Books, 1973.
An examination of the occupations becoming available to middle-class women during this period and the causes and consequences of the feminization of these occupations.

Houghteling, Leila. *The Income and Standard of Living of Unskilled Laborers in Chicago.* Chicago: The University of Chicago Press, 1927.
A working-class household budget study.

Hughes, Gwendolyn. *Mothers in Industry: Wage-Earning by Mothers in Philadelphia.* New York: New Republic Inc., 1925.
An early study of the households of working wives, which discusses why they work for wages.

Humphries, Jane. "The Working Class Family, Women's Liberation, and Class Struggle: The Case of Nineteenth Century British History," *The Review of Radical Political Economics,* 9 (Fall 1977), pp. 25-42.

An analysis of the causes of the historic survival of the privatized household that emphasizes class struggle, the role of the household with respect to the standard of living and the effects on the value of labour power of the involvement of several family members in wage work.

Inman, Mary. "Maternity as a Social Function," *Political Affairs,* 52 (Jan. 1973), pp. 56-60.

A response to LUMER that focusses on childbearing.

Katz, Michael. *The People of Hamilton, Canada West: Family and Class in a Mid-Nineteenth-Century City.* Cambridge, Mass.: Harvard University Press, 1975.

An intensive study of the primary sources from 1851 to 1861 indicating the occupational, household and family structures of Hamilton's workers.

Kolko, Gabriel. "Working Wives: Their Effects on the Structure of the Working Class," *Science and Society,* 42 (Fall 1978), pp. 257-77.

A discussion of the causes and consequences of the growing involvement of married women in wage work.

Kuhn, Annette and Ann Marie Wolpe, eds. *Feminism and Materialism.* London: Routledge and Kegan Paul, 1978.

An exciting anthology that explores the possibilities of studying patriarchy as it is shaped by class relations. Articles by Roisin McDonough and Rachel Harrison, Annette Kuhn, and Mary McIntosh are especially interesting; includes a critique of theories of domestic labour by Paul Smith.

Kyrk, Hazel. *Economic Problems of the Family.* New York: Harper, 1933.

A thorough discussion of the changing household and women's domestic labour, by an early home economist.

Landes, Joan. "Wages for Housework: Subsidizing Capitalism?" *Quest,* 2 (Fall 1975), pp. 17-31.

A Marxist theory of the household as a mode of production.

———. "Women, Labor and Family Life: a Theoretical Perspective," *Science and Society,* 41 (Winter 1977-78), pp. 386-409.

A critique of the domestic labour debate.

Larguia, Isabel and John Dumoulin. "Aspects of the Condition of Women's Labour," *Latin America and Empire Report,* 9 (Sept. 1975), pp. 4-13.

———. "Towards a Science of Women's Liberation," *Latin America and Empire Report,* 6 (Dec. 1972), pp. 3-20.

Two articles that raise the key questions involved in understanding women's productive role.

Lasch, Christopher. "The Emotions of Family Life," *The New York Review of Books,* 22 (Nov. 27, 1975), pp. 37-42.

A discussion of the historical evidence of changing family form and its importance with respect to personal life, with an emphasis on the changing roles of men and women and the changing sexual division of labour in the household.

———. "The Family and History," *The New York Review of Books,* 22 (Nov. 13, 1975), pp. 33-38.

A fine review of traditional sociological assumptions about historical changes in the family and the new historical-demographic evidence on household composition and structure; a discussion of the usefulness of modernization theory.

———. "What the Doctor Ordered," *The New York Review of Books,* 22 (Dec. 11, 1975), pp. 50-54.

A good critique of Edward Shorter's book, *The Making of the Modern Family.*

Laslett, Peter. *The World We Have Lost.* London: Methuen, 1965.

A simplified description of family and household in pre-capitalist societies.

——— and Richard Wall, eds. *Household and Family in Past Time.* Cambridge: Cambridge University Press, 1972.

A scholarly anthology of important findings on household and family size and structure in early centuries in Europe.

Leacock, Eleanor. "Introduction" to Engels' *The Origin of the Family, Private Property and the State.* New York: International Publishers, 1942.

An excellent discussion and interpretation of anthropological evidence relevant to Engels' theory of the origins of private property, class society and women's oppression; includes a discussion of anthropological evidence on sexual hierarchy.

Lebowitz, Michael. "The Political Economy of Housework: a Comment," *Bulletin of the Conference of Socialist Economists,* 5 (Mar. 1976).

A sketch of a Marxist analysis of the household as a sphere of production.

Lenin, V. I. *The Emancipation of Women.* New York: International Publishers, 1966.

Lenin's statement about the reasons for women's oppression and the conditions necessary for their liberation.

Little, Esther and William Cotton. *Budgets of Families and Individuals of Kensington, Philadelphia.* Lancaster, Pa.: The New Era Printing C., 1920.

A study of the household budgets of early twentieth-century textile mill workers' families.

Lopata, Helena. *Occupation: Housewife.* London: Oxford University Press, 1971.

A bourgeois sociologist's examination of the roles of wife, housewife and mother; discusses typical role changes over the life cycle and the way women see themselves and their husbands. Useful empirical material from in-depth interviews carried out in the 1950s in the United States.

Lumer, Hyman. "On the Economic Status of the Housewife," *Political Affairs,* 53 (Mar. 1974), pp. 1-6.

A statement of the classical Marxist argument that domestic labour is a form of private service separate from capitalist production.

Luxton, Meg. *More Than a Labour of Love: Three Generations of Women's Work in the Home.* Toronto: The Women's Press, 1980.

A study of the domestic labour of three generations of working-class women living in a Canadian mining community; informed by a Marxist theory of domestic labour and generously punctuated with quotes from the women themselves.

Lynd, Robert S. and Helen Merrell Lynd. *Middletown: A Study in Modern American Culture.* New York: Harcourt, Brace and World, 1929.

———. *Middletown: A Study in Cultural Conflicts.* New York: Harcourt, Brace and World, 1937.

Community studies that discuss women's work in the home.

Malos, Ellen. "Housework and the Politics of Women's Liberation," *Socialist Review,* 8 (Jan.-Feb. 1978), pp. 41-73.

A discussion of theory and strategy.

McBride, Theresa. *The Domestic Revolution: the Modernization of Household Service in England and France, 1820-1920.* London: Croom Helm, 1976.

A social history of domestic service.

Meissner, Martin, Elizabeth Humphreys, Scott Meiss and William Scheu. "No Exit for Wives: Sexual Division of Labour," *The Canadian Review of Sociology and Anthropology,* 12 (Nov. 1975), pp. 424-40.

An analysis of data on the hours wives, husbands and children spend doing housework—and the consequences of wives' work outside the homes.

Milkman, Ruth. "Women's Work and Economic Crisis: Some Lessons of the Great Depression," *The Review of Radical Political Economics,* 8 (Spring 1976), pp. 73-98.

A discussion, with an examination of data, of the validity of the notion that women are a reserve army of labour.

Millett, Kate. *Sexual Politics.* New York: Doubleday, 1969.

A bourgeois feminist analysis of women's oppression, with a review of male writers' treatments of women.

Mitchell, Juliet. *Woman's Estate.* New York: Vintage Books, 1971.

A Marxist (influenced by Althusser) analysis of women's oppression under capitalism, which discusses the four (separate) structures defining women's position: production, reproduction, sexuality and the socialization of children.

_______ and Ann Oakley, eds. *The Rights and Wrongs of Women.* Harmondsworth: Penguin, 1976.

A fine anthology on women's social history that includes articles on women's work in the home, and their involvement in wage work in nineteenth-century London and in the American trade union movement.

Molyneux, Maxine. "Beyond the Domestic Labour Debate," *New Left Review,* 116 (July-Aug. 1979), pp. 3-28.

A Marxist critique of theories of domestic labour.

More, Louise Bolard. *Wage-Earners' Budgets: A Study of Standards.* New York: Henry Holt and Co., 1907.

An early working-class household budget study, which discusses the woman's contribution to household maintenance.

Morton, Peggy. "A Woman's Work is Never Done," in *Women Unite!* ed. The Women's Press. Toronto: The Women's Press, 1972.

An important early statement on women's oppression in the household and the wage work force; discusses women as reproducers of labour power.

Neff, Wanda. *Victorian Working Women: An Historical and Literary Study of Women in British Industries and Professions,* 1832-1850. London: George Allen and Unwin, 1929.

A study of mid-nineteenth-century work roles and wage jobs available to women; relies largely on literary sources.

Oakley, Ann. *The Sociology of Housework.* New York: Pantheon Books, 1974.

Reports the results of a survey of housewives.

_______. *Woman's Work: The Housewife, Past and Present.* New York: Pantheon Books, 1974.

A feminist sociologist's history of women's domestic labour with a focus on changes consequent to the industrialization of commodity production; an analysis of domestic labour; the results of in-depth interviews with housewives; explorations of myths about women.

On the Political Economy of Women. London: Stage One, n.d.
A collection of articles by British Marxist feminists.

Pinchbeck, Ivy. *Women Workers and the Industrial Revolution, 1750-1850.* London: Frank Cass and Co., 1930.
A description of the changes in women's work that accompanied the industrialization of the capitalist production of commodities in England.

Proulx, Monique. *Women and Work: Five Million Women—A Study of the Canadian Housewife.* Ottawa: Advisory Council on the Status of Women, 1978.
Presents data obtained in a recent study.

Quick, Paddy. "The Class Nature of Woman's Oppression," *Review of Radical Political Economics,* 9 (Fall 1977), pp. 42-54.
An analysis of women's oppression that examines the social relations under which women biologically reproduce the next generation and situates male dominance entirely within capitalist class relations.

Rabb, Theodore and Robert Rotberg, eds. *The Family in History: Interdisciplinary Essays.* New York: Harper and Row, 1971.
An interesting anthology; contains Robert Well's article on changes in women's typical life cycle since the late eighteenth century, Virginia Yans McLaughlin's study of the relationship between the wage work patterns of Italian women and the organization of their households in 1900-30 in Buffalo, articles on adolescence and women's history.

Rainwater, Lee, Richard Coleman and Gerald Handel. *Workingmen's Wife: Her Personality, World, and Life Style.* New York: Oceana Publications, 1959.
A study of working-class and middle-class housewives—their work and self-images—commissioned by a woman's magazine for purposes of better advertising!

Rapp, Rayna. "Family and Class in Contemporary America: Notes Toward an Understanding of Ideology," *Science and Society,* 42 (Fall 1978), pp. 278-301.
An interesting discussion of the relation of family and household, women's role in each and the results in terms of family structure of the differential access to resources of the households of different classes in North America.

Reeves, Pember. *Round About a Pound a Week.* London: Virago Limited, 1979.
A British working-class household budget study.

Reid, Margaret. *Economics of Household Production.* New York: John Wiley and Sons, 1934.
A textbook on the changing American household and women's domestic labour, by an early home economist.

Reiter, Rayna, ed. *Toward an Anthropology of Women.* New York: Monthly Review Press, 1975.
An anthropological anthology. Useful articles: Lila Leibowitz on the behavioural effects of sex differences in nonhuman primates, Sally Slocum on women's role in the development of human society, Kathleen Gough on the origin of the family, Rayna Reiter on public and private domains in a village in southern France.

Robinson, John, Phil Converse and Alexander Szalai. "Everyday Life in Twelve Countries," in *The Use of Time: Daily Activities of Urban and Suburban Populations in Twelve Countries,* ed. Alexander Szalai. The Hague: Mouton, 1972, pp. 113-43.
Evidence on the number of hours spent in various household tasks, focussing on the effects of women's employment outside the home.

Rosaldo, Michelle and Louise Lamphere, eds. *Woman, Culture, and Society.* Stanford, California: Stanford University Press, 1974.
An anthropological anthology; Michelle Rosaldo's, Nancy Chodorow's and Sherry Ortner's articles present theories of women's oppression that assume its universality.

Rowbotham, Sheila. *Hidden From History: 300 Years of Women's Oppression and the Fight Against It.* London: Pluto Press, 1974.
An historical sketch of changes in women's position and feminist struggles for liberation, from early capitalist development to the post-World War I period, in Britain.

———. *Woman's Consciousness, Man's World.* Harmondsworth: Penguin, 1973.
A provocative, insightful Marxist feminist analysis of women's position under capitalism; discusses the impact of capitalism on the family, women's work and their personal lives.

———. *Women, Resistance and Revolution: A History of Women and Revolution in the Modern World.* New York: Vintage Books, 1972.
A history of struggles for women's liberation, from the colonial period in North America, through the Russian and Chinese revolutions, to 1960s struggles against imperialist powers.

Rowntree, Mary and John Rowntree. "More on the Political Economy

of Women's Liberation," *Monthly Review*, 21 (Jan. 1970), pp. 26-32.
A response to BENSTON on domestic labour.

Rubin, Lillian. *Worlds of Pain: Life in the Working-Class Family*. New York: Basic Books, 1976.
A sensitive study of working-class family life in North America.

Scott, Joan and Louise Tilly. "Women's Work and the Family in Nineteenth-Century Europe," *Comparative Studies in Society and History*, 17 (Jan. 1975), pp. 36-64.
A discussion of the changes in the sexual division of labour in the household and commodity production with the destruction of the peasant mode of production, in Europe.

Seccombe, Wally. "The Housewife and Her Labour Under Capitalism," *New Left Review*, 83 (Jan.-Feb. 1974), pp. 3-24.
A Marxist theory of domestic labour as independent commodity production.

______. "Domestic Labour—Reply to Critics," *New Left Review*, 94 (Nov.-Dec. 1975), pp. 85-96.
Involves an explanation of the influx of married women into the wage labour force.

Silveira, Jeanette. *The Housewife and Marxist Class Analysis*. Pittsburgh: Know Inc., 1975.
A radical feminist critique of the Marxist debate on domestic labour.

Simeral, Margaret. "Women and the Reserve Army of Labor," *Insurgent Sociologist*, 8 (Fall 1978), pp. 164-81.
An argument, with empirical support, that women have functioned as a reserve army of labour (in the sense of a secularly and cyclically activated labour pool) in the United States since 1950.

Smith, Dorothy. "Corporate Capitalism," in *Women in Canada*, ed. Marylee Stephenson. Toronto: New Press, 1973, pp. 5-35.
A class analysis of domestic labour that emphasizes middle-class households and discusses the ideological functions of domestic labour.

Smith, Joan. "Women and the Family," *International Socialism*, Nos. 100 and 104, n.d.
A discussion of strategy for ending women's oppression in the household.

Smuts, Robert. *Women and Work in America*. New York: Schocken Books, 1959.
An essay that describes the changes in women's work lives in the United States since the nineteenth century.

Stack, Carol. *All Our Kin: Strategies for Survival in a Black Community.* New York: Harper and Row, 1974.

An analysis of family and kinship organization in an American black ghetto.

Stearns, Peter. "Working-Class Women in Britain, 1890-1914," in *Workers in the Industrial Revolution: Recent Studies of Labour in the United States and Europe,* eds. Peter Stearns and Daniel Walkowitz. New Brunswick, N.J.: Transaction Books, 1974, pp. 401-25.

An examination of evidence on the changing household position of the married working-class woman at the turn of the century.

Strasser, Susan. "The Business of Housekeeping: The Ideology of the Household at the Turn of the Twentieth Century," *Insurgent Sociologist,* 8 (Fall 1978), pp. 147-64.

A discussion of the historical development (in the twentieth century) of ideology about the household, as it reflected changes in the productive activity occurring in the household and the transition from competitive to monopoly capitalism.

Szymanski, Al. "The Socialization of Woman's Oppression: A Marxist Theory of the Changing Position of Women in Advanced Capitalist Society," *Insurgent Sociologist,* 6(Winter 1976), pp. 31-61.

A discussion of the causes and implications of women's increased involvement in wage work.

________. "Reply to the Feminist Theory Collective," *Insurgent Sociologist,* 6 (Spring 1976), pp. 40-47.

Tilly, Louise and Joan Scott. *Women, Work, and Family.* New York: Holt, Rinehart and Winston, 1978.

An analysis, based on the use of primary and secondary data sources, of the position of women in the "popular classes" under independent commodity production, in early industrial capitalism and monopoly capitalist society.

Vanek, Joann. "Time Spent in Housework," *Scientific American,* 231 (Nov. 1974), pp. 116-20.

A review of the results of time budget studies of domestic labour, covering 50 years in the United States.

Vogel, Lise. "The Earthly Family," *Radical America,* 7 (July-Oct. 1973), pp. 9-50.

A discussion of domestic labour as use value production.

Walker, Kathryn. "Homemaking Still Takes Time," *Journal of Home Economics,* 61, pp. 621-24.

A study of hours spent at domestic tasks.

Weinbaum, Batya and Amy Bridges. "The Other Side of the Paycheck: Monopoly Capital and the Structure of Consumption," *Monthly Review*, 28 (July-Aug. 1976), pp. 88-103.

A Marxist discussion of women's domestic labour.

Young, Michael and Peter Willmott. *Family and Kinship in East London.* London: Routledge and Kegan Paul, 1957.

A community study that describes women's role in the household in an old and stable working-class community in Britain.

Zaretsky, Eli. *Capitalism, the Family and Personal Life.* Santa Cruz: Loaded Press, 1973.

A provocative social history of the family and women's productive role in the household; discusses the emergence of the sphere of "personal life."

Zetkin, Clara. "Proletarian Women and Socialist Revolution," reprinted in *Socialist Register,* eds. Hal Draper and Anne Lipow, 1976.

An essay by one of the first revolutionaries to recognize the role of the privatization of the household in women's oppression.

I am grateful to Linda Briskin and Meg Luxton for their help in preparing these annotations. B.F